The Representation and Processing of Compound Words

For Oda and Konstantinos

The Representation and Processing of Compound Words

Edited by
GARY LIBBEN AND GONIA JAREMA

UNIVERSITY PRESS

OXFORD
UNIVERSITY PRESS

Great Clarendon Street, Oxford OX2 6DP

Oxford University Press is a department of the University of Oxford.
It furthers the University's objective of excellence in research, scholarship,
and education by publishing worldwide in

Oxford New York

Auckland Cape Town Dar es Salaam Hong Kong Karachi
Kuala Lumpur Madrid Melbourne Mexico City Nairobi
New Delhi Shanghai Taipei Toronto

With offices in

Argentina Austria Brazil Chile Czech Republic France Greece
Guatemala Hungary Italy Japan Poland Portugal Singapore
South Korea Switzerland Thailand Turkey Ukraine Vietnam

Oxford is a registered trade mark of Oxford University Press
in the UK and in certain other countries

Published in the United States
by Oxford University Press Inc., New York

© Editorial matter and organization Gary Libben and Gonia Jarema 2006
© The chapters their several authors 2006

The moral rights of the author have been asserted
Database right Oxford University Press (maker)

First published 2006

All rights reserved. No part of this publication may be reproduced,
stored in a retrieval system, or transmitted, in any form or by any means,
without the prior permission in writing of Oxford University Press,
or as expressly permitted by law, or under terms agreed with the appropriate
reprographics rights organization. Enquiries concerning reproduction
outside the scope of the above should be sent to the Rights Department,
Oxford University Press, at the address above

You must not circulate this book in any other binding or cover
and you must impose the same condition on any acquirer

British Library Cataloguing in Publication Data
Data available

Library of Congress Cataloging in Publication Data
Data available

Typeset by SPI Publisher Services, Pondicherry, India
Printed in Great Britain on acid-free paper by
Antony Rowe Ltd., Chippenham, Wiltshire

ISBN 0-19-928506-3   978-0-19-928506-8

Contents

Preface and Overview	vi
Notes on Contributors	xii

1	Why Study Compound Processing? An overview of the issues *Gary Libben*	1
2	Compound Types *Wolfgang U. Dressler*	23
3	Compound Representation and Processing: A cross-language perspective *Gonia Jarema*	45
4	The Neuropsychology of Compound Words *Carlo Semenza and Sara Mondini*	71
5	Preschool Children's Acquisition of Compounds *Elena Nicoladis*	96
6	Doghouse/Chien-maison/Niche: Approaches to the understanding of compound processing in bilinguals *Erika S. Levy, Mira Goral, and Loraine K. Obler*	125
7	Conceptual Combination: Implications for the mental lexicon *Christina L. Gagné and Thomas L. Spalding*	145
8	Processing Chinese Compounds: A survey of the literature *James Myers*	169

References	197
Index	223

Preface and Overview

It has been claimed that the mental lexicon is the backbone of human language processing, encompassing the manner in which words are represented and processed in the mind. As such, the study of the mental lexicon is in a privileged position to reveal properties of the human ability to create, store and mobilize both simple and complex cognitive representations. Compound words such as *handbook* and *tablecloth* are perhaps the most fundamental of such complex representations. Compound words are extremely widespread among the world's languages and represent perhaps the easiest way to form a new cognitive representation from two or more existing ones. The two compounds cited above represent words that have already been incorporated as fixed expressions in the English language. However, novel combinations of the constituents of these compounds are also quite easily comprehended by native speakers of the language. Thus, *table-book* and *book-cloth* can also be said to be potential words of English that are made available by the compounding word formation process.

A consideration of the above leads naturally to a set of fundamental questions: What are the psychological mechanisms that allow such free lexical creation? Are the production and comprehension processes involved the same for both existing lexicalized words and novel combinations? How are these processes related to other lexical and non-lexical processes? When are they acquired? How are they compromised by damage to the brain? How might they differ across languages? What shape might compound processing take among bilinguals?

Until quite recently these questions had hardly been asked, let alone answered. Over the last two decades, however, the psycholinguistic and neurolinguistic study of compound representation and processing has seen great advances. From just a handful of studies in the 1970s, we now have a substantial body of research both within and across languages. To the best of our knowledge, this volume is the first to bring this research together in order to provide the reader with a comprehensive overview of the current state of knowledge and to synthesize the implications of compound processing research for our broader understanding of language processing, acquisition, and breakdown across languages.

The eight chapters of the book each represent an overview of the state of knowledge in key areas of current compound research. The authors are all members of the International Mental Lexicon Research Group, which is supported by a Major Collaborative Research Initiative Grant from the Social Sciences and Humanities Research Council of Canada. They have undertaken to provide synthetic state-of-the-art reports in the domains of compounding research in which they are expert. The research material between and across chapters has been sequenced and cross-referenced with the goal of providing the reader with an overview of the field that is accessible, current, and complete.

In the initial chapter of this book, Gary Libben presents an overview of the key psycholinguistic issues in the study of compound representation and processing. Against the background of these issues, Libben presents a case for the view that morphological processing, in general, and compound processing, in particular, is characterized by the principle of 'maximization of opportunity'. In this view, the lexical processing system seeks neither computational efficiency nor storage efficiency. Indeed, he claims that the language processing system is not guided by considerations of efficiency at all. Libben argues that morphological processing is better captured as a system that seeks to maximize the opportunities for activation at all levels. Thus, he proposes that the activation of a compound word such as 'strawberry' involves the activation of all constituents as well as the whole word. Where such massive activation creates conflict between the meanings of the compound constituents and that of the whole word, a set of post-activation 'cleanup' procedures resolves this conflict by deactivating spurious representations.

The chapter by Wolfgang Dressler begins by addressing the question of the manner in which compounds may be defined. Dressler notes that it is by no means a simple task to present an intensional definition of the notion 'compound'. He focuses therefore on an extensional definition as well as a discussion of the prototypical properties of compounds. Compound prototypes in Dressler's formulation are characterized by the absence of a set of features that are known to be properties of syntactic phrases. At the outset of his chapter, Dressler states that his discussion will focus on 'regular compounds, i.e. rule governed, particularly productive compound formation'. This emphasis leads him naturally to discuss the definition of morphological productivity, which in turn leads to a consideration of the role of morphological headedness in compound formation. He cites evidence that compounding shows a preference for right-headedness and endocentricity. The chapter concludes by summarizing the properties of prototypical compounds, and listing the structural preferences that one may observe across languages.

What implications do the cross-linguistic differences addressed by Dressler have for our ability to develop a comprehensive theory of compound processing? In her chapter, Gonia Jarema stresses from the outset that, to date, the needed comparative studies are still scarce. The author therefore focuses on investigations in both the monolingual and multilingual literature that have led to a consensus with respect to central questions in the study of compound representation and processing across at least two languages. Issues reviewed in the chapter include constituent activation, as evidenced by semantic transparency effects, by distributional effects, and by patterns of performance in aphasia. Other issues included in the chapter are the role of position-in-the-string and headedness in the activation of compounds across languages. Finally, Jarema addresses the problem of the lexical status of compounds and discusses the role of elements that intervene between compound constituents in some languages.

The chapter by Carlo Semenza and Sara Mondini begins by pointing out the fact that neuropsychological evidence can be more revealing of language representation and processing because the effects obtained from the study of brain-damaged populations are often of a much greater magnitude. Semenza and Mondini review the state of the art in the neuropsychology of compound processing. They claim that this evidence, taken together with current evidence from the psycholinguistic literature, points to the functional independence of different types of lexical knowledge and that all compound processing involves morphological composition and decomposition. Evidence from Italian also points to the independence and dissociability of mechanisms of gender assignment. The authors cite neuropsychological evidence that is consistent with the view that both compound constituents as well as whole-word representations are routinely and automatically activated in compound processing.

Elena Nicoladis addresses the question of how compound words are acquired by preschool children. She reviews the current state of knowledge on the extent to which cross-linguistic differences exist in the ages at which compounds can be said to be acquired and how structural differences among compounds within a language may affect age of acquisition. Nicoladis focuses on morphological headedness direction as a major distinguisher of compound structure, cross-linguistically. She reviews research on how bilingual children deal with headedness clashes and the effect that this has on both their production and comprehension of novel compounds. A dominant theme in the chapter is that children's compound acquisition is very much influenced by properties of the linguistic input that they receive. There is evidence that input frequency is related to the age of compound acquisition across languages. Nicoladis notes, however, that a fuller understanding of the relation between input frequency and compound acquisition will require more fine-grained measures of input frequency and a consideration of the manner in which input to the child is modulated by perceptions of the child's proficiency.

What are the implications for research on compound representation and processing for bilingual processing? This is the question that is addressed by Erika Levy, Mira Goral, and Loraine Obler. They present both an overview of what is currently known about the representation and processing of compounds among bilingual children and adults and correlate this knowledge with the evidence currently available on the differences in compound processing across languages. This overview enables the authors to identify the domains in which future research on compound representation and processing in bilinguals might proceed and to identify the questions which would be most revealing in future research.

The chapter by Gagné and Spalding introduces a construct that has not yet been considered in the psycholinguistic literature on compound processing. This construct, conceptual combination, is argued to be fundamental to our ability to interpret novel compounds. Gagné and Spalding claim that information that specifies how compound constituents are related is carried by the modifier and that, in essence, the processes that account for head-modifier relations in phrases are comparable to those that may be needed to account for conceptual relations within compounds. This position is elaborated through a discussion of the CARIN (Competition-Among-Relations-in-Nominals) model. The authors further argue that the computation of conceptual relations is not limited to the production and comprehension of novel compounds, but is also operant in the processing of existing, lexicalized, compounds.

The final chapter by James Myers concentrates on a single language, Chinese. As the author notes at the outset, Chinese has a rather special role to play in our understanding of compound processing. Chinese is often cited as the language that has extensive compounding as the dominant word-formation process. But yet, the role of compounding in the language is not without its complications. As Myers argues, there is great difficulty in defining the concept of word in Chinese, which he relates closely to the nature of Chinese orthography. Myers brings together, to our knowledge for the first time, the research to date on how Chinese compounds are represented and processed, focusing both on language-specific effects and on other effects such as constituent frequency and transparency that have been central in the non-Chinese psycholinguistic literature.

In concluding this overview, the editors wish to thank all the authors for the hard work and creativity that they have put into their contributions. We would also like to thank our anonymous reviewers and Ray Jackendoff who have played an important role in helping us to present material as clearly and accurately as possible. Finally, we thank Oxford University Press for supporting this project and for working with us to bring this body of research to the scientific community.

Notes on Contributors

Wolfgang Dressler is Professor and Chair of Linguistics at the University of Vienna. He studied Linguistics and Classical Philology in Vienna, Rome and Paris, taking his M.A., Ph.D. and Habilitation at the University of Vienna. Wolfgang Dressler's research combines diachronic and synchronic perspectives on phonological and morphological structure across languages. He is the author of 25 books and over 300 articles that span

Christina L. Gagné received her PhD in Cognitive Psychology from the University of Illinois at Urbana-Champaign in 1997 and is currently Associate Professor at the University of Alberta. Her research focuses on the representation and use of conceptual knowledge. She also examines how language is used to convey information about conceptual structures. Her past work has shown that information about the relations among conceptual representations plays an important role in the creation and comprehension of novel noun phrases as well as in the comprehension of compound words.the field of linguistics.

Mira Goral, Ph.D., CCC-SLP, is a Research Assistant Professor in the Department of Neurology at the Boston University School of Medicine and the Project Manager of the Language in the Aging Brain Laboratory of the Harold Goodglass Aphasia Research Center at the Boston VA Healthcare System. She is an Adjunct Professor in the Program in Speech and Hearing Sciences at the Graduate Center of the City University of New York. Her research includes work on multilingualism, aphasia, aging, and language attrition.

Gonia Jarema is Professor of Linguistics at the University of Montreal and Director of the Mental Lexicon Laboratory at the Research Centre of the Institut universitaire de gériatrie de Montréal. She specializes in the psycho- and neurolinguistics of the mental lexicon from a cross-linguistic perspective. She is co-editor with Gary Libben of the journal *The Mental Lexicon* (John Benjamins Publishing Co.).

Erika Levy, Ph.D., CCC-SLP, is Assistant Professor in the Department of Biobehavioral Sciences at Teachers College, Columbia University in New York City, where her research focuses on cross-language speech production and perception. She wrote a series of three books entitled Baby's First Steps (2001) on infant perception of speech sounds in a foreign language. She has also published on topics involving adult cross-language vowel production and perception in the *Journal of the Acoustical Society of America* with Winifred Strange, and authored "Neurolinguistic aspects of bilingualism" in the *International Journal of Bilingualism* (2002) with Goral and Obler.

Gary Libben is Professor of Linguistics and Director of the Centre for Comparative Psycholinguistics at the University of Alberta. His research focuses on the representation and processing of morphologically complex words in the mind. He is Director of the project "Words in the Mind, Words in the Brain" and is co-editor with Gonia Jarema of the journal *The Mental Lexicon* (John Benjamins Publishing Co.).

Sara Mondini is Assistant Professor at the Department of General Psychology, University of Padua, where she teaches Psychobiology and Neuropsychological assessment techniques. Her research focuses on language processing in aphasia and cognitive impairment in dementia. She obtained her PhD in Psychology at the University of Padova (Italy) and been a visiting doctoral student at the National Hospital for Neurology and Neurosurgery of London, the Centre de recherche de l'Institut universitaire de gériatrie de Montréal (Université de Montréal), and McGill University.

James Myers is Professor in the Graduate Institute of Linguistics, National Chung Cheng University, Taiwan, where has worked since 1997. He obtained his Ph.D. in linguistics from the University of Arizona in 1993 and previously taught at the University of Michigan,

Ann Arbor. He specializes in morphological and phonological representation and processing.

Elena Nicoladis is an Assistant Professor in the Psychology Department at the University of Alberta, Canada. She received her undergraduate education at the University of California, Berkley, and graduate education in Psychology at McGill University (PhD, 1995). Her research interests include morphological acquisition and manual gestures.

Loraine K. Obler, Ph.D., is Distinguished Professor in Speech and Hearing Sciences, and in Linguistics, at the Graduate Center of the City University of New York. Research in her Neurolinguistics Laboratory there is on topics including the neurolinguistics of bilingualism, effects of stress on second-language performance, dyslexia, and language in aging. Her books include *The Bilingual Brain: Neuropsychological and Neurolinguistic Aspects of Bilingualism* (with Martin Albert, 1978), *Agrammatic Aphasia: A Cross-Language Narrative Sourcebook* (edited with Lise Menn, 1990), and *Language and the Brain* (with Kris Gjerlow, 1999).

Carlo Semenza is Professor of Psychology at the University of Trieste, Italy where he teaches Neuropsychology and Cognitive Neuroscience. He graduated in medicine at the University of Padova, where he also obtained a Psychiatry Diploma. Carlo Semenza has been visiting fellow and professor at the VA Hospital in Boston, Melbourne University, Victoria University and Universitad Complutensis of Madrid. He is the author of over 200 articles on neuropsychological topics and has published in journals such as Nature, Brain, and Cortex.

Thomas L. Spalding (PhD 1994, University of Illinois at Urbana-Champaign has taught and conducted research at the University of Iowa and the University of Western Ontario and is currently Associate Professor in the Department of Psychology at the University of Alberta. His research interests relate to the issue of how people combine information in the course of learning, comprehension, and inference. This overarching interest has led to research on concepts, conceptual combination, memory, word meanings, analytic reading, and expository writing, as well as peripheral interests in spatial cognition, conceptual development, and consumer loyalty.

1

Why Study Compound Processing? An overview of the issues

GARY LIBBEN

The 1960s and 1970s were years of debate over fundamental issues in almost every field of scholarship. In the field of linguistics, one of the most fiercely debated issues was whether language was a species-specific genetic endowment or an advancement built upon lower forms of animal communication. Although it did not seem at the outset that this could ever be an actual empirical issue, a long-term study by Allen and Beatrix Gardner made it one. They raised a female chimpanzee named Washoe and taught her American Sign Language (ASL) in an effort to level the playing field that gave humans an insuperable advantage in the production of speech sounds. Could Washoe display any of the properties of human language? Could she use ASL to creatively combine the form–meaning relationships that characterize words in order to produce new units of meaning? For much of the decade of the 1970s (and a good number of years thereafter) the answer to this question seemed to hinge on a single compound word, 'waterbird', which Washoe reportedly created upon seeing a swan.

We may never know whether 'waterbird' was the first novel multimorphemic word ever formed by a non-human primate, or whether Washoe was simply acknowledging that she saw both a bird and the water upon which it swam. But it is hardly surprising that this putative linguistic invasion into human exclusivity should have involved a compound. Indeed, this could have been predicted.

The reason for this predictability is that compounding might be considered to be the universally fundamental word formation process. Under the assumption that the purpose of novel word formation is to communicate, compounding offers the easiest and most effective way to create and transfer new meanings. By building new lexical items upon the meanings of existing items, novel compounds can, in principle, be understood upon first presentation.

If we feel free to speculate about the prehistory of the first multimorphemic words that language would possess, we might also imagine that, for humans as well, the first word formation process in language might have been compounding. Although it is unclear whether compounding would have preceded morphological processes such as reduplication, it seems very likely to have preceded derivational affixation. Although derivational affixation also represents a powerful means by which new words can be created from old morphemes, it is associated with a substantial bootstrapping problem. It is hard to imagine how the derivational enterprise could have started without positing an intermediate step of grammaticalization, whereby roots become affixes. Thus, it seems reasonable to assume that the dawn of derivation must have been preceded by the dawn of compounding. This line of reasoning is also employed by Dressler (this volume) and by Jackendoff (2002).

Jackendoff (2002, p. 250) argues that the synchronic character of compounds reveals their early role in the history of human language development. Compounds may be seen as the result of a simple merging of two elements, with the exact relations between constituents being highly variable. As such, Jackendoff claims that they may be regarded as 'protolinguistic "fossils"', a structural type that has survived from the earliest forms of human language (cf. Bickerton, 1990) and which are characterized by syntactically less constrained relations between elements. This claim is consistent with the role of compounding in the languages of the world that we see today. As noted by Dressler (this volume), languages may have compounding without affixation, but the reverse does not seem evident. Thus, when we study compounds, we examine the fundamental characteristics of morphology in language and the fundamentals of the human creative capacity for morphological processing and representation.

This fundamental capacity would seem to have two sides. On the one hand, compound words need to be easily segmentable into their constituent morphemes in much the same way as sentences need to be segmentable into their constituent words. If this were not the case, new compound forms that children and adults encounter would not be interpretable (as we know they are). On the other hand, the compound sequence as a whole must be stored in memory so that it becomes a new lexical item that can be retrieved as a single entity for production and whose idiosyncratic meaning can be stored in the mind (as we know it often is).

Seen in this light, compound words are structures at the crossroads between words and sentences reflecting both the properties of linguistic representation in the mind and grammatical processing. As such, they offer us a unique opportunity to understand the interplay between storage and computation in the mind, the manner in which morphological and semantic factors impact the nature of storage and the manner in which the computational processes serve the demands of on-line language comprehension and production.

In the sections below, the nature of these opportunities for understanding are discussed both with reference to the insights that have already been gained, as well as with reference to those insights that stand to be gained by the psycholinguistic enterprise.

1.1 The interplay between storage and computation

For both monomorphemic words and sentences, the question of storage vs. computation is really not very much of a question. It seems quite clear, for example, that monomorphemic words must simply be memorized. With the exception of relatively few onomatopoeic items, simple words represent arbitrary associations of sound and meaning. Thus, the fact that the word *dog*, for example, refers to a four-legged domesticated animal is simply a fact that must be stored. The meaning of *dog* cannot be computed from the meanings of its phonological components because its phonological subcomponents are not meaningful. Quite the opposite is true of sentences. Although some sentences can, of course, be committed to memory, human language is such that this is not a strategy that is very likely to result in success in either language comprehension or production. The reason for this, as pointed out by Chomsky (1988, p. 5), is that most sentences that one encounters in the normal process of language comprehension are unique events and that the number of distinct possibilities is virtually infinite.

It seems, then, we stand to gain little insight into the relative advantages of storage vs. computation in the mind by studying either of these structures because, for both of them, the linguistic system has no choice. Where the system does have a choice, however, is in the domain of multimorphemic words. An inflected verb such as *going*, for example, seems like an ideal candidate for the preference of computation over storage. Although the word could easily be stored as a whole in the mental lexicon, it could also easily be computed from the meanings and forms of its constituent morphemes *go* and *-ing*. The fact that this is much more the case for regular forms such as *coming* and *going* than for irregular forms such as *came* and *went* has been the subject of considerable debate in both the psycholinguistic and popular literature, and forms the basis of claims made by Pinker (1999), for example, that the lexical processing system shows a duality of processing, whereby regular forms are computed and irregular ones are stored in the mental lexicon.

Pinker's framework for the representation of affixed words has been very valuable in offering a well-defined domain for fundamental debate between proponents of a symbolic approach to language modeling and proponents of a connectionist approach who claim Pinker's distinction between words and rules to be artifactual. However, the framework has been somewhat less useful in offering a domain in which to test the interplay between storage and computation because it presents the difference between them as correlated

Why Study Compound Processing? An overview of the issues

with a difference between types of words (regular vs. irregular). Compounds, in contrast, allow for plausible storage and computation for the same set of words. In principle, a compound such as *houseboat* could be either stored as a whole or computed from its constituent morphemes (or both). By examining which one of these options is actually preferred, we stand to learn something about whether the language system as a whole seeks to maximize storage efficiency or to maximize computational efficiency.

If the human mind were constructed such that it sought to maximize computational efficiency, we would imagine that there would be great pressure for compound words to be represented as whole atomic lexical forms as soon as possible after they are initially recognized as organizations of root morphemes. The reason for this is that such an approach would limit the need for morphological composition to the times when a speaker constructs a novel compound and would limit the need for morphological decomposition to the times when a listener encounters a novel compound. At all other times, a compound word would simply be extracted from memory or matched to an existing lexical representation that was functionally indistinguishable from a monomorphemic word. Such an arrangement is depicted in Fig. 1.1a.

At the opposite extreme, we might imagine a mental architecture that seeks only to maximize storage efficiency (as depicted in Fig. 1.1b). In this case, compound words would never be represented in the mind as distinct from their constituent morphemes so that, in principle, they would entail no additional storage cost. Thus, for example, if a speaker's vocabulary consisted of 100 monomorphemic lexical items (with no restrictions on their combinability), compounding (assuming the bi-directionality that allows *boathouse* and *houseboat* to be distinct compounds) would allow for the creation of $(N!/(N-2)!)$ or 9,900 new words for free. Such an architecture would, of course, not be cost free in terms of computation. Every time a compound word was recognized, it would need to be decomposed into an ordered arrangement of morphemes and interpreted anew in terms of those constituents and that ordering. Similarly, because they could not simply be extracted from memory, all compounds

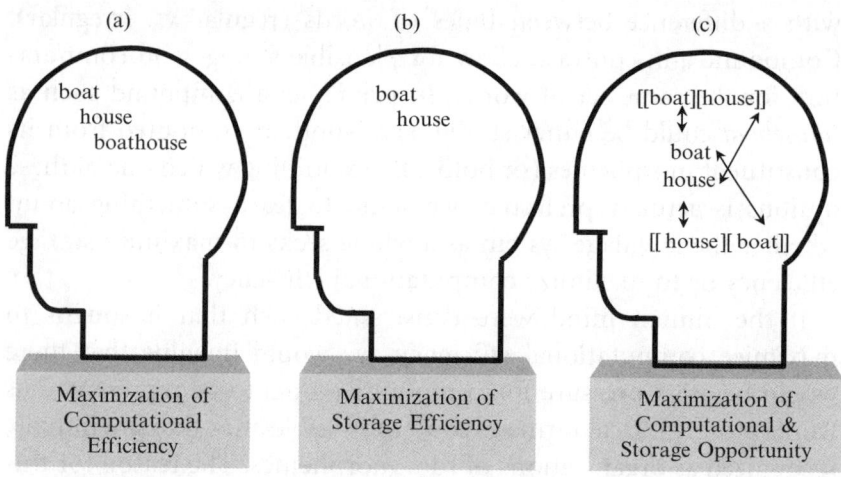

FIG. 1.1 Three representations of compound words in the mental lexicon

In (a) compounds are represented as full forms independently of the representations of their constituents. In (b) only the constituents are represented. In (c) both constituents and morphologically structured compounds are represented and linked.

would need to be produced as an ordered sequence of morphemes in much the way that phrases are.

The results of recent research into compound recognition (see Jarema, this volume) have suggested that the human lexical system seeks neither of these extreme alternatives. We see no evidence of the maximization of either computational or storage efficiency but, rather, the maximization of the opportunities for both. It seems that the human mind does not seek to maximize efficiency, by either computing less or storing less. Quite to the contrary, the mind seeks to both store and compute as much as possible. If a compound word has been presented often enough so that it can be lexicalized, it is stored as a representation that can be retrieved as a whole. This, however, does not shut down the process of morphological decomposition for that word, nor does it sever links between the whole compound word and its constituent morphemes. As can be seen in Fig. 1.1c, this *maximization of opportunity* suggests that both compound words and their constituents must be represented in the mental lexicon both with morphological structure and with links to monomorphemic representations. This representation is, by definition, considerably more complex than the representations in Figs. 1.1a and 1.1b because any system that maximizes opportunity is going to possess redundancy and complication that would be avoided in a system that seeks efficiency. This observation leads us to the next point of discussion: How could an inefficient and redundant lexical processing system have advantages over an efficient and elegant one?

In all probability, the expectation that the human mind would strive for efficiency derives from the *zeitgeist* of the 1970s, in which models of mental operations were couched in computer program-like terms. In the design of programs, computational elegance is highly valued, and it seemed perhaps reasonable to assume that the same value of elegance might exist within the functional architecture of the lexical processing system. In addition, because storage space was always at a premium in the early days of computer design, it could have been assumed that a system that was space efficient would have considerable advantages over one that was not. Some three decades later, both these assumptions appear to be anachronistic.

However, even if the *zeitgeist* of the 1970s might account for the erroneous expectation that the lexical processing system would strive for the maximization of efficiency, we are still left with the need for a separate account as to why the system might be inclined to maximize opportunity instead. Although, as yet, there is no conclusive evidence on this point, a reasonable speculation would make reference to the time frame in which the lexical system must operate. Words that one encounters or produces must be processed in well under a second. In the case of word recognition, in particular, the language user has no control over what type of word is to be accessed and can therefore be certain of very little, except the fact that the word must be processed rapidly. Under such environmental demands, it seems plausible that a pre-sorting mechanism, which would have to decide whether a word is one of those to be processed in terms of its constituents or one of those to be processed as a whole word, would either operate too slowly to be effective or would generate so many errors that frequent backtracking would also result in an insufficiently fast system.

Now, what about systems that would not possess an executive front-end but rather a default initial strategy for dealing with constituents vs. whole words? One such system would first recognize words as wholes and then, if necessary, process them in terms of their constituent morphemes. While this may indeed be the architecture underlying the processing of real words in languages like English and French, it seems impossible that this architecture could tell the whole story. One reason for this is that such a system would be incapable of dealing with novel compounds. As is discussed by Dressler (this volume) compounding is a very productive word-formation process, so that the likelihood of encountering a compound that one has neither seen nor heard before is very high. Consider, for example, the difference between an existing compound such as *blackboard* and seemingly exotic novel compounds such as *yellowboard*, *pinkboard*, *orangeboard*, and *brownboard*. Although all of these register as errors in Microsoft Word and none are represented in the CELEX database, each showed between 50 and 1,000 hits on Google at the time of writing. A whole-word first architecture would be incapable of processing such words. The fact that they are easily comprehended, however, suggests that a whole-word first architecture would require a backup parsing system (as will be discussed in greater detail below) or the return to a pre-sorter as described above. For languages such as German, that show extensive novel compounding, such a system would simply not meet everyday processing demands.

An alternative, apparently efficient, system is one that would have obligatory decomposition as the default initial strategy. Such a system would easily be able to handle both existing and novel compounds. However, the disadvantage of this architecture is that it would seem to pass up an obvious speed advantage by having to process a relatively frequent word such as *blackboard* in the same manner as a novel compound that was encountered for the first time. We might also imagine that such a system, uncorrected by a whole-word processor, would have a great deal of difficulty with monomorphemic words such as *carpet* that just happen to contain morphemic substrings (i.e. *car-pet*) in the orthography.

To summarize to this point, it seems likely that a lexical system that would seek to maximize either storage efficiency or computational efficiency might simply be too slow because it would either have to pre-sort words or deal with a substantial number of mis-analyses. In addition, if the assumption that the system ascribes an independent value to elegance is incorrect, there is no reason to reject redundancy as a viable alternative.

A 'maximization of opportunity' system certainly has redundancy in abundance. As represented in a number of models that may be described as horse-race models, such a system would simply allow (on the recognition side) for both whole-word processing as well as morphological processing to occur simultaneously. Thus, under such an architecture, a word such as *blackboard* would be simultaneously processed as a whole as well as in terms of its constituents *black* and *board*. Assuming the representational architecture such as the one shown in Fig. 1.1c, the processing of the word *blackboard* as a whole word and as an ordered set of constituents will result in bi-directional activation, such that the constituents of *blackboard* receive activation both from the process of morphological parsing, as well as from the structured representation of the compound in the mental lexicon. This situation is depicted in Fig. 1.2.

Now, why might such a complicated functional architecture be preferred? The main reason is that it does not require anything to be decided. Rather, all representations that can be activated, will be activated. Novel words will only be processed in terms of their constituent morphemes because there is no whole-word representation to activate, and real words may show graded trade-offs between whole-word and constituent activation. For very frequent words, whole-word activation would be expected to be both stronger and faster. For less frequent words, the morphological route might, in fact, 'get there first'.

The above considerations may then offer an answer as to why the lexical processing system shows no tendency to seek efficiency. Activating everything possible appears to be the easiest and most

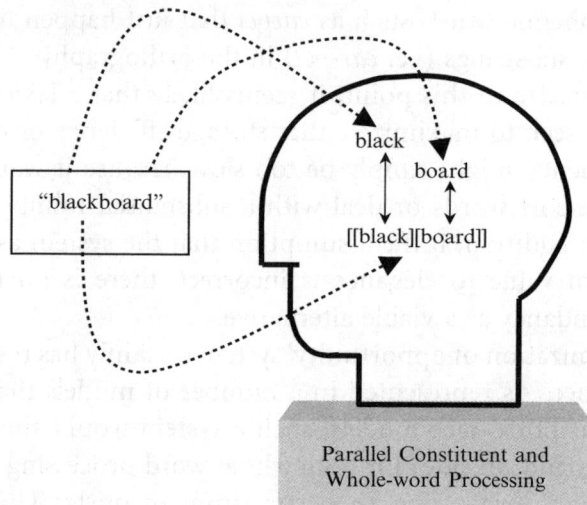

FIG. 1.2 Parallel constituent and whole-word processing
Dual inputs allow whole-words to activate their constituents in the mental lexicon and vice versa.

generally applicable mental architecture for the processing of multimorphemic words under the conditions of uncertainty that characterize word recognition. However, if, as has been suggested, both whole words and constituent morphemes are routinely activated during language processing, then the system will be characterized by redundant activation in the best case and by competing activation in the worst case. As is discussed below, this will create substantial problems for compounds that show a discord between the meanings of their morphemes as independent lexical entries and as constituents within a multimorphemic string.

1.2 The problem of meaning

The compound structures that we have considered so far, such as *blackboard, houseboat,* and *boathouse,* all have relatively straightforward relationships between their constituent and whole-word representations. In this way, they seem much like words such as *going,* for which decomposition of the string into its constituent morphemes poses no problem at all. However, even for the relatively uncomplicated compounds above, some reflection leads us to the conclusion that the meaning of the compound word cannot simply be derived from the meanings of its parts. Whereas *going* is really no more than the combination of the meanings of *go* + *ing*, there is nothing in the meaning of the morphemes *black* + *board* that would lead to the conclusion that their combination would be something upon which one writes. Similarly, once one knows that a *houseboat* is a boat that one can sleep and cook in, the contributions of its morphemes to that meaning seem clear. However, a priori, *houseboat* could just as easily be a boat that you cannot sleep in, but is rather shaped like a house (e.g. with a triangular bow and a square stern). It is also not obvious why other types of boats, such as arks and cruise ships, are not called *houseboats*. These considerations strengthen the case for the implausibility of a lexical processing system that would represent compound words solely in terms of their constituents. They also suggest that lexicalized compound words are never semantically transparent in the sense that their whole-word meanings are fully predictable from the meanings of their constituents. In the best cases, only the reverse is true: that the semantic functions of the constituents can be predicted from the meaning of the whole word.

The worst cases are quite a bit worse indeed. A surprising number of compounds across languages that have been studied have non-transparent meaning relations between their constituents and their whole words. In English, for example, most of the members of the *berry* family of compounds have this property. The contribution of the meanings of *blue* and *berry* in *blueberry* seem clear (again, only in retrospect), but for other members such as *boysenberry, cranberry, elderberry, gooseberry, loganberry, raspberry*, and *strawberry*, it is exceedingly unlikely that the meaning of the first constituent as an independent morpheme contributes to the meaning of the whole word.

The first psycholinguistically revealing fact concerning the semantic opacity of these forms is that it is so rarely noticed by native speakers. Thus, the system will extract constituents from compounds but does not depend on doing so. This appears to be consistent with a 'maximization of opportunity' framework that posits a mental architecture in which all representations that can be activated will be activated. Under such an architecture, the system remains relatively crash-proof by being able to extract all that it can—namely, the whole meaning for each word as well as the fact that they are all berries. This in itself may be quite revealing of cognitive processing in general, but the exact mechanisms that are involved for stimuli such as these have not yet been investigated.

It would appear, however, that an account of how the lexical processing system deals with semantic opacity would have to make reference to a fundamental distinction within the class of *berry* compounds described above. For some compounds (e.g. *boysenberry, cranberry, loganberry*) the initial constituent simply does not contribute to the meaning of the compound because it is treated as though it were a Proper Noun. In this case, we would want to know the exact mechanisms that underlie the system's ability to posit two morphemes in the compound, where only one is a known word. Understanding how this is done would very likely have application to a number of domains in cognitive science as well as to our understanding of lexical acquisition, which for many languages crucially depends on the ability to extract new roots from both compound and affixed forms.

The second type of semantic opacity shown in the *berry* compounds is one that has been more studied in the psycholinguistic literature. This is the type in which both constituents are known morphemes (e.g. *elderberry, strawberry*), but the meaning of at least one morpheme is not consistent with the meaning of the whole word, so that there is no meaning of *elder* in *elderberry*, for example. As is discussed in Jarema (this volume), there is experimental evidence that semantically opaque compounds such as these do not show the normal pattern of cross-activation between the constituents of a compound and its whole-word representation. What is less clear, however, is what representational or processing factors account for this change in activation pattern and how they might

Why Study Compound Processing? An overview of the issues

interact with the functional architecture posited in Fig. 1.2. One possibility (e.g. Sandra 1990; Zwitserlood, 1994) is that such words do not undergo morphological decomposition. Another possibility (e.g. Libben, 1998) is that their representations are not structured in the same way as those for more transparent compounds such as *blackboard*. A third possibility is that the links between the whole word and its constituents in the mental lexicon are either less strong or absent. If any of these explanations are correct, we would have evidence that the architecture depicted in Fig. 1.2, or any other architecture for that matter, is not fixed and universally applicable to all types of compounds. Thus, research into the effects of semantic transparency has implications for the adequacy of a universally applicable lexical processing architecture vs. one that is free to be organized differently depending on the system's experience with individual words and word types. Clearly, the latter case would favour a connectionist rather than a symbolic approach to modeling.

In Fig. 1.3, the three possibilities above are represented as modifications to the architecture in Fig. 1.2. In all three cases,

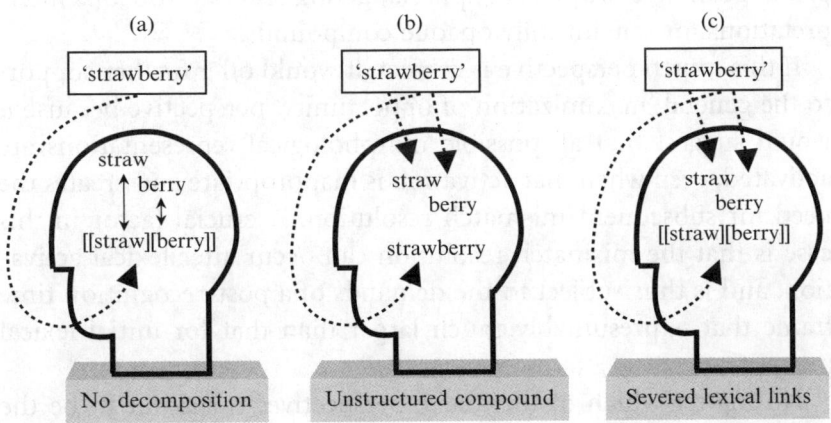

FIG. 1.3 Three possible effects of semantic opacity

In (a) the input is not broken down into morphemes; in (b) the internal representation is not structured (and therefore can have no links); in (c) only the links between the whole word and its constituents are absent.

a semantically, partially opaque compound has diminished constituent activation resulting from either the absence of morphological parsing, diminished morphological structuring, or the lack of connections between representations. Thus, what the models have in common is that they all account for the effects of semantic opacity by assuming that, for one reason or another, compound constituents receive less activation. A fourth possible line of explanation takes an entirely different approach. Following the line of reasoning in Libben and de Almeida (2001) and Libben, Buchanan, and Colangelo (2004), it is also possible that semantic opacity does not diminish constituent activation at all, but rather creates a mismatch of activation whereby the semantic representations activated by *elder* as an independent morpheme is non-overlapping with the semantic representations activated by *elderberry*. Under such circumstances, there is semantic incongruity that requires resolution through the inhibition of inappropriate semantic activation. These inhibitory processes elevate response times giving the appearance, in priming experiments, of a failure to activate. However, under this account, activation is initially full, and only diminished in a later stage of processing. Libben *et al.* (2004) argue that this inhibitory process can be disrupted in aphasia, giving rise to erroneous interpretations for semantically opaque compounds.

If this fourth perspective is correct, it would offer further support to the general 'maximization of opportunity' perspective because it would suggest that all possible morphological representations are activated, even when that activation is inappropriate and creates the need for subsequent mismatch resolution. A crucial factor in this case is that the mismatch resolution can occur after lexical activation, and is thus subject to the demands of a post-recognition time frame that is presumably much larger than that for initial lexical processing.

No matter which of the above perspectives turns out to be the most profitable way to understand the effects of semantic transparency, it seems clear that stimuli of this sort offer an important window to fundamental issues in how words are represented in the mind, and how morphology and semantics interact in lexical processing. As noted above, one important factor to be considered in this research is that, although the system may show sensitivity to semantic transparency under certain task conditions such as primed lexical decision, this opacity does not seem to disrupt everyday language processing and, indeed, may be invisible to other experimental paradigms that do not have a decision component, such as eye-tracking. Thus, a resolution of the issues surrounding semantic opacity needs to account for the exact nature of the processing challenges that semantic opacity creates, as well as the means by which those challenges are overcome so that both transparent and opaque words can be processed with ease.

Two other important considerations, which have not been addressed above, are whether we need to look outside the specific characteristics of individual compounds to account for semantic opacity effects and whether semantic opacity is fundamentally a property of the compound word or a property of its individual morphemes.

With respect to the first issue, it seems at least possible that the nature of a compound's morphological family as defined in Schreuder and Baayen (1997) and de Jong et al. (2002) needs to be taken into consideration. For example, it may be the case that, because so many *berry* compounds are semantically opaque, native speakers have a higher tolerance for opacity in compounds with *berry* as their morphological and semantic head, as compared to words that have a morpheme such as *stick* as the final constituent. In the latter case, a semantically opaque word such as *joystick* may really stand out, because most other members of the family are relatively transparent (e.g. *broomstick, candlestick, drumstick, lipstick*). If this were the case, our understanding of transparency effects would need to take into account the connections between whole compound words in the mental lexicon, in addition to the connections between compounds and monomorphemic constituents.

The second issue, whether opacity is a property of whole words or constituents, is taken up in three chapters of this volume (Dressler, Jarema, and Levy, Goral, and Obler). At issue is whether the opacity of a word such as *strawberry*, for which the locus of opacity is the initial non-head constituent, differs from the opacity of a word such as *jailbird*, in which the opacity is localized in the morphological head. If transparency is a property of the entire word, it will matter little where the opacity is localized, but rather only how much there is. If this turns out to be the case, it would suggest that the postulation of separate bi-directional arrows between constituents and compounds in Fig. 1.2 must be wrong. Such a representation assumes that each constituent contributes independently to the relationship between the compound and its constituents. If, however, semantic opacity is a property of the relationship between the meaning of a constituent in isolation and its meaning within the multimorphemic string, it seems very likely that we will need to consider both the semantic and morphological roles that a constituent plays within the compound's overall structure. In order to make any headway on that issue, we need to address the question immediately below.

1.3 Is morphological structure represented in the mind?

One of the key opportunities provided by the study of compounds is the opportunity to study the representation of linguistic structure in the mind. The reason for this brings us back to the differences between sentences, which we assume cannot be profitably stored *en masse*, and multimorphemic words, most of which we assume must be stored. When we speak of the syntactic structure of sentences, then, we are speaking of a potentially fleeting structure that must be computed on-line during comprehension and production. The linguistic structure of a compound, in contrast, must be represented in the mind in a relatively stable form. But, what is the nature of this representation? Here we would want to gain an understanding both of how much morphological detail is associated with the representation of compound words in the mind and how that knowledge is instantiated in the functional architecture of the mental lexicon.

At the simplest level, we can think of the morphological structure of *houseboat* as a specification that the word is made up of two morphemes, the first of which is *house* and the second of which is *boat*. This structural determination would capture the important fact that *boathouse* and *houseboat* do not mean the same things.

The problem with the representing of compounds such as *houseboat* and *boathouse* as simply an ordered set of morphemes, however, is that such a representation would fall short of accounting for the fact that a speaker of English, even one who had perhaps never heard either word before, immediately knows that *boathouse* is a type of *house* and that *houseboat* is a type of *boat*. In order to account for this latter fact, we need the concept of morphological head. Now, how could such a concept be represented in the mind? One possibility is that the concept of head is not represented in the word at all. It might be derived from what the speaker knows about the properties of the English language in general because, in English, all compounds have their heads as the last (rightmost) constituent. This approach, however, would not work for languages such as French, which can have both right-headed (e.g. *grandmère*, 'grandmother') and left-headed compounds (e.g. *Maison Blanche*, 'White House'). Let us assume, then, that morphological headedness is a property of the word and proceed to ask how this morphological property might be represented.

As indicated above, there seem to be two possibilities: one is that headedness falls out from how compounds and their constituents are linked in the mental lexicon so that, for example, there is a stronger link between the head and its monomorphemic representation than for the modifier and its monomorphemic representation. The second possibility posits some explicit representation of morphological headedness. To date, there have been no psycholinguistic or neurolinguistic studies that have addressed these alternatives directly. It seems, however, that the resolution of these accounts would have important consequences. If it turns out that morphological structure is explicitly represented, this would suggest that the mental lexicon cannot simply be an organization of lexical representations. Rather, those representations would need to be augmented by the structural properties that characterize each particular multimorphemic word.

For compounds, such augmentation would minimally include headedness specifications as well as possibly a specification of the lexical category of each constituent. If this were the case, the implication would be that compounds such as *belltower* and *watchtower*, despite the fact that they are both nouns, would have different psychological properties because *watchtower* has a verb as its initial constituent and *belltower* has a noun as its initial constituent. As is discussed by Semenza and Mondini (this volume), it seems to be the case that this difference in the lexical category of the non-head constituents indeed affects the performance of Italian aphasics who have difficulty in the production of verbs. This finding clearly offers support for the view that compounds cannot simply be processed in terms of their whole-word representations.

Finally, we might consider whether, in addition to the above, compounds show evidence of the hierarchical linguistic structure that is captured by tree diagrams in theoretical treatments of both morphology and syntax.

This question has been addressed in only a handful of studies so far. The reason for this is most probably that the investigation of hierarchical morphological structure requires that words with at least three morphemes be investigated, as the examples below will illustrate. At present, however, there seem to be so many unresolved issues in the processing of bimorphemic words that researchers have tended to shy away from yet more complicated word types.

Nevertheless, those studies that have been carried out suggest that compound processing might offer our best opportunity to explore the hierarchy phenomenon. As discussed in Libben (2003), the question of whether hierarchical structure is relevant to the processing of affixed words such as *refillable* can be very elusive. Although there is a well-understood linguistic reason why this word must be assigned the structure *refill + able* rather than *re + fillable*, namely that the prefix *re-* can only attach to verbs, this linguistic analysis does not seem to constrain participants' on-line processing. One possible reason for this is that the morphological structure of such a prefixed and suffixed word does not have any overt semantic consequences. Such is not the case for compounds, however. Whereas *refillable* can plausibly be parsed as either *refill+able* or *re+fillable* with the same meaning, there is little doubt that a triconstituent compound such as *basketball hoop* is composed of *basketball+hoop* rather than *basket + ballhoop*, which would have a novel and entirely different meaning. While it is true that English orthographic conventions make this structural configuration clear by only allowing a space at the major morpheme boundary, compound constituent structure is no less clear in languages such as German, which represents multiconstituent compounds without spaces, or in languages such as Chinese, which represents all compounds with spaces throughout.

We can thus be reasonably confident that native speakers are able to perceive triconstituent compounds such as *basketball hoop* as being hierarchically structured. But is it not possible that this is simply a result of the fact that *basketball* is an existing word and *ballhoop* is not? Some recent research (e.g. Baayen *et al.* 2002) suggests that this cannot be the whole story. They found that there is a marked tendency by native speakers of both Dutch and German to prefer left-branching compounds (i.e. those with the major morphological boundary between the second and third constituents) and that this structural tendency is mirrored in the processing of triconstituent novel compounds for which neither the individual constituents nor their bi-constituent pairings are real words. In this case, the resulting hierarchical structure cannot make reference to the presence or absence of constituent words in the mental lexicon, and must be computed on-line.

To summarize then, early evidence concerning the morphological structuring of compounds suggests that ordering, headedness, constituent category, and hierarchical structure may all play roles in how compound words are represented in the mind and how they are processed. Exactly what the processing and structural correlates of these facts are is still unclear. What is clear, however, is that compound words offer an important opportunity for their understanding because, unlike affixed morphological structures, almost anything can combine with anything. This means that morpheme reversals are licensed in a way that they are not for affixed words (e.g. *unhappy*, but not *happy-un; *happiness*, but not *ness-happy). It also means that the lexical category of one constituent cannot be predicted from the category of another constituent.

This morphological freedom, which seems to characterize compounding in all languages that have been studied psycholinguistically, leads us to the last question to be discussed in this chapter—the question of morphological parsing.

1.4 How do we find words within words?

If indeed, as has been claimed above, compounding is a very productive morphological process such that the probability of encountering a novel form such as *yellowboard* is very high, and if it is also true that such novel forms are only comprehensible in terms of their constituents, we are left with the question which is at the center of this section: How do we find those constituents?

This is considerably less of a problem for affixed words because, for these words, the system can capitalize on the fact that languages have few prefixes and suffixes, relative to the number of roots. Thus, the system could keep such affixes 'in its back pocket' as a short list and use that short list to strip affixes from their stems as required (see Taft and Forster, 1975). Such a strategy will simply not work for compounds, however. Because, as we have said, almost anything can combine with anything in compounding, there is no short list that a morphological parsing system could make use of. Although this may not seem like an insurmountable problem for English compounds such as *yellowboard*, it is a very substantial problem in the visual domain for languages such as German in which compounds are written as single words without spaces and for which many morphemes can be easily compounded to yield words such as *Sonntagnachmittagspaziergang* (*Sonn+tag+nach+mittag+spazier+gang* = 'Sunday afternoon stroll') as both lexicalized and novel structures.

So, how are such compounds parsed into their constituents, and what can this tell us about the mind? As is discussed in Jarema (this volume), this issue was addressed for English by Libben (1994) and Libben *et al.* (1999) who presented evidence that the lexical processing system searches for morphemes in a beginning-to-end fashion. What is most relevant for the discussion here, however, is that this beginning-to-end parse does not simply construct a single compound representation for a series of morphemes, but rather appears to find all available morphemes. This suggests that the parsing system, like the rest of the lexical system, seeks to maximize opportunity by extracting all possible morpheme sets from an input string and by constructing all possible morphological representations. Although such a parsing system is less efficient than one that would seek from the outset to find the correct parse of an input string, it seems the one that is best adapted to the indeterminate nature of compound words and, perhaps more importantly, to the overall nature of the lexical processing system.

1.5 Conclusions

This chapter began with the observation that compounding represents the fundamental word-formation process across the world's languages and, as such, it affords a unique opportunity to understand fundamental aspects of mental architecture. In all probability we have just begun to exploit this potential for understanding. Nevertheless, as has been stressed throughout this chapter, some conceptualizations seem to better accommodate the available facts than others. In particular, it has been claimed that compound processing, as a whole, points to a view of mind that is characterized by redundancy rather than efficiency, and by a propensity to create as many distinct representations as possible.

It has also been claimed in this chapter that compound processing allows us to better understand some of the dominant issues in the psycholinguistic study of the mental lexicon—issues such as semantic transparency, morphological structure, morphological parsing, and the interplay between storage and computation. The contribution of these perspectives is twofold: On the one hand, they aid us in piecing together how the mind handles the on-line demands of everyday language processing. On the other hand, they reveal to us just how complex that processing may be. In the long run, this may turn out to be the enduring contribution of the research. Recent advances in the investigation of compound processing, in particular, and of lexical processing, in general, have done much more than help us to evaluate the merits of one hypothesis over another. They have made it possible to reveal mental phenomena that until recently have been completely shielded from scientific scrutiny.

As is often noted, the recognition of words is extraordinarily fast and almost entirely effortless under conditions of normal language use, in which we are concentrating on anything but the lexical processes that allow us to carry on a conversation, read a novel, or evaluate road signs while driving. This effortlessness is almost certainly made possible by a computational encapsulation that allows complexity without conscious intervention. As is evident throughout this book, the methods, theoretical constructs, and data made available through the past quarter-century of research have enabled us break through that encapsulation, bringing to the fore the fact that, in human cognition, not all things that appear to be easy are necessarily simple.

2

Compound Types

WOLFGANG U. DRESSLER

2.1 Introduction and definitions

2.1.1

Compounds are important objects of morphological investigations, because compounds are present in all languages of the world (as far as described in grammars). Thus compounding is the widest-spread morphological technique. This may be formulated in two transitive implications: if a language has inflection, it also has derivation and compounding, and if a language has derivation, it also has compounding, but not vice-versa. Keeping different types of compounding apart is essential for psycholinguistic investigations, in order to guarantee comparability of results both within the same language and in a cross-linguistic perspective. What is normal within the system of compounding may differ considerably from one language to another. Still there exist universal or, at least, general preferences, a subject for psycholinguistic explanations in itself.

The term compounding or composition goes back to the Latin *vocabulorum genus quod appellant compositicium* 'the word class which is called composite' (Varro) and *figura nominum composita* 'composed structure of nouns' of the Ancient Roman grammarians Priscianus, Donatus, etc., where Latin *com-positum* is a literal translation of Greek *sýn-theton*. This focus on noun-noun compounds corresponds to a general preference for this type of compound in most languages.

Compounding is part of grammar, governed by non-conscious rules. Thus we exclude extragrammatical combinations of so-called expressive morphology, such as echo-word formation, as in English *hip-hop* or contaminations (blends) as in *smog* (from *smoke* and *fog*) or German *jein* (from *ja* 'yes' and *nein* 'no'), cf. Dressler (2000).

2.1.2

Compounds thus can be loosely defined as grammatical combinations of words, that is of lexical items or lexemes, to form new words. More explicit universal definitions of the intensional type are not only theory-dependent (cf. ten Hacken, 1994; Fabb, 1998; Olsen, 2000) but also cross-linguistically never watertight—in many languages there are exceptions or fuzzy transitions to non-compounding. The same holds for internal classifications of compounds. Therefore we will focus on extensional definitions (cf. Olsen, 2000; ten Hacken, 2000) and on the descriptions of compound prototypes (cf. also Mel'čuk, 1997, pp. 87ff). In our exemplification we will concentrate on regular compounds, that is rule-governed, particularly productive compound formations, which account for those compounds which are of primary interest to psycholinguistic investigations.

In a first approximation, a prototypical compound is a word which consists of two prototypical lexical words. This excludes combinations of clitics, such as It. *glielo* = *gli* 'to him' + *lo* 'it', because clitics are non-prototypical words or, according to Anderson (1992) phrasal affixes. As a consequence, combinations of a lexical word and a clitic are also excluded, for example It. *darlo* 'to give it'. Derivations from compounds are derivations, not compounds, for example E. *high-land-er*, although an exact distinction may be difficult. For example, E. *generative grammarian* is a compound in form, but a derivation in meaning, because it is derived from *generative grammar* (on such so-called bracketing paradoxes cf. Lieber, 1992, pp. 87ff; Rainer, 1993, pp. 102ff). Moreover, different theories distinguish compounding and derivation in different ways (cf. ten Hacken, 1994).

Prototypically all members of a compound recur as free forms (i.e. autonomous words). This is not the case with so-called cranberry morphs (cf. Aronoff, 1976, p. 10). The first members of E. *cran-berry, boysen-berry, huckle-berry* do not occur independently, but they can be assigned a lexical meaning which distinguishes them from those of other berries. Neoclassical compounds (cf. Bauer, 1998) may also contain non-autonomous parts, so-called combining forms, for example *helio-graphy, biblio-therapy, biblio-graphy* (cf. Iacobini, 1998). For Chinese, see Myers (this volume).

2.1.3

Next, compound members prototypically belong to major lexical categories (especially nouns, verbs, and adjectives, see below section 3); grammatical function words are only marginally involved, for example Ge. *Ich-sucht* 'selfishness' (lit. 'I-mania'), E. *Yes-man*, the conscious feminist occasionalism *her-story* (as an analogical adaptation of *history*). Combinations of function words, such as *which-ever, in-between, with-in, on-to* are rare and not productive, as is expected for closed-class items. Higher numerals, for example *21, 35*, are a very special type of compounds; note that compounding of non-natural numbers (e.g. *a, b, c...; x, y*) is not possible (except in mathematical formulae), in contrast to potential derivation, as in ordinal number formation (e.g. *the nth, x^{th}*).

2.1.4

How can compounds be distinguished from multi-lexical units in the format of syntactic phrases? (called *polirematiche* in Italian, cf. Grossmann and Rainer, 2004). In general, the simple syntactic criterion of separability distinguishes compounds from syntactic phrases, viz. the impossibility vs. possibility of: (1) changing linear order (see the end of section 1); and (2) inserting another word between the members of a compound vs. a syntactic phrase. Thus the adjective *big* may be inserted within the phrase *a high school* (→ *a high, big school*), but not within the compound *high-school* (→ *a *high-big-school* vs.

correct *a big high-school*). However, fixed idiomatic phrases (called constructional idioms by Booij, 2003, 2005a, p. 83) may not be interrupted either. For example, the idiomatic verb-phrase *to kick the bucket* may be inflected on the head verb *kick* but not on the dependent noun *bucket* and does not allow insertion between the definite article and the head noun of the noun-phrase itself (*he kicked the *old *buckets*) without losing its idiomatic meaning. A second syntactic criterion is, in principle, the inaccessibility of the internal structure of compounds to syntax (cf. ten Hacken, 1994; Bisetto and Scalise, 1999): compounds are 'anaphoric islands' or atoms (Scalise, 1992, p. 195). Thus the sentence 'Truck drivers do not fill *them up' is ungrammatical if the anaphoric pronoun *them* corefers to the compound-internal, non-referential noun *truck* (for exceptions cf. Dressler, 1987).

2.1.5

Semantic distinctive criteria are less obvious. Thus, syntactic phrases may be idiomatically lexicalized in ways similar to compounds. Note the German formal equivalents of E. *high-school*: the compound *die Hoch-schule* 'the university, polytechnic' vs. the noun phrase *die Hohe Schule* which may refer to any high-level school or routine, but not to a tall school building, which would be orthographically distinguished (*die hohe Schule*). The above-mentioned syntactic criterion is distinctive here: one may insert something within the idiomatic phrase, but not within the compound. For example one may say sarcastically *Die Hohe, allzu Hohe Schule* 'the high, all too high school'.

2.1.6

Phonological distinctions are valid in languages (e.g. English, Turkish) where prosodic criteria distinguish compounds from phrases, such as the compound stress rule which assigns a single compound stress to the first member of E. *bláck-board* vs. the sequence minor and major stress in *blàck bóard*. But not all of English compounding follows this rule, for example *blue-green* with level stress or *apple píe* vs. the expected pattern in *ápple cake* (Lieber, 1992, p. 83). Segmental phonological deletions or assimilations may be obligatory in compounds but excluded or optional in phrases, for example It. *lung-arno* 'street along the river Arno' with deletion of the final vowel in the first member adjective *lungo* 'long' (Scalise, 1992).

2.1.7

A morphological distinction is relevant in those languages where all members of a phrase are inflected by agreement, whereas parts of a prototypical compound are not (cf. Booij, 2005a, p. 82). For example, the plurals of the above-mentioned German minimal pair are *die Hoch-schule-n* vs. the constructional idiom *die Hohe-n Schule-n*, where both the adjectival modifier and the head noun are pluralized.

2.1.8

However neither the prosodic nor the morphological criterion may hold for so-called juxtapositions, non-prototypical compounds which are distinguished from phrases only by the syntactic criterion. For example, Ge. *der Hohe-priester* 'the (Jewish) high-priest' with main stress on the first member (modifier) and secondary stress on the second (head) may inflect either only the final part, as in Gen. *des Hohe-priester-s* or both members, that is *des Hohe-n-priester-s*, without any meaning difference. The second variant is more phrase-like, the first more compound-like. The prototypical compound would be (potential) *Hoch-priester*. Compare the single or double inflection of the Polish toponym *Biały-stok* (lit. 'white slope'), Gen. *Biały-stok-u* or *Biał-ego-stok-u* (cf. adj. masc. *biały*, Gen. *biał-ego* 'white'). A partially similar difference exists between more phrase-like Italian 'loose compounds' vs. prototypical 'strict compounds' (Scalise, 1992, pp. 180–1), for example *mezza-luna* 'half-moon', Pl. *mezze-lune* vs. *lung-arno*, Pl. *lung-arn-i*.

Most contributions to this volume include any multilexical unit with idiomatic meaning into the category of such loose compounds instead of syntactic phrases, that is constructional idioms. This may be conceptually warranted, but it is in contradiction with the mainstream in theoretical morphology.

2.1.9

Thus syntactic phrases (including those with idiomatic meanings) should be assumed whenever they are syntactically well-formed and include unmistakably syntactic indicators which are not allowed within compounds (cf. Booij, 2005a, pp. 83f, pace Zwanenburg, 1992a; Jarema, Semenza, & Mondini, Nicoladis this volume). A case in point is Fr. *sortie de secours* 'emergency exit' (lit. 'exit of help'), It. *mulino a vento* 'wind-mill' as opposed to the loose compounds Fr. *homme grenouille* 'frogman' (lit. 'man frog'), Sp. *hombre anuncio* 'poster man' without a syntactic indicator of the relation between head and modifying non-head, thus not a well-formed syntactic phrase (cf. Rainer, 1993, p. 42; Moyna, 2004). French and the other Romance, as well as Slavic, languages often have such syntactic phrases where Germanic languages have compounds, for example E. *rail-way*, Ge. *Eisen-bahn* (lit. 'iron-path') vs. Fr. *chemin de fer* lit. 'way of iron', Ru. *Železnaja daroga* (with an adjective derived from 'iron'). In this case Italian and Spanish have neoclassical compounds: It. *ferro-via*, Sp. *ferro-carril*. Syntactic indicators may occur in phrasal compounds (cf. Bisetto and Scalise, 1999), such as It. *tira-l-oro* 'gilder' (lit. 'draws the gold'), which would be a well-formed verb phrase, but is a noun and thus not a well-formed noun phrase and therefore classifies as a compound. More on the distinction between compounds and syntactic phrases can be found in Spencer (1991, pp. 319ff).

Juxtapositions may be understood as diachronic transition stages in the grammaticalization of syntactic phrases to compounds. Within the further grammaticalization process of compounds into derivatives, whereby one part of the compound changes into an affix, we also find a transition stage, the so-called semi-affixes or affixoids (cf. Wolff, 1984, pp. 89ff; Bauer, 2005; Booij, 2005b).

2.1.10

Let us begin with semi-suffixes/suffixoids as transition towards suffixation: the German productive suffixoid-*tum*, cognate of E. *doom* and the suffix-*dom*, derived from it, was originally identical with an independent, now obsolete noun. It is a prima-facie suffix, but with the two following characteristics of compound heads: (1) it carries secondary stress (vs. primary stress); (2) it is preceded by the compound-linking (interfix)-*en*- (see below section 6, cf. Fuhrhop, 1998). The same holds for the suffixoid-*schaft* (cognate of E.-*ship*), for example in *Fráu-en-schàft* 'women's organization' (lit. 'women-ship'), *Fráu-en-tùm* 'women-dom', cf. the compounds *Fráu-en-àrzt* 'women's doctor, gynecologist', *Fráu-en-fèind* 'woman hater' vs. the derivatives *Frau-chen* 'little woman', *frau-lich* 'womanly'. Thus, synchronically, suffixoid formation lies between prototypical compounding and prototypical suffixation, diachronically it represents a transition stage in the grammaticalization of compounds to derivatives.

For corresponding cases of prefixoids it is even harder to decide between prefixes, initial members of compounds and transitional prefixoids, as the debate about English prefixation has shown (cf. Bauer, 1983; Iacobini, 1998; Ralli, 2003). For example, is *over-ripe* a compound of a preposition with an adjective or is it a case of prefixation?

2.1.11

Separable 'prefixes' (or particles) of German and Dutch belong to the category of juxtapositions rather than to the category of compounds (cf. Booij, 2005a, pp. 84f; Bauer, 2005), as in Ge. Inf. *áus-geh-en* 'to go out', 3.Sg.Pres. *geh-t...áus*, past participle *áus-ge-gang-en*, according to the criterion of partial separability, because in finite forms long syntactic constituents may be inserted between verb and particle, whereas in the past participle only the prefix *ge-* is inserted. The same holds for separable compound verbs (cf. Wurzel, 1998), such as Ge. *Schi-fahr-en* 'to ski (lit. ski-drive)', 3.Sg.Pres. *fährt...Schi*, past participle *Schi-ge-fahr-en*. For corresponding Dutch compound verbs see Ackema (1999).

As we can see, an intensional definition of compounds must be preferential, by referring to prototypes, rather than discrete. Accordingly, an extensional definition leads to the identification of several transitions between compounding and adjacent areas of grammar (cf. Olsen, 2000; ten Hacken, 2000; Dressler *et al.*, 2005).

2.2 Productivity

2.2.1

Our intention of focusing on productive compounding (cf. also Levy *et al.*; Nicoladis, Myers, this volume) necessitates a definition of morphological productivity (cf. Bauer, 2001; Kiefer, 2001), including degrees of productivity. Morphological productivity, on the level of the potential system of grammar, can still be defined in H. Schultink's way (as translated by van Marle 1985: 45) as: 'the possibility for language users to coin, unintentionally, a number of formations which are in principle uncountable.'

Combined with lexical and pragmatic factors, productivity therefore accounts for actual type and token frequencies of compounds and compound types (cf. Dressler and Ladányi, 2000; Fuhrhop, 1998). Type frequency not only concerns the number of compounds of a certain type, but also the family size of compound members, that is the number of compounds which share the same member, especially if they occur in the same (initial or final) position (cf. Schreuder and Baayen, 1997), for example all compounds starting with *land-*. This is positional family size. The token frequencies of such family members are also relevant for productivity on the level of performance (Myers, this volume).

2.2.2

Compounding rules are, *ceteris paribus,* most productive when they also apply to words of foreign origin, that is to recent loan words, especially if these have to be morphologically adapted to indigenous patterns (cf. Dressler and Ladányi, 2000). If a rule only generates new compounds from indigenous bases, then it is less productive. For example, the Italian compound noun formation with a verbal stem as first part and a singular or plural noun as the second part is not only productive with indigenous parts, such as *porta-disch-i* '(instrument/object which) carries records'. It also integrates loan words, as in *porta-sci* 'ski carrier' and even allows for hybrid neologisms, such as *porta-container-s* 'container carrier' (with an English plural noun) and its literal translation *porta-contenitor-i*. In contrast, the typologically corresponding English type *pick-pocket, kiss-granny, dare-devil* is unproductive.

In regard to the inflection of compounds and compound members, often the notion of productivity is lumped together with notions of default (or generality) and transparency under the concept of regularity (e.g. in Clahsen, 1999, with critique by Dressler, ibidem p. 1021; cf. Jarema, Semenza, and Mondini, this volume).

2.3 Heads and compound classification

2.3.1

The oldest systematic classification of compounds goes back to the ancient Indian grammarian Pāṇini (sixth century BC). Although most of his terms are still used today, this classification is non-homogeneous, because it lacks an explicit notion of head. A head is the most important member of a compound, since, prototypically, it assigns its relevant semantic, syntactic, and morphological properties to the whole compound or, in other words, the whole compound inherits its basic properties (including referentiality) from the head. Thus a *black-board* is a type of board, with which it shares its syntactic and semantic features of being an inanimate, concrete noun of neuter gender (whereas the non-head *black* is a quality adjective). Semantic headedness is most evident in so-called pleonastic compounds (cf. Bloomer, 1996), where the head is a hyperonym of the non-head, as in G. *Eich-baum* = E. *oak-tree*.

Morphologically the whole compound inflects in its head (plural in English, also case in languages which possess this morphological category).

2.3.2

As a consequence we can classify compounds first of all according to the morphologically relevant basic properties of the head (cf. also Jarema, this volume). The most important criterion is the word class of the head, which results in the large classes of nominal, verbal, and adjectival compounds, depending on whether the head is a noun (e.g. *black-board*), a verb (e.g. *to dish-wash*) or an adjective (e.g. *war-weary*), and analogously with minor word classes. Similar classifications of the non-head are secondary and subordinated to classification of the head. The largest subclass in most languages is represented by noun-noun compounds (e.g. *peace treaty*), smaller ones in terms of type frequency are adjective-noun compounds (e.g. *mad-man*), noun-adjective compounds (e.g. *leaf green*), verb-noun compounds (e.g. *draw-bridge*), adjective-adjective compounds (e.g. *dark blue*), verb-verb compounds *(to stir-fry)*, adjective-verb compounds (e.g. *to dry-farm*), etc. Most languages show a clear preference for noun compounding, especially noun-noun compounds.

2.3.3

All of the above compounds have their head on the right, which corresponds to a universal preference, called the right-hand head rule by Williams (1981, p. 248). A minority of languages has large classes of left-hand heads as well (cf. Zwanenburg 1992a, 1992b; Scalise 1992, pp. 179ff; Rainer, 1993, pp. 57; cf. Semenza and Mondini, and Levy *et al.*, this volume). A left-headed compound, such as It. *capo-stazione* 'station-master' (lit. 'head-station'), inherits its masculine gender from its head (whereas *stazione* is feminine) as well as the inflection class: original Pl. *cap-i-stazione*. Since, however, Italian plural endings attach to the right edge of words, there is the substandard alternative Pl. *capo-stazion-i*. This is an instance of non-uniformity of head properties (cf. Di Sciullo and Williams, 1987, p. 26; Rainer, 1993, pp. 57ff): the first member *capo* still has the semantic and syntactic head properties (including gender determination), but the inflectional head is at the right-hand side of the substandard variant. Moreover, we again see that the preference for right-hand heads creeps in even in generally left-hand-head compounds. Another consequence of the preference for righ-hand headedness is the prohibition (Haider, 2001) or, at least, rareness of recursive left-headedness. One of the rare Italian examples of a doubly left-headed compound of the pattern *porta-bagagli* 'carrier' (lit. 'carry-luggages') is *porta-stuzzica-denti* 'tooth-pick carrier' (lit. [carry [pick teeth]]).

2.3.4

All of the compounds of this section have their head within the compound, thus they are endocentric compounds. Exocentric compounds have their head outsides or, more precisely, the head has to be inferred. Thus a *loud-mouth* is a person who, metaphorically, has a loud mouth, *bare-foot* is an adjective derived from a noun-phrase, a *pick-pocket* is a person who picks pockets, and a *pass-port* was originally a document which allows to pass a port. Pāṇini had called them in Sanskrit *bahu-vrihi* '(having) much rice', another current term is possessive compound. Sometimes endocentric and exocentric compounds are morphologically differentiated. For example, the plural *sabre teeth* refers to teeth (endocentric), the plural *sabre tooth-s* to animals having *sabre teeth* (exocentric). Endocentric compounds are by far preferred to exocentric compounds in the languages of the world, because they allow much easier access to the head.

2.3.5

All endocentric and exocentric compounds dealt with so far are subordinate compounds, that is one member (the non-head) is semantically and structurally subordinate to another one (the head). This holds, secondarily, even among the actual members of exocentric compounds: *loud* is subordinated to *mouth* in *loud-mouth*, whereas in *pick-pocket* we again find non-uniformity (of secondary head-hood): although the primary, semantic head designating the person who picks pockets is not expressed, *pocket* is, secondarily, the morphological head determining gender and inflection, whereas syntactically *pocket* is subordinated to *pick*.

The universally dispreferred alternative of coordinate compounds has two or more semantic and syntactic heads (cf. Wunderlich, 1986, p. 241). Thus in *speaker-hearer* both members are of equal status, although the plural ending attaches only to the right member, another example of non-uniform headhood and of the right-hand head preference (cf. Plag, 2003, p. 147). Coordinate (or coordinative) compounds may again be endocentric, such as *speaker-hearer* or the adjective *bitter-sweet*, also called appositional compounds, or they may be exocentric, such as *morphology=syntax interface*, where the two coordinated compound members have their semantic heads outside: it coincides with *interface*, the syntactic head of the whole noun-phrase. More subtle properties of coordinate compounds may differ considerably from language to language (cf. Olsen, 2001): the linear order of members in coordinate compounds is not grammatically determined (since all members are equipollent), but pragmatically (e.g. the most important first) or stylistically, for example prosodically (e.g. the longest last). The first reason explains the order of *speaker-hearer* (because linguists tend to think more of the speaker than of the hearer, cf. the term *native speaker*), the second explains why the order of the synonym *speaker-listener* is even more difficult to reverse (?*listener-speaker*) than in the case of *speaker-hearer*. The distinction between subordinate and coordinate compounds is not always easy to draw, thus Scalise (1992, p. 183) interprets It. *caffe-latte* 'coffee with milk' (lit. coffee-milk) as coordinate. However, since the order cannot be reversed without a change of meaning, it must be a left-headed subordinate compound. The same holds for the right-headed German equivalent *Milch-kaffee*: the potential, inverted *Kaffee-milch* would mean 'milk with a drop of coffee'.

2.3.6

Coordinate compounds are preferentially binary, that is, they consist of just two members, therefore called *dvandva* 'pair' by Pāṇini. Multiple membership is possible when real-world concepts require it, such as in adjectival compounds denoting flags (e.g. *blue-white-red* for the French *tricolore*).

Subordinate compounds appear to be always structured in a binary way, although this structuring may be recursive. For example, a *three-star general* is a general (head) who has three stars (subordinated noun phrase as non-head). This subordinated noun-phrase has the secondary head *stars*, modified by its non-head *three*. Thus subordinate multi-member compounds consist of binary compounds of binary compounds, that is, they are due to recursive binary compounding. Recursive compounding may result in left-branching, for example in bracketing notation *[[three-star] general* or *[[foot-ball] team]*, or right-branching, as in *[family [[drug-store]]*. In general, left-branching compounds appear to be preferred (cf. Krott *et al.*, 2004).

2.4 Other structural classifications

2.4.1

Incorporation as an extreme case of compounding found in many polysynthetic Amerindian, Australian, etc. languages can be understood as a radical way of morphologizing the majority of syntactic relations in a sentence (Baker, 1988; Mithun and Corbett, 1999; Rood, 2002; Launay, 1998). This is mainly achieved by incorporating objects into verbal compounds, so-to-say by elaborating on the English patterns of *to dish-wash* (for German cf. Wurzel, 1998).

2.4.2

A special type of compound is represented by synthetic compounds (opposed to root compounds), such as *street-sweep-er* (cf. Lieber,

1994, 1992, pp. 81 f; Booij, 2005a, pp. 91 ff). The second member is a noun which is derived from a verb. The prevailing interpretation of such synthetic compounds considers them to be nominalizations of verb phrases, that is 'someone who/a machine which sweeps streets', with the agentive suffix -*er* representing the head.

2.4.3

This leads us to the question of the semantic interpretation of compounds in general (cf. Lieber, 2004, pp. 45–60). Potentially, most compounds are polysemous (and thus ambiguous), that is they allow multiple interpretations (cf. Heringer, 1984). Let us start with a German example highlighted by Coseriu (1975) the structure of which is parallel to that of the preceding synthetic compound: Ge. *Straße-n-verkäuf-er* lit. 'street seller'. This may be a builder who sells streets to a third-world country, but its usual interpretation is 'someone who sells something on a street'. Moreover, parallel compounds may have different accepted meanings. For example an *iron pipe* is a pipe made of iron, whereas a *stove-pipe* is a pipe of a stove. This might induce us to think that the meaning of compounds is largely indeterminate, and that the actual meaning of a compound may be contextually or pragmatically determined, insofar as it is highly improbable that, for example in the case of *iron pipe*, a pipe would be used for producing iron or, in the case of *stove-pipe*, a pipe would be produced by melting old stoves.

2.4.4

There have been several attempts to provide restricted lists of potential meanings of compounds, especially for the largest class, viz. nominal compounds (e.g. Levi, 1978; Bauer, 1978; Fanselow, 1985; Meyer, 1992, pp. 12 ff, 102 ff; Gagné and Spalding, this volume). If the head of a subordinate compound has a relational meaning, then any non-head allows at least a potential interpretation as an argument of the relation governed by the head, including secondary heads of exocentric compounds, provided that the non-head is a potential argument of that relation (cf. Lieber, 1992, pp. 89 ff; Gagné and Spalding, this volume). This is the case with relational adjectives (e.g. *war-weary*, as opposed to the non-relational head of *dark-blue*) and with transitive, that is at least bivalent verbs (e.g. *to dish-wash*). This also holds for nominalized verbs, as in synthetic compounds, including exocentric compounds, such as *pick-pocket*. Also non-derived relational nouns follow this pattern, as in *tree surgeon, city father, sound engineer*. In contrast, the non-head excludes a relational interpretation in *house-surgeon, step-father, civil engineer*. Difficulties arise, however, with compounds such as the above-mentioned Ge. *Straße-n-verkäuf-er* 'street seller': in the interpretation as 'someone who sells streets', the first member is clearly an internal argument of the underlying verb. In the interpretation of 'someone who sells on the streets', however, the first member assumes the thematic role of a locative, which many grammatical theories do not count as an argument, whereas Lieber (1983) calls it a semantic argument.

Moreover, even in its first reading, *street seller* may be interpreted as a 'seller of streets', whereby the first member becomes a modifier of the head. This represents the second basic meaning structure of compounds, which is the only possibility for the above-mentioned compounds *dark-blue, house-surgeon, step-father, civil engineer, black-board*, but also allows an alternative interpretation for *tree-surgeon, city father, sound engineer*. In which way may the non-head modify the head? Here Brekle's (1984, 1986) notion of stereotypical relation is pertinent, that is the cognitive scheme that sets the meaning of a head in relation to the meanings of possible subordinated non-heads (cf. also Gagné and Spalding, this volume). For example, *factory* evokes the cognitive scheme of a place where something is produced. Thus the non-head of *car factory* is easily construed as the internal argument (direct object) of what is produced. And again, when we take German neologisms, such as *Küsten-fabrik, Sommer-fabrik* 'coast factory, summer factory', investigated by Brekle (1984, 1986) and his team (cf. Fanselow, 1985; Wildgen, 1987), then the non-heads are assigned, within this cognitive relational scheme, the thematic roles of locative and time, respectively, that is where or when the factory is functioning.

This assumption of cognitively-based stereotypical relations, however, leads back to the strategy of Levi (1978) and others to construct certain basic relations applicable to the meaning of compounds. In fact, no comprehensive description of nominal compounds works without relational notions, such as 'consisting/made of, similar to' or metaphor, if compounds such as *potato chips, blood orange, velvet voice, fire-eater* have to be accounted for (cf. Fanselow, 1985; Motsch, 1994).

2.5 Bases of compounds

2.5.1

Universally preferred bases of morphological rules are autonomous words (Dressler, 1988; cf. Rainer, 1993, pp. 98 ff). This preference for word-based morphology applies to compounding even more than to inflection and derivation. Nearly all examples given so far are unequivocal representatives of word-based compounding, that is the bases are the autonomous citation forms of words, such as singular nouns in English, Dutch, Hebrew, and Romance languages, singular nouns in the nominative case in German and in Slavic languages. Larger and less-preferred bases are represented by inflected words which are not identical with citation forms. Such bases are very rare and restricted in English, for example *sport-s-girl, income-s tax* with a pluralized first base (cf. Jensen, 1990), as well as in Dutch (Booij 1992, pp. 44) and other languages (cf. Nicoladis, this volume). Pluralized second bases (non-heads) are widespread in the Romance type of It. *porta-contenitori/container-s* 'container carrier' (section 2.2, cf. Rainer and Varela, 1992, pp. 127 ff, 136, 139; Gather, 2001; Levy *et al.*; Nicoladis, this volume).

2.5.2

Still larger bases, namely phrases, appear in synthetic compounds (section 4) in the type *three-star general, three-phase motor, three-*

color process, etc., where the modifier of the noun-phrase in the non-head position is often difficult to omit (e.g. *star general* belongs to a different compound type and designates a 'general who is a star'). For other phrasal-compound patterns cf. Lieber (1992, pp. 92 ff), Booij (1992, pp. 45 ff), Bisetto and Scalise (1999). Whole sentences as first members of a binary compound occur only in consciously formed occasionalisms, such as *an oh-what-a-wicked-world-this-is-and-how-I-wish-I-could-do-something-to-make-it-better-and-nobler* (J. K. Jerome: *Three Men in a Boat*).

2.5.3

The smallest possible bases are roots, the smallest carriers of lexical meaning which are smaller than autonomous words. Examples of root-based compounding in English are neoclassical compounds, such as *bio-chemistry, bio-acoustical*. They have a wider occurrence in other languages, for example in the German unproductive pattern *Fried-hof* 'cemetery (lit. peace-court)' or *Kirsch-baum* 'cherry-tree', where the citation form of the first base is *Friede(n), Kirsche*. The alternative of assuming phonological deletion of the final vowel (cf. section 1) is less attractive in view of the compounds *Fried-en-s-vertrag* 'peace treaty', *Kirsch-e-n-baum* (with interfixes, see below § 6), of the variation between *fried-liebend* and *fried-en-s-liebend* 'peace-loving' and of the derivative *fried-lich* 'peaceful'.

2.5.4

Between root-based and word-based morphology there is stem-based compounding/morphology. Stems are defined in different ways (cf. Matthews, 1972, pp. 63 f, 165 ff; Fuhrhop, 1998; Rainer, 1993, pp. 93 f; Mel'čuk, 1997, pp. 81 ff). One definition of stem is root plus a thematic vowel, as in Lat. *pont-i-fex* 'pontiff (lit. bridge-maker)', where the first member is a stem (root plus thematic vowel *-i-*), the second member a root plus Nom.Sg. *-s*, cf. It. *port-a-bagagli* (sections 2.2, 3.3) with the thematic vowel /a/ and Pol. *baw-i-damek* 'ladies' man (lit. entertain-ladies)' with thematic vowel /i/.

2.6 Transparency

2.6.1

Most linguists and psycholinguists assume that actually existing, accepted compounds are stored in the lexicon (Bauer, 1983; Wolff, 1984, p. 61; Brekle, 1984; Meyer, 1992; Baayen and Schreuder, 2003; and all chapters of this volume). This is called lexicalization and is the source of idiosyncratic changes of individual compounds which affect varying degrees of lexicalization in its second sense, that is properties of meaning and form which are in principle unpredictable from meanings and forms of compound members. In this sense, one can speak of degrammaticalization as infringements in the grammatical derivability of meaning and form. The end point is fossilization, where members and their combination are hardly visible, if at all. For example, E. *lord* and *lady* are not recognizable as compounds any more, E. *nostril* barely. In contrast, E. *dandelion* may be recognized as a compound, whose first member is difficult to identify, whereas its second is semantically totally opaque (diachronically a loan from Fr. *dent de lion* 'lit. tooth of lion'). Less lexicalization means more transparency, more lexicalization more opacity. More transparency implies more motivation of the compound via its members.

2.6.2

We start with (morpho)semantic transparency, a topic dealt with by all contributions to this volume. Due to lexicalization (lexical storage), actual compounds are never fully transparent in the sense of the logician Frege's principle of compositionality. Thus the meaning of a non-idiomatic noun-phrase, such as *a high school* (section 1) is fully compositional and thus transparent, the cognate compound *high-school* is not. Still, for the purpose of psycholinguistic investigations, *high-school* may be classified as a morphosemantically transparent compound, because the meaning of the head is fully transparent and because the semantic motivation by its first member (non-head) is still evident: a *high-school* is high in a metaphorical sense, that is relatively high in contrast to elementary and grade school. In fact, a *high-school* is a specific instance of what a 'high school' may mean potentially. Thus, in a first approximation, we may define an actual transparent compound as one whose meaning is a subset of the set of potential meanings of the compound as constructed grammatically via the combination of the meanings of the two members. This is more precise than Shaw's (1979) criterion that the head must be an hyperonym of the compound. This is also relevant for psycholinguistic research on non-existing, but potential compounds. They are always transparent, but their use depends on the possibility of instantiating a pragmatically plausible potential meaning.

2.6.3

Based on this approach and following Libben (1998) we can differentiate the following four fundamental degrees of morphosemantic transparency (which are clearer and more systematic than Shaw's 1979):

(i) transparency of both members of the compound, e.g. *door-bell*;
(ii) transparency of the head member, opacity of the non-head member, e.g. *straw-berry*;
(iii) transparency of the non-head member, opacity of the head member, e.g. *jail-bird*;
(iv) opacity of both members of the compound, e.g. *hum-bug*.

This scale of transparency presupposes that transparency of the head is more important than of the non-head.

Further refinement is possible, if we differentiate between direct and indirect, that is metaphoric motivation (cf. de Knop, 1987; Nicoladis, this volume), which would allow the dividing of degrees (ii)–(iv) above into subdegrees with metaphorically motivated vs. unmotivated opacity. Thus German *Löwe-n-zahn* 'dandelion' (lit. 'lion's tooth', translated from Fr. *dent de lion*) would have an opaque first member, but a metaphorically motivated second member (the leaves are compared with teeth), thus belonging to the more transparent variant of transparency degree (iii).

Another refinement refers to the degree of descriptiveness of compounds, that is the degree to which the meanings of the parts 'describe' and thus motivate the meaning of the whole (cf. Seiler, 1975; Semenza and Mondini, this volume). Thus, on the average, syntactic phrases are more descriptive than compounds and affixal derivations even less, cf. *bread-cutting machine* vs. *bread-knife* vs. *cutt-er*. But compounds may also be more or less descriptive, and opaque idiomatic phrases are usually less descriptive than transparent compounds.

2.6.4

Boundaries between compound members may be marked by linking elements or interfixes (cf. Dressler and Merlini Barbaresi, 1991; Booij, 2005a, p. 88; Jarema, Semenza, and Mondini, this volume). For example, in E. *gas-o-meter*, the interfix *-o-* goes back to a thematic vowel in Latin and Ancient Greek. It is widespread in Romance languages and Modern Greek, for example It. *sessu-o-fobo* 'sex-o-phobic', Gk. *xart-o-péktis* 'card player' (← *xartí* 'card' and *péktis* 'player', Ralli, 1992, pp. 152 ff), as well as in Slavic languages, for example Pol. *kraj-o-znawstwo* = Ge. *Land-es-kunde* 'study of national customs (lit. country science)'. In Germanic languages, other than English, interfixes, going back diachronically (and synchronically often homophonous) to inflectional suffixes, are frequent, for example interfixes *-s-* and *-(e)n-* in Ge. *Frau-en-feind* 'woman hater', *Frieden-s-vertrag* 'peace treaty', Du. *schaap-s-kop* 'sheep's head', *aardbei-en-jam* 'strawberry jam' (cf. Becker, 1992, pp. 10 ff; Fuhrhop, 1998, pp. 185–218; Booij, 1992, pp. 41 ff; Dressler *et al.*, 2000). Interfixes do not contribute to the meaning of the compound and thus reduce morphosemantic transparency.

2.6.5

Interfixes also reduce morphotactic (or phonological) transparency of compounds and thus ease of parsing (cf. Libben, 1994; Jarema, Nicoladis, this volume), because 'the less a word changes, the simpler it is' (Clark and Berman, 1984, pp. 548). Thus phonological truncations, as mentioned in section 1.6, also diminish morphotactic transparency.

2.7 Conclusion

This brief survey of compound types and of some of their properties may have shown the multiplicity of patterns and the necessity of choosing judiciously among available compounds for establishing test stimuli. As is evident in the psycholinguistic and neurolinguistic studies represented in this volume, this multiplicity of patterning informs our understanding of compound processing across languages, the acquisition of compounds, and the representation and processing of these stimuli in bilinguals, who must develop a single system that can represent disparate patterns in one mind.

The various properties and subtypes discussed in this chapter can be summarized in the two following schemes (with cross-references to paragraphs):

1. Properties of prototypical compounds. Prototypical compounds are:
    lexicalized (2.6.1) thus at least slightly idiomatic (2.1.4, 2.1.5)
    non-separable (2.1.4, 2.1.11)
    atoms (internally non-referential: 2.1.4)
    polysemous (2.4.3)
    noun–noun compounds (2.1.1, 2.3.2)
    have a binary structure (2.1.2, 2.3.6)
    consist of prototypical words (2.1.2)
    consist of words of major lexical categories (2.1.3)
    lack internal agreement (2.1.7, 2.1.8)
    lack internal syntactic well-formedness (2.1.9)
    may possess interfixes (2.1.10, 2.6.4)
    may apply recursively (2.3.3)
2. There are preferences for being:
    productive > non-productive (2.2)
    right-headed > left-headed (2.3.3)

left-branching > right-branching (2.3.6)
endocentric > exocentric (2.3.4, 2.3.5)
subordinate > coordinate (2.3.5)
word-based > stem-based > root-based (2.5.2)
word-based > phrase-based > sentence-based (2.5.3, 2.5.4)

Compounds may be classified beyond the above-mentioned properties of binarity, productivity, headedness, endo/exocentricity, sub/coordination, bases, interfixes. The following properties allow further classifications:

3. Further classificatory properties. Compounds may be
   nominal vs. verbal vs. adjectival (2.3.2)
   relational or non-relational (2.4.4)
   synthetic or root compounds (2.4.2)
   incorporating or not (2.4.1)
   morphosemantically transparent vs. opaque (2.6.2–2.6.4)
   morphotactically transparent vs. opaque (2.6.5).

3

Compound Representation and Processing: A cross-language perspective

GONIA JAREMA

The study of how compounded words such as *doormat* or *humbug* are represented and processed provides important insight into the way in which the human mind stores and organizes multimorphemic words and accesses them from the mental lexicon. Together with inflected words such as *washed* and derived words such as *washable*, compounds are characterized by a complex word-internal morphological structure (e.g. in the examples given above, each lexical item is composed of two morphemes: *door* and *mat*, *hum* and *bug*; *wash* and *-ed*; *wash* and *-able*). Compounding is a productive word formation process in many languages and involves structural complexity at both the semantic and the morphological levels. Indeed, compounds can feature different degrees of semantic transparency and vary in componentiality (Libben, 1998 and this volume). Thus, according to Libben, the word *strawberry* is only partially transparent, but componential (or endocentric), since only the meaning of berry is linked to the meaning of the compound as a whole, yet it designates a type of berry, while the word *bighorn* is fully transparent, but noncomponential (or exocentric), since the meanings of its constituents are transparently related to the meaning of the compound, yet a bighorn is not a type of horn. Furthermore, compounds can also vary in morphological complexity (for a comprehensive linguistic analysis, see Dressler, this volume), exhibiting simple concatenated structures comprised of two lexical categories (e.g. in German, *Hausfrau*, 'housewife'), or featuring, for example, linking elements attached to either full lexical base forms (e.g. in German *Königshof*, 'king's court'), or to the bound stem of lexical bases (e.g. in German, *Firmensitz*, 'head office', where the lexical base form of the first constituent is *Firma*; in Greek, *domatosalata*, 'tomato salad', where it is *domata*; in English, *liposuccion*, where it is is *lipid*). In sum, the meanings of compounds are not always straightforwardly constructed from the meanings of their constituents, nor can their morphological structure always be straightforwardly recovered. Because compounds can differ both language-internally and cross-linguistically along many dimensions, they are of particular interest to psycho- and neurolinguists who seek to determine how children, adults, and neurologically-impaired individuals presenting a linguistic deficit compute these variously combined lexical forms. Furthermore, research on compounds can shed light not only on the factors that play a role in their retrieval and production, but also more broadly on the manner in which multimorphemic words are being processed. That is, issues raised in the compounding literature, such as the role of semantic transparency of compounds and of their individual constituents, as well as of morphological structure and complexity, are all relevant to investigations of the mental lexicon in general, and in particular to the central question of whether and when lexical units are decomposed during word processing.

To date, only a handful of studies have addressed the issue of compound representation and access from a cross-linguistic perspective. In contrast, a much larger number of investigations have approached the problem of compound processing through the study of a single language. Importantly, a growing body of studies is being conducted in languages other than English, thus making it possible to compare findings across a variety of typologically-distinct linguistic systems. The goal of this chapter is thus to provide a comparative overview of the relevant psycho- and neurolinguistic literature on compounding in an effort to uncover convergences across languages and to determine whether any general principles emerge from the various studies reviewed. We do not aim to provide a comprehensive coverage of the literature to date. Rather, we will highlight those findings and interpretations that are validated across two or more languages, with reference to both monolingual and comparative studies. The chapter will be structured around a number of themes that are central to a better understanding of how compounds and, ultimately, multimorphemic words are represented and processed.

3.1 Constituent activation

3.1.1 Semantic transparency effects

A major question in the study of compounding is whether the individual constituents of compounded forms are activated during lexical access. This issue was addressed by Sandra (1990) and Zwitserlood (1994) for Dutch and by Libben and collaborators for English (Libben, 1998; Libben et al., 2003). Taking advantage of the fact that compounds show varying degrees of opacity, Sandra (1990) predicted that if compounds are parsed into their individual constituents, a semantic priming effect would be obtained in a lexical decision task[1] in which compounds such as *birthday* (transparent) or *Sunday* (opaque) would be primed by a semantic associate (*death* and *moon*, respectively). Results obtained showed that only semantically transparent compounds exhibited priming effects. This led Sandra to conclude that only semantically transparent compounds are decomposed into their constituents during word recognition. By

---

[1] In a lexical decision task, participants are required to decide as quickly and as accurately as possible whether a visually or auditorily presented string of letters is a word in their language or not by pressing a 'YES' or 'NO' response button; this technique allows the recording of reaction-time measures. Lexical decision paradigms can be simple or primed; in a primed lexical decision task, the presentation of the target word is preceded by the presentation of a related item, the prime, e.g. the presentation of *death* followed by *birthday* is a case of semantic priming, and that of *birth* followed by *birthday* is a case of constituent priming in compound recognition. Priming effects are calculated by comparison with an unrelated prime-target pair (e.g. *cloud-birthday*).

contrast, Zwitserlood (1994), who also investigated Dutch compounds—using a constituent priming paradigm—found priming effects for both transparent and opaque compounds. In another experiment, Zwitserlood employed a semantic priming paradigm and found priming effects for transparent as well as for partially transparent compounds, but not for fully opaque ones. This points to the view that even only partially transparent compounds are decomposed. Investigating English compounds of all four types (fully transparent, or transparent-transparent; partially opaque, or transparent-opaque and opaque-transparent; fully opaque, or opaque-opaque) Libben *et al.* (1997), however, found constituent priming effects for all types of compounds, including the fully opaque ones. Libben concluded that constituents are activated for both opaque and transparent compounds, but that the priming effects obtained derive from two different sources. An initial substring effect, as suggested by Taft and Forster (1996), in the case of first constituent priming, and a constituent activation and headedness effect in the case of second constituent priming. The author argues that Sandra's semantic priming technique targeted 'lines of associations within the lexicon', rather than units of activation during lexical recognition. Moreover, Libben (1998) proposes a model that accounts for constituent activation across all types of compounds by postulating three levels of compound representation and processing: the stimulus level, the lexical level and the conceptual level (see Fig. 3.1).

Libben argues that, at the lexical level, constituents are isolated through left to right parsing, as predicted by Libben's (1994) APPLE (automatic progressive parsing and lexical excitation) procedure. At the lexical level, compounds such as the fully transparent form *blueberry* and the partially opaque form *strawberry* have identical representations ([blue][berry] and [straw][berry]), however they differ at the conceptual level of representation, because only the word form *blue*, but not *straw*, is linked to its corresponding conceptual representation. In this view, the meaning of *straw* is inhibited because of the absence of a link between the two levels of representation. This accounts for the interpretability of compounds,

```
Conceptual level:   blue [blue][berry] berry        straw [straw][berry] berry
                         ╲  │  ╱                           │  ╱
Lexical level:      blue -[blue][berry] -berry      straw -[straw][berry] - berry
                         ╲  ↓  ╱                        ╲  ↓  ╱
Stimulus level:           blueberry                      strawberry
                              ▲                              ▲
                         APPLE Parse                    APPLE Parse
                             (a)                            (b)
```

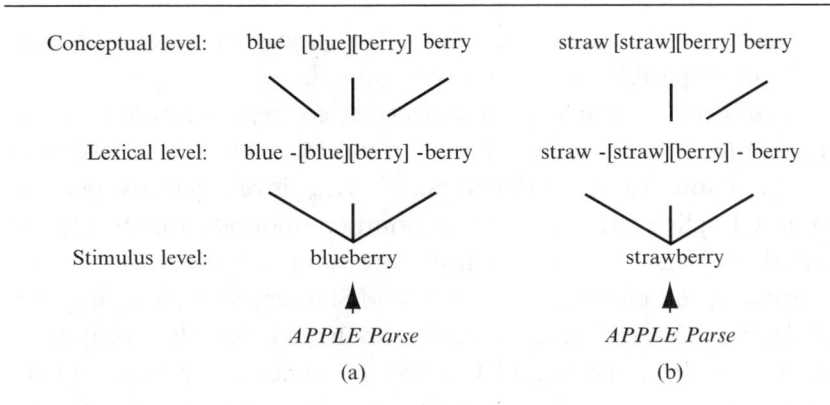

FIG. 3.1 The processing of transparent (a) and partially opaque (b) compounds
Source: Adapted from Libben, 1998.

mediated by an interplay of facilitatory and inhibitory links between the lexical and conceptual levels of interpretation and processing, as well as for constituent activation in opaque compounds (for a detailed account of compound parsing, see Libben, 1998).

To further probe the mechanisms of prelexical parsing, Libben, Derwing, and de Almeida (1999) devised a morpheme recall paradigm employing ambiguous novel compounds (e.g. *clamprod*) first used by Libben (1994). In the first experiment participants were requested to recall left or right constituents, whereas in the second experiment they were asked to recall constituent associates primed by ambiguous compounds (in this example *sea* and *hold*). Results showed that in the first experiment both parses were generated equally often, and in the second experiment compounds primed the semantic associates of both their parses. The authors concluded that compounds are not simply divided into one or the other possible parse (in this example *clam-prod* or *clamp-rod*), but are interpreted through a recursive parsing procedure that generates multiple interpretations. Similarly, Coolen, Jaarsveld, and Schreuder (1993) demonstrated interactive activation of the meanings of constituent nouns in Dutch novel compounds in which the meaning of the ambiguous head noun (e.g. *staal*) is either dominant (*zwaardstaal*, 'sword steel') or subordinate (*tapijtstaal*, 'carpet sample').

The account offered is that compatible meanings are enhanced, while incompatible meanings are inhibited.

Studies investigating other aspects of concept formation in the processing of compounded forms are also relevant to the question of whether compounds are decomposed. Thus investigations focusing on how English attributive noun-noun compounds are interpreted have shown that thematic relations, for example 'MADE OF' for the compound *chocolate bunny* (Gagné and Shoben, 1997), and property attribution, for example, 'mushroom-shaped' for the compound *mushroom cloud* (Estes and Glucksberg, 2000) are relevant to semantic interpretation. These results provide further evidence for the parsing of compounds into constituents during lexical processing. They also bring to the fore knowledge of modifier–head relations and constituent properties (for a discussion, see Dressler, this volume), a knowledge that can only emerge after decompositional processes have taken place.

Constituent activation has also been evidenced in languages that are typologically distinct from both Germanic and Romance languages. A paper and pencil decomposition task—perhaps the simplest way to tap the role of constituent structure in the processing of compounds—was employed by Kudo (1992) who tested aphasic patients' ability to decompose three-character kanji compounds that are either of the head (1+2 3, or left-branching, e.g. the word for winter landscape) or tail (1 2+3, or right-branching, e.g. the word for entrance fee) type with respect to position of the correct parse. All aphasic patients (7 Broca's, 5 Wernicke's, and 6 anomics) demonstrated performance that was comparable to that of unimpaired participants, despite the fact that their word formation and word selection was impaired, suggesting that knowledge of word-internal structure is preserved in aphasia. Results from another non-Indo-European language also support the salience of constituents in processing compounds. In a series of auditory lexical decision experiments, Zhou and Marslen-Wilson (1994) investigated the representation of disyllabic compounds in Mandarin Chinese, varying word frequency, morpheme frequency (where each morpheme corresponds to a unique character), and syllable frequency (a morphemic frequency that includes all the homophones of a morpheme, as homophonic morphemes are prevalent in Chinese). Robust whole-word frequency effects that did not interact with morphemic and syllables frequency effects led the authors to conclude that Chinese disyllabic compounds are represented whole, while being accessed syllable by syllable. They thus propose a network-based whole-word model (the Multi-Level Cluster Representation Model) that distinguishes a syllabic layer, a morphemic layer, and a word layer of representation. At the morphemic level, morphemes that share the same phonological form are connected to the same syllable node at the syllabic level and compete with each other, whereas at the word-level, words sharing the same first syllable compete with each other. Words sharing the same morpheme are connected indirectly via connections with the morphemic level. Word-level representations are thus hypothesized to be structured, that is marked to indicate morpheme boundaries and to allow access via decomposed forms.

As has been stated above, cross-linguistic investigations of constituent activation in compound processing are still scarse. One such study is that of Kehayia *et al.* (1999) who probed compound recognition in Greek and Polish employing a primed lexical decision task and found that both first and second constituents primed target compounds in the two languages (e.g. in Greek, both *domata* and *salata* primed *domatosalata*, 'tomato salad'; in Polish, both *gwiazda*, 'star' and *zbiór*, 'collection' primed *gwiazdozbiór*, 'constellation'). First constituents, however, showed an advantage over second constituents, despite the fact that both languages are right-headed. This finding led the authors to conclude that position-in-the-string is a factor that influences compound processing. This factor will be addressed in the following section.

3.1.2 *Distributional effects*

Further support for a decompositional view of compound processing is provided by a study of Dutch and English compounds using measures related to the concept of morphological family, defined as the set of all the words in a language containing a given word as a morpheme (de Jong et al., 2002; for a more detailed discussion of the notion of morphological family see Dressler, this volume). Morphological family size, the type count of a morphological family, has been found to influence word recognition, while morphological family frequency (the summed frequencies of the family members, or token count of a morphological family) has not (Schreuder and Baayen, 1997). In view of the fact that contrasting results have been reported in the literature with regard to constituent activation in Dutch employing frequency effects as a diagnostic, de Jong et al. (2002) used a visual lexical decision paradigm to investigate whether the family size of the constituents of compounds affect response latencies. Results revealed that although larger left or right constituent family sizes decreased response latencies as predicted, the position family frequency ('the family frequency of a constituent constrained by position within the compound') proved to be a better predictor than the constituent family size. While similar results were obtained for concatenated Dutch and English compounds, English compounds written with a space between the constituents (termed 'open' by the authors) exhibited a position family size, rather than family frequency, effect. By contrast, artificial open Dutch compounds showed only an effect of positional family frequency, indicating that the differential results obtained for English open compounds are not due to a superficial orthographic effect. Evidence from an additional experiment was taken to suggest that English open compounds are phrase-like lexical items that do not belong to the morphological families of monomorphemic words. Taken together, these results led de Jong et al. (2002) to the conclusion that compound processing is sensitive to morphological structure, and that on-line decomposition takes place peripherally, that is at the level of access representations.

3.1.3 *Aphasiological evidence*

Of particular interest to the issue of constituent activation is Libben's (1998) re-analysis of the performance of a mixed aphasic (RS) on compound processing, previously reported in Libben (1993), who exhibited activation of compound constituents for all types of compounds (thus possessing a spared lexical level of representation and processing), but who was unable to inhibit representations at the conceptual level. When asked to paraphrase partially opaque compounds such as *blueprint*, RS would reply 'a print that is blue', indicating that she was unable to inhibit the link between the form *blue* and its meaning. This resulted in an erroneously transparent reading of the compound. A paraphrase that Libben (1998) underscores as particularly revealing is RS's response to the compound *dumbell*: 'stupid weights...Arnold', in which the patient demonstrates comprehension of the meaning as a whole, activation of a constituent and lack of inhibition of its meaning, as well as activation of a semantic associate (Arnold Schwarzenegger) of both the first constituent and the compound as a whole.

Aphasiological evidence showing patients' sensitivity to the compositional nature of compounds has also been reported in other studies and across a variety of languages. Rochford and Williams (1965), for English, and Ahrens (1977), for German, were among the first authors to report omissions of compound constituent in aphasia and to stress, among other factors, the importance of constituent frequency. Using a picture-naming paradigm, Hittmair-Delazer *et al.* (1994) and Blanken (2000) tested German-speaking aphasic patients, while Semenza, Luzzatti, and Carabelli (1997) and Delazer and Semenza (1998) studied Italian-speaking patients and all found that when patients produced errors on compounds, they systematically provided a compounded structure (crucially, even when targets were semantically opaque). In the case of Broca's aphasia, they omitted one of the constituents of the target compound. Badecker (2001) reports on an English-speaking aphasic who systematically produced only one of the compound's constituents and argues that the prosodic structure of these incomplete productions, as well as the observation that they were often followed by either a correct response or by a compounded form, point to the fact that the patient was aware of the morphological structure of the target. These converging neurological findings across English, German, and Italian provide strong empirical evidence for morphological parsing during compound processing. (For a comprehensive discussion of compound processing in aphasia, see Semenza and Mondini, this volume.)

This section presented psycho- and neurolinguistic evidence from several languages (Chinese, Dutch, English, German, Greek, Italian, and Polish) that brings converging support to the position that individual constituents are activated during the processing of compounds. Below, variables that come into play across languages as a consequence of constituent retrieval are considered in turn.

3.1.4 Position-in-the-string effects

Akin to the issue of constituent activation is the question of whether one of the activated constituents of a compound plays a more prominent role in lexical access procedures. This question has been addressed both cross-linguistically and in individual languages. As mentioned above, Kehayia et al. (1999) found a clear position-in-the-string effect in the significantly greater magnitude of priming of first constituents as compared to second constituents in the recognition of both Greek and Polish compounds.

Pathological data stressing the stability of first constituents in compound production by aphasic patients were, to our knowledge, first reported by Ahrens (1977) for German. Probing the issue of compound processing in the reading performance of a deep dyslexic patient (HH) in Finnish, a language in which compounding is highly productive, Mäkisalo, Niemi, and Laine (1999) made the following observations: in his reading of compounds, HH exhibited preserved compound structure, and although first and second constituents were quantitatively equally impaired, noteworthy qualitative differences emerged from the data. Thus, when the first constituent was produced correctly, HH mostly produced another existing Finnish compound. In contrast, when the second constituent was correct, forms given were significantly less frequently compounds. Moreover, the compounded forms produced in the latter case were overwhelmingly neologistic in nature. In other words, correct first constituents prompted productions of existing compounds (on the basis of legally combined, but erroneously selected, second constituent substitutions), while correct second constituents prompted the productions of neologistic compounds (on the basis of first constituent substitutions yielding nonexistent, semantically implausible, forms). From these results, Mäkisalo *et al.* (1999) conclude that first constituents easily lead to plausible lexical items and thus guide compound access. Stark and Stark (1990) report on a German-speaking Wernicke's aphasic who tended to omit the second constituent of twin compounds, such as *Orangensaft*, 'orange juice' and *Saftorangen*, 'juice oranges', while exhibiting awareness of compound structure, as evidenced by the patient's approximations of the whole compounds. Taken together, these aphasiological findings support evidence from psycholinguistic studies that suggest an advantage of the first constituent in compound processing.

To summarize, the significance of the first constituent in the left-to-right processing of compounds has been evidenced in typologically distinct languages (Finnish, German, Greek, and Polish) and in both neurologically unimpaired and impaired populations. The variable first-position-in-the-string thus clearly contributes to the complexity of phenomena involved in compound recognition and production.

Compound constituent position and compound headedness must, however, be teased apart to fully evaluate their respective influence on the processing of compounds. This is of particular relevance because headedness varies across languages. Some languages, such as English, German, and Greek, are right-headed, while others, such as Hebrew, are left-headed. Moreover, some languages, such as French, feature compounds that are either right- or left-headed. The relative effect of headedness will be discussed in the next section.

3.1.5 *Headedness effects*

Comparing results across a variety of languages suggests that the importance of the first constituent may be independent of the role of headedness in the processing of compounds. Thus, although not only in English, but also in languages such as Finnish, German, Greek, and Polish, compounds are right-headed (e.g. *mat* is the morphological head of the compound *doormat* and assigns grammatical category, here Noun, and other lexical features to the full form), the studies reviewed above demonstrate that the first, left-most, constituent plays a more central role during access procedures, at least in some languages. Crucially, the relative importance of first position in the string vs. headedness can best be tested in languages featuring both right-headed (RH) and left-headed (LH) compounds. In a study comparing French (RH and LH) and Bulgarian (RH only), Jarema *et al.* (1999) investigated the role of headedness, using a primed lexical decision task, precisely to verify whether, in contrast to languages such as English or Bulgarian, French—a language in which headedness is not predicted positionally, would enable the disentanglement of the effects of position-in-the-string vs. headedness. French adjective-noun compounds such as *garçon manqué*, 'tomboy', which is left-headed, and *grasse matiné*, 'sleep-in', which is right-headed, were used and constituent transparency was varied employing Libben's (1997) four-way classification. For both French and Bulgarian, results showed robust priming effects, that is constituent activation, for all types of compounds tested (with the exception of opaque-opaque compounds in Bulgarian, which the authors postulated to be accessed whole in the language). Furthermore, the finding that first-constituent primes yielded significantly greater magnitudes of priming when compared to second-constituent primes for left-headed transparent-transparent, transparent-opaque, opaque-transparent, and opaque-opaque compounds, was interpreted as reflecting the combined effects of position-in-the-string and headedness. The claim that headedness and position interact was further confirmed by the finding that, in French, right-headed opaque-transparent compounds (the only right-headed category tested, as left-headed compounds are more frequent in the language) failed to yield the differential priming pattern obtained for left-headed compounds, when comparing first- and second-constituent primes. Contrary to French, differential priming was not found for Bulgarian, a language that is right-headed, as is English, and which patterns with results obtained for English by Libben (1997), with only one exception. The category that did exhibit a significant difference between first- and second-constituent priming, for both Bulgarian and English, was the transparent-opaque category, which showed a greater magnitude of priming with first (transparent) constituent primes as compared to second (opaque) constituent primes. This result highlights the role of constituent transparency, as in this case the opaque head is a weaker prime than the transparent initial constituent.

In light of the evidence presented thus far, we can conclude that, position-in-the-string, headedness and constituent transparency interact in the processing of compounds across languages. Other structural factors, however, have also been demonstrated to come into play cross-linguistically and will be discussed below.

3.2 The lexical status of compounds

The fact that constituent activation has been unequivocally shown to be at play in compound retrieval of course begs the question of whether compounds constitute distinct lexical units at all. The status of compounds has been widely debated by theoretical linguists and remains controversial (see Dressler, this volume), particularly in view of the fact that, in many languages, putative compounds are not simple concatenations of elements but, rather, contain structures that are analogous to phrases. Examples of such structures are compounds containing prepositional phrases (e.g. in Italian, *mulino a vento*, 'windmill', literally 'mill by wind'), or compounds featuring genitive-like structures (e.g. in German, *Königshof*, 'king's court'). In fact, historically, such structures originated as phrases and became lexicalized over time. Synchronically, those forms that are productive in the language in turn serve to coin novel compounds by analogy. This diachronic evolution in the lexical status of combined words corresponding to a single concept is also reflected in the changing, and sometimes varying, orthography of compounds (i.e. whether they are written as two words, in hyphenated form, or as one word). In the psycholinguistic literature, however, the lexical nature of compounds has been repeatedly attested across languages, even in the case of the more controversial structures, and independently of the issue of orthographic convention (but see de Jong et al. 2002, discussed above). In particular, it has been demonstrated that compounds *behave* differently from their constituents and from monomorphemic words in general.

3.2.1 Awareness of structure

Using a novel compound comprehension and production task to probe the acquisition of compounds in Hebrew, Clark and Berman (1987) demonstrated that from age four, children could identify head nouns in interpreting novel compounds out of context, as well as various relations between head and modifier (possession, location, containment, material, and purpose). Furthermore, although some Hebrew nouns may require stem changes when used as bound forms in compounding, the morphological form of the head noun—the initial constituent in the language—had no significant effect on their comprehension. Although, in production, knowledge of morphological form did play a role in the acquisition of compounds by Hebrew-speaking children (i.e. the simpler the form, the earlier it was produced), their early mastery of the structural constraints on compounds in comprehension indicates that, even in a language in which the morphology is more complex than in English and in which compounding is concurrently less productive, morphological patterns unique to compounds are acquired early on.

Other studies have also examined how linguistic knowledge affects the acquisition of compounds. In a effort to determine how linguistic form and conceptual hierarchies determine the acquisition of labels, Gelman, Wilcox, and Clark (1989) have shown that for English-speaking children subordinate compounds (e.g. *dingo-dog*) were easier to learn than simple subordinate nouns (e.g. *dingo*). In her conclusions, Clark underscores the role of compound form in how children learn the skill of labeling hierarchical categories and suggests that 'the ubiquity of compounds to express subordination in languages of the world may have evolved for functional reasons, to help the language learner'.

Comparing normal to impaired children's performance has also contributed to elucidating the issue of constituent awareness in children's processing of compounds. Employing a task requiring unimpaired and SLI (specific language-impaired) Greek-speaking children to produce compounds when presented with base constituents, Dalalakis (1999) showed that, contrary to SLI participants, unimpaired children were always aware of constituent boundaries. Their errors were mostly overgeneralizations in the production of the linking vowel -*o*- before vowel-initial second constituents, where it is not required in the language (e.g. *podikoanthropos*, the target novel compound being *podikanthropos*, 'mouseman'). They thus demonstrated correct abstraction of the structural representation of compounds in Greek.

Taken together, these acquisition data from English, Greek, and Hebrew clearly indicate that children (even of pre-school age, as shown by Gelman *et al.*, 1989) are sensitive to compound structure and treat compounds differently from other lexical items, again confirming their distinctiveness (for a discussion of compound acquisition see Nicoladis, this volume).

Evidence from aphasic performance also supports the distinct status of compounds. Luzzatti and de Bleser (1996) report two cases of Italian-speaking agrammatic patients who exhibited a selective disturbance in inflecting compounds and in choosing compound-internal prepositions, in the absence of an impairment in inflectional and derivational morphology. The selective nature of impairments, reflected in the breakdown of one linguistic process and the sparing of another, has widely been interpreted as evidence of their psychological reality. In the case in point, compounding is thus a word-generating process of its own and distinct from other such processes, that is derivation and inflection.

Mondini *et al.* (2002) compared gender agreement within left-headed noun-adjective and right-headed adjective-noun compounds and their phrasal counterparts in the production of two Italian-speaking aphasic patients. Thus compounds such as *natura morta*, 'still life' and *prima donna*, 'prima donna' were compared to nouns phrases such as *natura bella*, 'beautiful nature' and *vecchia donna*, 'old woman'. Results revealed that both patients could produce inflected adjectives within compounds correctly, but were unable to do so in noun phrases. Mondini *et al.*'s study again demonstrates that dissociations in impaired speech reflect awareness of differential structural properties and procedural mechanisms between compounded and non-compounded lexical sequences (see the discussion in Semenza and Mondini, this volume).

3.2.2 *Regularity effects in compound processing*

A pervasive issue in the psycho- and neurolinguistic literature on the mental lexicon concerns the processing of regular vs. irregular forms. A major focus of inquiry has been regular vs. irregular past-tense formation, and investigations of the performance of language-impaired individuals have revealed dissociations between regularly and irregularly inflected past-tense forms (e.g. Ullman, 1998, for English). In a study of the acquisition of regularly and irregularly inflected German noun plurals, Clahsen *et al.* (1992) observed that in longitudinal data from both an unimpaired child (data collected by Miller, 1976) and 19 dysphasic children, the plural affixes *-n* and *-s*, used in over-regularizations, were left out in compounds. Clahsen *et al.* argue that, in German, the default plural suffix *-s* is regular, while the other plural allomorphs (-o, and *-en*, *-e* and *-er* and their stem variants with an umlaut) are irregular. They further argue that 'a regular plural form created by an inflectional rule may not enter into a compound, whereas irregular plurals which are stored in the lexicon are accessible for compounding' and, furthermore, that the affix *-s* in compounds can be analyzed as a linking morpheme, rather than as a plural marker, because nouns correctly marked with the plural *-s* never appear in compounds (e.g. *Autobahn* 'highway', but not *Autosbahn*) and compounds containing an *-s* feature first-constituent nouns that do not take the -s plural (e.g. *Freundeskreis*, 'circle of friends' where the plural of *Freund* is *Freunde*). Crucially, children who misanalyzed -*n* as a regular affix and used this form as the default plural in simple nouns would omit the -*n* in compounds (e.g. *Blume_kohl, 'cauliflower'), whereas children who used -*s* as the default plural form would omit the -*s* in compounds (*Autobahn*). The children did, however, systematically provide the irregular plural markers required on the first constituent of compounds (e.g. *Kinderwagen*, 'picture book'). Similarly, Gordon (1985, cited in Clahsen *et al.*) found that English-speaking 3–5 year-olds who would produce the default plural form -*s* in simple words such as *mouses*, would never produce them within compounds (*mouses-eater*), but would sometimes produce the irregular form *mice-eater*. Clahsen *et al.* (1992) conclude that the distinction between regular and irregular morphology is available not only to unimpaired, but also to dysphasic children. Adopting Kiparsky's (1982, 1985) level-ordered morphology, the authors also conclude that since compounding takes place at level 2 and since -*n* and -*s* are level 3 affixes for children, they are left out, while irregular, level 1 affixes are intact. Clahsen *et al.*'s (1992) study thus provides evidence that universal morphological constraints involved in compounding are at play in the productions of not only unimpaired, but also impaired, children.

For English-speaking children, Kim *et al.* (1994) have shown that regularizations such as the ones found in plural formation (e.g. *gooses* instead of *geese*), are more likely to occur in exocentric compounds, that is compounds that are not 'a kind of X' (where X is the head of the compound), than in endocentric structures. Thus, children would tend to produce more regular plurals for exocentric compounds (e.g. *Mother Gooses* and *snaggletooths* > *Mother Geese* and *snaggleteeth*) than for their endocentric phrasal counterparts (e.g. *little geese* and *shark teeth* > *little gooses* and *shark tooths*). This points to the 'wordhood', or word-like nature, of compounds and, as Kim *et al.* (1994) argue, to their underlying hierarchical structure and to the principle that lexical features such as irregularity can only be inherited by the compound through its head. If there is no head, as is the case with exocentric compounds, regular plural formation applies by default. Again, acquisition data reveal that, cross-linguistically, young children are already sensitive to the distinctiveness of compounds and their structural characteristics.

Thus, across languages (English, German, Greek, Hebrew, and Italian) compounds have shown to be perceived and processed differently from other multimophemic words. The robustness of this finding is enhanced by the fact that similar results were obtained not only across languages, but also across populations (linguistically unimpaired and impaired children and aphasic patients).

3.3 The role of linking elements

As demonstrated by Dressler (this volume), compound structure varies substantially across languages. In some languages, one of the characteristics of compounds is that constituents are linked together by an intervening vowel or vowel-consonant sequence, called an interfix, linking morpheme, or linking element. Thus, for example, in Polish and Greek, compounds generally feature the linking vowel -*o*- (e.g. Polish: *wod*o*spad*, 'waterfall'; Greek: *domat*o*-salata*, 'tomato salad'). In German, by contrast, interfixed compounds make use of a much larger variety of frequently used forms (-*e*(*n*)-, -*er*-, -*s*-). Furthermore, stem+linking element combinations can be homophonous with inflected forms. Thus the form *Frauen* in the compound *Frauenheim*, 'women's home', is identical to the plural form of the word *Frau*, 'woman', while *Geschichts*- in *Geschichtsband*, 'history book', does not correspond to any existing form of the word *Geschichte*, 'history'. The question arises, therefore, whether these elements play a determining role in compound processing, or whether they merely serve as a type of 'glue' that both binds constituents and signals constituent boundaries. In the first case, linking elements would be morphemic in nature, while in the second case they would be considered morphologically 'empty'. Within- and cross-language evidence tends to concord with the view that these items are linking elements rather than morphemes, as the following review demonstrates.

An example of an early study that shed some light on the nature of linking elements is that of Kehayia *et al.* (1999) who used a constituent priming paradigm to probe compound processing in Greek and Polish. Although these two highly inflected languages differ typologically, they both feature the linking vowel -*o*- within compounds. Of particular interest to the question of the status of interfixed elements is the fact that in Greek all stems are non-words, while in Polish they can be homophonous with existing inflected words. Thus, Greek words such as *domatosalata*, 'tomato salad' or *hortokoptis* 'lawnmower' (lit. grass cutter), contain the stems *domat-* and *hort-*, which are nonwords when used in isolation. In contrast, in the Polish word *gwiazdozbiór*, 'constellation' (lit. star collection), the stem *gwiazd-* is homophonous with the word *gwiazd* (genitive plural form of the word *gwiazda*, 'star'), while *mebl-* in *meblowóz*, 'moving van' (lit. furniture car) is not. Although Greek and Polish differ with respect to the wordhood of their initial constituents, the two languages are identical with respect to the wordhood of stem+linking vowel combinations. In both Greek and Polish, the stem+linking vowel combinations can be either word-homophonous or non word-homophonous. The finding that in both languages the word-homophonous stem+linking vowel combinations (*horto* and *gwiazdo*) primed compounds as much as the free-standing citation forms of bound stems (*domata*, 'tomato' and *mebel*, 'piece of furniture'), combined with the finding that the magnitudes of priming were significantly greater with word-homophonous than with non word-homophonous primes (*horto* and *gwiazdo* > *domato and *meblo), was interpreted by Kehayia *et al.* (1999) as showing that homophony can create a word-effect in priming, and not as evidence that linking vowels function as morphemes. In fact, synchronically, the linking vowel -*o*- does not appear to be morpheme-like in either Greek or Polish, precisely because it is used productively even with stems that can never be inflected with the suffix -*o*. Whether they are derived by rule or by analogical processes, compounds with pseudo-affixed stems cannot be analyzed as featuring inflectional relics. In both languages, the historically driven de-morphologization of linking vowels may thus have been statistically enhanced by the concurrent presence of such forms, limiting their role to that of a 'concatenator' or 'linker'.

The issue of the status of linking elements in the processing of compounds was specifically addressed by Dressler *et al.* (2000) and Libben *et al.* (2002). In these studies, the processing of German interfixed compounds was investigated employing a series of off-line and on-line experiments. Results suggest that the diversity of interfixes in the language creates a computational cost and that this cost is influenced by speakers' knowledge of the forms that lexical items can take as initial constituents and by their knowledge of associated patterns of interfixation. Compound processing is thus, at least in part, driven by analogical principles. Further support for the view that interfixes are not morphemes comes from Dressler *et al.*'s (2000) and Libben *et al.*'s (2002) observations that compounds in which linking elements yield initial strings that are homophonous with inflected words do not differ from non-homophonous ones.

In an effort to investigate the role of typological variation in the processing of interfixed compounds, Jarema, Libben, Dressler and Kehayia (2002) compared results from a primed lexical decision experiment on German with those of Kehayia *et al.*'s (1999) study on Greek and Polish compound processing. In contrast to Greek and Polish, where, as indicated above, priming was facilitated in cases where the morphological prime was homophonous with a word, a wordhood effect was obtained for German un-interfixed primes (e.g. *Firma*, 'company', the base form of the first constituent of *Firmensitz*, 'head office'), but not for German interfixed primes (e.g. *Firmen*, 'companies'). The authors note that Greek and Polish cluster together in that they both feature the same productive linking vowel (*-o-*). German, on the other hand, clusters with Polish in that first constituents can be free-standing or bound, yet it dissociates from both Polish and Greek in the richness of its interfixational system. Jarema *et al.* (2002) conclude that access to the base form of first constituents is crucial across languages, that linking elements merely signal concatenation and that language-specific morphological properties influence compound processing.

Probing another Germanic language, Schreuder *et al.* (1998) investigated the problem of the functional role of the linking schwa -*e*- and its variant -*en*- in Dutch nominal compounds. In Dutch, both linking elements are homographs of inflectional markers (a semantically empty agreement marker used on adjectives and a regular and productive plural marker on nouns and verbs, respectively). Note that -*en*- appears in compounds in which a semantic plural reading is plausible (e.g. *boekenkast*, 'bookcase'), while -*e*- appears elsewhere (e.g. *slangebeet*, 'snake bite'). In 1996, however, in order to uniformize the spelling system, the (more frequent) *en* spelling was officially prescribed for compounds featuring *e* by the Dutch government. The question addressed by Schreuder *et al.* (1998) was, therefore, whether plural semantics would be activated when the *e* is written as *en*. Results from a series of experiments revealed that this is indeed the case: the newly prescribed *en* spelling for compounds in which a plural reading is meaningless induced activation of plural semantics. The authors argue that a plural interference effect is compatible with a dual-route approach to morphological processing in which the parsing route is an autonomous process. The parsing route thus automatically provides the plural interpretation of the first constituent, while the direct access route provides the meaning of the compound as a whole. Schreuder *et al.* (1998) conclude that the plural realization of the linking schwa is a morpheme, rather than a meaningless phoneme/grapheme in Dutch. It thus appears that Dutch spelling conventions, and the teaching thereof (before 1996: insert *en* only when a plural reading is plausible, for example *bookenkast*, 'bookcase', but not *slangenbeet*, 'snake bite'; from 1996: use *en* everywhere, for example *slangenbeet*, 'snake bite'), have biased speakers of the language toward plural interpretations of first constituents ending in -*en*, as well as hampered the shift from inflectional morphology to meaningless linkers observed in other languages. An important contributing factor may be that in Dutch -*en* is also an extremely productive plural suffix for verbs. Thus, this apparent counterexample to the position that linking elements are functionally empty can be interpreted as a language-specific (and perhaps item-specific) exception to the historical development of inflections into linking elements, some of which can be highly productive in compound formation (see Dressler, this volume).

Crucially, in later studies using a fill-in-the-blanks task (cloze procedure), Krott, Baayen, and Schreuder (2001) and Krott, Schreuder, and Baayen (2002a) demonstrate that in both off-line and on-line processing, the choice of linking elements in novel Dutch noun-noun compounds can be predicted probabilistically on the basis of the distribution of linking elements in what they call the left and right constituent families, that is the set of compounds that share the left-or right-constituent with the novel compound. In both off- and on-line experiments, the authors found that distributional biases influenced the choice of linking elements. However, the left-constituent family had a stronger effect than the right-constituent family. Moreover, the on-line experiment (Krott *et al.*, 2002a) also revealed that although right-constituent families do influence choice, albeit to a lesser degree than left-constituent families, they do not, in contrast to the latter, influence response latencies. The authors propose that, in Dutch, linking elements in novel compounds are chosen on the basis of analogy, not symbolic rules. Taken together, these results suggest that linking elements are not morphemic in nature and that initial constituents play a crucial role in compound processing. It is worth noting that although Krott *et al.* (2002a) do not directly address the issue of the status of interfixes in Dutch, the fact that they adopted the term 'linking element', rather than using the term 'linking morpheme' employed in Krott *et al.* (2001), may be indicative of a shift in their conceptualization of the role of interfixes. Moreover, the authors now use the term 'linker' (Krott *et al.*, 2002b), which suggests even more emphatically the morphologically 'empty' quality of intervening elements in compounds.

Bilingual children's productions of novel compounds have also shed light on the nature of intervening elements within compounds. Nicoladis (2002) administered a novel compound picture naming task to French–English bilingual children and observed that they produced more noun-preposition-noun (e.g. *fauteuils à fleurs*, 'chairs with flowers') than the less highly productive noun-noun structures in French (*fauteuils-fleurs*, literally 'chairs-flowers', meaning 'flower-chairs'), while the reverse was true for English (*flower chairs* > *chairs with flowers*). They however chose target prepositions only 50 percent of the time and were least accurate in ordering French prepositional compounds. Nicoladis concluded that prepositions within compounds are in the process of becoming linking elements in French. Important to the issue at hand is that Nicoladis' study reveals that even in the most phrase-like structures, that is nouns modified by prepositional phrases, intervening elements, in this case full lexical items (prepositions), tend to become devoid of meaning over time (for a full discussion, see Nicoladis, this volume).

In summary, with the exception of the Dutch study by Schreuder *et al.* (1998), investigations probing French, German, Dutch, Greek, and Polish suggest that linking elements are not morphemic in nature. However, both in the linguistic and psycholinguistic literature, this issue remains controversial and needs to be further explored across different languages, tasks, and populations.

3.4 Conclusion

In this chapter, we aimed to bring together cross-language evidence that would shed light on the issue of how compounds are represented and processed in the mental lexicon. More specifically, our main objective was to uncover whether the principles underlying the cognitive processes involved in the storage and access of compounds are generalizable across languages.

We first observed that cross-linguistic studies *per se* are still surprisingly rare. Indeed it has been demonstrated that the vast majority of studies on the mental lexicon concentrate on phenomena in a single language (Libben and Jarema, 2002). In this chapter, we reviewed five cross-linguistic investigations that included the following comparisons: Greek vs. Polish, German vs. Greek vs. Polish, Dutch vs. English (2), and French vs. Bulgarian. Other monolingual studies reviewed probed Chinese, Dutch, English, Finnish, Greek, Hebrew, Italian, and Japanese, while one study investigated French–English bilinguals. The twelve languages used in these studies vary typologically, as they represent different language families: Germanic (Dutch, English, German), Greek, Romance (French, Italian), Slavic (Bulgarian, Polish), Sino-Tibetan (Chinese), Japanese-Korean (Japanese), Semitic (Hebrew), and Uralic (Finnish). Thus one-third of the languages studied were non Indo-European. It must be noted, however, that monolingual studies of the mental lexicon in a poorly-inflected language such as English have been instrumental in uncovering many phenomena, indicating that critical distinctions need not rely on the study of languages with complex morphological systems. Ultimately, bringing such distinctions to the fore in languages at both ends of the continuum, that is with extremely poor morphological systems (e.g. Chinese, a language of particular interest because of its logographic writing system) and extremely rich morphological systems (e.g. Finnish, in which nouns can have up to 2000 inflected and cliticized forms) provides the critical test for uncovering universal lexical phenomena. The studies reviewed above, although limited in number, are nevertheless distributed along this continuum. Moreover, they include a language that is nonconcatenative in nature (Hebrew), offering a window into lexical representation and processing not only as a function of number and regularity of word-generating concatenative operations, but also as a function of structural constructs themselves.

In this cross-language overview, only phenomena that have been demonstrated to come into play across two or more languages were discussed. Unsurprisingly, issues raised across and within languages in studies on compounding relate to central questions in mental lexicon research. Are constituents activated during lexical access? What is the role of word-internal structure? Are there positional effects in lexical processing? Do distributional factors affect storage and access procedures? What is extraordinary, however, is that although actual comparative studies are scarce, there appears to be converging cross-language evidence that points to commonalities in the architecture of the mental lexicon. In particular, with respect to the issue of the representation and processing of compounds, the studies reviewed in this chapter provided a testing ground for the generalizability of individual approximations of the architecture of this lexical sub-system and, ultimately, of the lexical system as a whole.

The first and primary question discussed concerned constituent activation during compound processing. Whether structural, distributional, or semantic transparency effects were investigated, results obtained strongly support the view that the constituents of a compound are activated during compound processing. This general consensus emanates from studies in seven structurally-different languages investigating unimpaired as well as impaired populations. The second issue addressed was whether or not there are processing differences associated with the position of a constituent in a compound. Again, studies across several languages and in both non-brain-damaged and aphasic populations underscore the privileged status of the first, as compared to the second, constituent of a compound. A third and related issue is that of the role of the morphological head in access procedures. A single cross-linguistic study cannot lead to any conclusive claim. However, the data point to the view that headedness, position-in-the-string and semantic transparency interact in compound processing. The fourth question was whether compounds are cognitively akin to other polymorphemic lexical units. Acquisition and aphasiological data from four languages clearly indicate that children as well as aphasic patients are aware of compound structure. Moreover, linguistically unimpaired and impaired children show sensitivity to distinct structural characteristics of compounds, as evidenced in their use of regular vs. irregular plurals within compounds. The fifth and last issue raised was that of the status of linking elements. Results from unimpaired adult and child performances from comparative as well as monolingual studies suggest that linking elements are not morphemic in nature, that is that their main role in compound processing is that of a 'linker' and of a 'flag' signaling that the string is evolving into a compounded structure.

To conclude, the studies of the representation and processing of compounds across languages reviewed in this chapter have offered converging evidence concerning issues that are at the core of current research on the mental lexicon. We have seen that comparisons across languages offer both more challenging tests of hypotheses and more compelling conclusions when converging evidence is indeed found. It is hoped that these advantages will encourage more researchers to engage in cross-linguistic investigations.

4

The Neuropsychology of Compound Words

CARLO SEMENZA AND SARA MONDINI

The rationale for studying cognitive tasks via neuropsychological methods and observations is grounded in the fact that brain damage offers a unique opportunity to observe the working of particular psychological processes in isolation from other processes. The undisturbed flow of normal performance makes the components of a complex cognitive process opaque to external scrutiny. In experimental psychology a special repertory of techniques and standardized methods of observation is normally used to overcome this problem. However, in many cases, neuropsychology has the non-negligible advantage over experimental psychology of obtaining effects of a considerably greater order of magnitude. Thus, exploring linguistic processing in the relatively limited domain of compounds, through, for example, collection and analysis of errors or through priming techniques, may prove very laborious in normal subjects, at the present time. Errors may be scarce and the effects of reaction time experiments may be dubious and may depend on factors that are difficult to control. It is the case, therefore, that, before this book, compounding has been mentioned only occasionally within psycholinguistics. Relatively few investigations, almost exclusively concerned with recognition, have provided relevant empirical evidence on the subject. In contrast, aphasic patients can provide investigators with copious errors in easily controlled experimental settings. The nature of these errors may be revealing *vis-à-vis* psycholinguistic theories. Indeed, especially in the past decade, aphasiology has produced a number of studies focused on the processing of compound words. These studies are the object of the present review.

4.1 Early descriptive aphasiological literature on compounds

The earliest aphasiological works concerned with compounds were more interested in assessing aphasics' behavior than in trying to draw inferences about normal processing from pathological findings. Frequency, descriptiveness, transparency, word length, and position of component morphemes were the factors of interest, insofar as they posed a variety of difficulties for aphasic patients.

For example, Rochford and Williams (1965) compared the naming performance of English-speaking aphasics on compound nouns, varying the relative frequency of their component parts. Compounds of high-high, high-low, low-low, and low-high frequency combinations were used. The frequency of the first component seemed to determine the retrieval performance of aphasics, independently of the frequency of the second component: compounds with high-frequency first components were more easily retrieved than compounds with low-frequency first components. This result has been confirmed by Blanken (2000) in a study of German aphasics.

Another investigation concerned with frequency was conducted by Ahrens in 1977. Three groups of German-speaking aphasics (Broca's, Wernicke's, and anomics) were compared in a confrontation naming task. Targets were simple nouns and compounds of the noun-noun and verb-noun types, the components of which had high or low word frequency. In this study as well, there were fewer errors for compounds with a high-frequency first component, whereas the effect of high frequency of the second component was less evident. When only one part of the compound was successfully named, it was usually the first one, that is, the one that in German specifies the meaning of the second, more general word (this effect, however, was not replicated in other group studies of German aphasics reported by Hittmair-Delazer *et al.*, 1994 and by Blanken, 2000). Ahrens attributed this somewhat unexpected finding to the fact that the compound's first component has a more specific meaning and also that it is the stress-bearing part. He also speculated that the grammatical unit of the compound noun is not very stable. The use of productive word-building rules would depend on the frequency of the compound, whereby frequent ones would be lexicalized and less frequent ones would be composed by rule. The patient groups behaved differently: Broca's aphasics often had trouble in connecting the two parts, while Wernicke's aphasics produced a large number of phonemic paraphasias. More interestingly, anomic aphasics tried to build the whole compound, a strategy leading to compound paraphasias.

Stachowiak (1979) investigated the influence of predicative processing. In a picture-naming task, target words were simple and compound words, varying in their amount of 'descriptiveness'. According to Stachowiak's distinction, a 'descriptive' word indicates in its form that it is derived from a predication, while a word that expresses no predication has the character of a label. Examples of strongly descriptive nouns are those derived from verbs like *boxer* (someone who *boxes*) or transparent compounds such as *nutcracker*. According to Stachowiak's hypothesis, strongly descriptive words should elicit descriptive responses rather than simple semantic paraphasias. The four groups of targets were: (a) low descriptive compounds: *Hubschrauber*, 'helicopter'; (b) high descriptive compounds: *Nagelfeile*, 'nail file'; (c) simple nouns, not descriptive: *Koffer*, 'suitcase'; (d) nouns derived from a verb: *Boxer*, 'boxer'. The highest error rate was observed for the descriptive compounds and the lowest for the 'label' nouns. As Stachowiak had hypothesized, descriptive compounds induced descriptive responses more frequently. No interaction of aphasia type is reported.

Dressler and Denes (1989) later explained the higher error rates for descriptive transparent compounds by arguing that transparent descriptive words are easier to analyze into their components and may therefore present a greater source of errors (namely, the parts plus the whole compound) than simple nouns. Dressler and Denes' own study investigated comprehension and identification of transparent and opaque compounds in Italian-speaking Broca's and Wernicke's aphasics. Patients were found to apply two basic strategies to identify and explain compounds: a 'morphological' strategy using one or both parts of a given compound, suitable only for transparent items, and a 'semantic' strategy using synonyms of the whole compound or descriptions. An example of a morphological strategy would be to say, instead of *portalettere*, postman (lit. 'carry letters'), 'someone who carries letters' or 'who brings mail'. An example of a semantic strategy is providing a synonym or a semantic description without morphological connection to any part of the compound (e.g. 'employee of the post office'). All patients performed better in dealing with transparent compounds and Broca's aphasics were always superior to Wernicke's aphasics. Broca's aphasics applied the appropriate strategy more often, while Wernicke's aphasics tended to rely on the easier, but often inadequate 'morphological' strategy.

A single case study of a German-speaking Wernicke's aphasic with a particular difficulty in processing compound nouns was reported by Stark and Stark in 1990. The patient's repetition of 'twin compounds' was assessed. 'Twin compounds' are those in which the serial order of the components can be reversed to form another compound: for example, *Hauskonzert*, 'house concert' and *Konzerthaus*, 'concert hall'. The first component of the twin compound was always repeated much more accurately and the second part was very often dropped: thus, *Hauskonzert* tended to be repeated as *Haus* and *Konzerthaus* as *Konzert*. When both components were repeated, phonological errors appeared in both. The patient made use of phonemic approximation to improve his first response in about one-third of his attempts. He often repeated the first word while trying to repeat the second. Although a word length effect was clearly present, it could not entirely explain the pattern of performance: the word boundary indeed proved to be the crucial point for errors. Further tasks (naming, reading, and writing) and spontaneous speech provided evidence that allowed for excluding both a selective semantic and a selective phonological deficit. Stark and Stark argued that the patient's pattern of performance was better explained by a 'faulty interaction between the lexical-semantic and the phonological levels.'

4.2 Knowledge of the compound status of a word

Knowledge of the compound status of a word seems to be stored independently of the ability to use compounding rules and to retrieve the appropriate phonological form. Evidence for this fact comes from a number of aphasiological studies: in picture–naming tasks, patients frequently replace compound words with verbal paraphasias (errors consisting of existing words that, however, do not apply to the target) and neologisms that reflect the compound structure of the target, while they replace single words for single-word targets. This effect first emerged as a group tendency in a study reported in Semenza, Butterworth, Panzeri, and Hittmair-Delazer (1992). In this study fifteen German-speaking aphasic patients, free from severe articulation disorders, were administered a naming test where the stimulus material consisted of forty-nine pictures which are correctly named by compounds, interspersed with distracter items whose name is a simple word. The analysis of errors revealed the following: when the error was a compound word (e.g. *Zuckerdose*, 'sugar jar'; *Lautsprecher*, 'loud speaker') or a compound neologism (e.g. *Spindelgrammophon*,[1] 'spindle gramophone'), the target was also a compound word (e.g. *Salzstreuer*, 'salt shaker'; *Plattenspieler*, 'record player') in ninety-one cases and it was a simple word, in just one case. When the error was a simple word, the target was a compound in thirty-three cases and a simple word in twenty-one cases.

A study in Italian (Semenza, Luzzatti, and Carabelli, 1997), using the same number of items but testing a much larger population (thirty-six patients), replicated the effect. The analysis was repeated

[1] Nonexisting word.

for each aphasia subgroup participating in the study. Wernicke's aphasics and, more clearly, a single anomic aphasic, showed the overall group trend. Broca's aphasics, instead, were slightly different because they gave more simple than compound responses for compound stimuli: this was largely due to the fact that they tended to drop the first part of the compound (e.g. the item *portalettere*, 'postman', [lit., carry letters] was replaced with *lettere*, 'letters', see below for a discussion of this effect); on the other hand, they never provided compound responses to a simple stimulus.

In Blanken's (2000) group study the effect was less marked. According to the author, this may be due to the fact that he considered only first naming responses. Interestingly, in this study, opaque compounds attracted a larger number of other compounds than transparent ones.

The group effect has been replicated in detailed single-case studies (Badecker, 2001; Delazer and Semenza, 1998). Badecker (2001) has also observed that omissions of one component (a very frequent error in his patient) were very often followed by correct responses or other compounding responses; furthermore, in his patient's speech output, the prosodic form of the component errors virtually always suggested that the patient was aware that the response was incomplete and that there was a word missing.

Badecker has argued that the fact that compound neologisms are evoked by compound targets (but not non-compounds) indicates that some feature of the compounds initiates the compositional procedure evident in these errors. Note that it cannot be the prosodic structure of the compound that accounts for this asymmetry, because polysyllabic monomorphemic words did not induce this error type. The morphological structure of the target is the clear candidate.

Delazer and Semenza's (1998) Italian-speaking patient seemed to have a particularly selective problem with compounds. Indeed, when presented with compounds, his error rate was 60 percent in confrontation naming, 52 percent in naming on description, 22.5 percent in repetition, 22.5 percent in reading and 7.5 percent in writing to dictation. In contrast, he produced only 5 percent errors with monomorphemic words in confrontation naming and none over all the other conditions. While there were no errors in simple words, all errors on compounds maintained the compound structure.

Interestingly, this effect is not limited to languages with highly productive compounding processes (such as German or English), but it is also found in Italian where compounding plays a less important role in creative word formation. Of course, nothing in the pictorial stimulus might have provided patients with reliable cues about whether the corresponding word was a compound or not. What is named with a compound word in one language may, in fact, be named by a simple word in another language. Note also, that many compounds have monomorphemic synonyms in the same language.

The fact that the morphological information of compound status could be intact when a word is inaccessible is not easily explained. It is indeed the case that aphasics with naming problems often retain control of morphological knowledge such as inflectional or derivational rules (Caplan *et al.*, 1972; Semenza *et al.*, 1990). However, bound morphemes such as inflections are part of the closed-class vocabulary and are classically thought to build, with other function words, a framework for sentences independent of their phonological specification (Garrett, 1990a). Most compounds (and indeed those used in the above-mentioned studies), on the other hand, belonging to the open-class vocabulary have neither the function of labeling specific semantic nor specific syntactic categories, and frequently denote contents that are named by monomorphemic words in other languages.

4.3 Knowledge of the compound structure and of word-building rules

Patients substituting compounds with compound paraphasias also most often seem to be aware of the particular structure of the compound. Indeed, in available investigations (Hittmair-Delazer *et al.*, 1994; Semenza *et al.*, 1997), most aphasics tended to replace noun-noun compounds with other noun-noun compounds (or noun-noun neologisms) and verb-noun compounds with other verb-noun compounds (or verb-noun neologisms). In this respect, no difference was found between Broca's and Wernicke's aphasics. This trend is confirmed in the case where only one part of the compound target is replaced. For instance, in the Hittmair-Delazer *et al.* corpus, in substitutions, the correctly named components kept their original position in the majority of cases (40/44), the first component being spared as frequently as the second component. For example: *Schneefrau**, 'snowwoman', instead of *Schneemann*, 'snowman'; *Wasserspieler**, 'water player', instead of *Plattenspieler*, 'record player'.

Aphasics' neologistic production of compounds was also found to be well-formed and to respect word-building rules. For example, in Hittmair-Delazer *et al.*'s (1994) collection of errors in German aphasics, in all the verb-noun neologisms, the verb stem appears in first position correctly dropping the *-en* ending of the infinitive. In noun-verb derivation, for example as in *Tischklapper**, lit. 'table folder', substituting for *Bügelbrett*, 'ironing board', there is a correct verbal derivation ending with *-er*.

In this respect, the following example is particularly instructive: the target *Rollschuh* (lit. 'roll shoe', 'roller skate', is replaced with *Schuhroller**: the word *Roller* appears in the target as the verb-stem roll-, while in the neologism it is correctly derived as the nominal form *roll_er_*. In Hittmair-Delazer *et al.*'s (1994) error collection only two out of twenty-six compound neologisms were not well-formed with respect to German compounding rules. The two exceptions are, however, worth discussing. The first is:

*Feuerschwimm**, lit. 'fire swim', instead of *Regenschirm*, lit. 'rain umbrella'.

Schwimm is the verb stem of *schwimmen*, and, according to German grammar rules, could not be in the second position. However, considering the target, Hittmair-Delazer *et al.* argued that the error in the second component may not have been lexical, but rather, phonological (*schwimm* instead of *schirm*).

The second is:

Spinnenrad* instead of *Spinnrad*, 'spinning wheel'.

The error may be a morphological one, since the stems are correctly produced: what is wrong is the particle *-en* between the two components of the compound. There are at least two explanations for this error. The first is that the patient may have chosen *Spinnen* as the plural form of the noun *Spinne*: indeed *spinnen* appears in some compounds (i.e. *Spinnennetz*, 'spider web'). According to the second explanation *spinnen* is the infinitive form of the verb *spinnen*, 'to spin'.

A remarkable finding in Hittmair-Delazer *et al.*'s (1994) study was that no linking morphemes appeared to connect the first and the second part of the compound neologisms, except in the particular cases where the first component was the plural form of a word whose singular form ends with -e. According to the currently productive German rules, such words take the plural form -n when appearing in compounds. Some old words stand as exceptions: consider, for example, *Mühlenrad*, lit. 'mill wheel', substituted by *Windmühle*, 'wind mill'. The lexical item *Mühlrad*, without the -en ending, does indeed exist. In the error, the patient appears to have applied the productive rule. The very rare word *Mühlenrad* also exists in German dictionaries: however, all the judges in Hittmair-Delazer *et al.*'s study considered it to be a neologism. These findings may suggest that the patients build their compounds using rules rather than using analogies with existing compounds.

4.4 Compositional processes

One central issue of the theory of lexical processing is the question of whether the composite nature of a word form is reflected directly in its recognition, storage, and production. Neuropsychological data have offered an unequivocal answer to the question of whether compounds undergo compositional processes when being produced.

In the case of compounds, as with other complex words, three different hypotheses compete with each other. First, compounds are stored as whole words and are retrieved as such. Second, while having a listed lexical entry, they may also be generated by morphological rules. A third hypothesis, according to which compounds are generated by rules and have no single lexical entry, is less likely to be true, since many compounds are idiosyncratic in structure and have opaque meanings.

A study in Italian (Semenza *et al.*, 1997) specifically addresses this issue. The investigation was based on two given facts. The first is that Italian verb-noun compounds, the most productive type in the language, are grammatically nouns. These compounds have an *exocentric* structure and neither of the two elements is the logical and grammatical head of the compound. For instance, a *portamonete*, 'purse' [lit. 'carry-coins'], is neither a special type of coin, nor a special way of carrying something: this compound is a noun and refers to an object that is used to contain (carry) coins. The second fact is that anterior Broca's aphasics, as a group, as compared to other aphasics, tend to omit verb forms, both in spontaneous speech or in constrained naming. Semenza *et al.* (1997) found that, in naming verb-noun compounds, Broca's aphasics, unlike Wernicke's aphasics, showed a much higher proportion of omissions of the verb component (e.g. when naming the compound item *girasole*, 'sunflower', [lit. 'turn sun'], they would tend to tell *sole* omitting the verb *gira*). Since verb-noun compounds are nouns, if they were processed whole, there would be no reason for Broca's aphasics to omit the verb component more often than other aphasics do. Semenza *et al.*'s results have been recently confirmed using a multiple-single-case paradigm and a more balanced set of items (Mondini *et al.*, 2004). This finding cannot be attributed to a simple effect of position because the patients did not show the same effect in compounds other than that of the verb-noun type. This conclusion is also supported by the fact that no position effect was found with Broca's aphasics in the German study by Hittmair-Delazer *et al.* (1994). Taken together these findings, therefore, provide a strong indication that compound words are parsed into their component parts in the course of lexical retrieval.

Badecker (2001) has suggested that aphasiological findings on compounds could resolve the issue of how compositional processes in production are related to morphological productivity. He argues that, since morphological productivity typically entails semantic compositionality, it could be that compositional procedures are exploited only when the meaning of the complex word is exhaustively characterized in terms of the meaning of its morphological constituents. Alternatively, the lexical production system may take a compositional approach to processing morphologically complex forms in cases of productive word formation, even if the semantics of the word cannot be derived formally from the meaning of its constituents. Badecker presents evidence in favor of this last alternative from the analysis of errors in an anomic patient, who (like Delazer and Semenza's 1998 patient and, in general, patients in group studies: see particularly Blanken, 2000) showed signs of composition not only for transparent compounds but also for opaque ones. In the same work, Badecker also points out how misordering errors like 'box post' or 'tree shoe' or 'wood fire', instead of 'post box', 'shoe tree', and 'fire wood', respectively shown in his patient, do not seem compatible with the whole-word retrieval account, which would lead one to expect that the word order would be respected. This is valid especially since no ordering errors were observed in the patient's production of monomorphemic words. Badecker concluded that misorderings can be observed only when the morphological structure of the target provides two lexical slots for its components. The misordering of compound constituents can then be accounted for relatively straightforwardly by positing a deficit in a mechanism that composes compounds out of their lexical components. In particular, the compositional mechanism must associate each of the two retrieved lexical forms with a specific position in the compound structure, and the loss of information concerning the links between the lexical items and their target positions may result in misordering.

4.5 The sequence of events in processing

The issue of sequencing is strictly related to, although not overlapping with, the preceding one. The sequence of events in the production of compounds is unclear and little theory has been developed on how different portions of the necessary information become available during the process (see, however, Libben, 1998 and Levelt, Roelofs, and Mayer, 1999). A compound corresponds to an exactly defined lexical unit in a language vocabulary and its meaning may not correspond to the paraphrase of the single components. How and in what order do the meanings and the syntactic properties of the whole-word and of its separate components interact in retrieval? Some information on these issues comes from Delazer and Semenza's (1998) and Badecker's (2001) observations on anomic patients who exhibited a specific difficulty for naming compound targets with respect to a relatively intact (less so in Badecker's patient) ability to name non-compounds.

The origin of Delazer and Semenza's patient's naming problem did not lie in disturbances to the central semantic/conceptual system or to its input. The patient, in fact, could understand compounds, provide appropriate definitions and distinguish existing from non-existing compounds. He also retained a clear notion of compounding rules and could easily tell legal from illegal compound neologisms. In the output his difficulty was not simply with long or low-frequency words, since he could retrieve low-frequency monomorphemic words well and made no errors with complex number words.

The difficulty, therefore, lay at some level of production. The patient never answered compound targets with monomorphemic paraphasias. He often retrieved just one component, replacing the other. These frequent substitution errors may suggest separate lexical processing of the compounds' components. The semantic properties of most of the patient's semantic paraphasias, however, argue against this hypothesis. Many neologisms were, in fact, good semantic descriptions and made sense in their compound connection, while their single components were neither semantically nor phonologically related to the target's components, as for example, in the substitution of *parafulmine* (lit. 'against lightning', 'lightning-rod') with *salvaguida** (lit. 'save guide', neologism). In this case the neologism was a good circumlocution of the target's meaning. It is unlikely that the single parts of the neologism were substitutions of the respective components (*guida*, 'driver', was in no way related to *fulmine*, 'lightning'). Also, most single-component substitutions were related to the whole-word meaning, while they were not (or they were less) related to the single missing component, as for example in the substitution of *portarifiuti* (lit. 'carry rubbish', 'dustbin') with *bidonerifiuti** (lit. 'bin rubbish', neologism). Few substitutions were related to the single missing part, such as in *pescecane* (lit. 'fish dog', 'shark') replaced with *pescetigre** (lit. 'fish tiger', neologism); even in this example, however, the general meaning, a particularly ferocious fish, is respected.

In general, therefore, substitutions seemed to be chosen with respect to the whole-word's meaning. Word frequency was not a critical factor and inserted substitutions did not have a higher frequency than the missing parts. The head of a compound was substituted equally as often as the subordinate part. Obviously the head did not play a privileged role in the retrieval of compounds.

Single-component substitutions were also informative of other aspects of compound processing. First and second components were often equally preserved and kept their place in the paraphasia, that is when only the second component was accessible, a first component was inserted in the first position (*aspirapolvere*, lit. 'suck dust', 'vacuum cleaner', replaced with *scopapolvere*, lit. 'sweep dust', neologism). The fact that the first and the second component were often equally preserved suggests that the components of a compound are activated in parallel without a hierarchical serial timing. Note that within this framework, access time for each component may depend on the characteristics of each language. Blanken (1997), in fact, observed a German-speaking aphasic who produced many component-wise approaches to compound targets (e.g. *Teebeutel* was replaced with *Beutel Teebeutel*, 'bag tea bag'). In these errors it was mainly the more general, final component that was named first. Indeed, according to Blanken (2000), the salient role of the second, basic component in German can also be accounted for syntactically. As syntactic head, it determines the gender of the whole compound in German, and thus the preceding article. According to Blanken, the fact that a position effect is not evident with substitutions (see also Delazer and Semenza, 1998) can be accounted for by assuming that these errors are generated at a relatively early stage of processing, for example at the semantic conceptual level.

Delazer and Semenza (1998) conclude that the patient's problem arises when activating two separate forms with a single entry. Badecker's patient was somewhat similar, although he made several errors on monomorphemic words as well. He, too, did not seem to have compounding problems at the semantic level. In addition, his semantic substitution errors were related more to the whole word than to its components. Unlike Delazer and Semenza's patient, who did not show such errors, the dominant error type was lexical responses corresponding either to the first or second constituent of the target compound (e.g. *grasshopper* replaced with *grass*; *lighthouse* replaced with *light*). As reported above in this case, however, there were indications that the patient was aware of the compound nature of the target. Badecker suggests that his patient's problems result from the combination of different impairments: a deficit affecting word form retrieval, a breakdown in linking retrieved forms to positions in the target frame, and possibly also from the amplifying effect that this linking difficulty has on the deficit that influences form retrieval in general. On this account, Delazer and Semenza's purer patient's deficit seems to lie mainly in the linking problem.

Both Delazer and Semenza's (1998) and Badecker's (2001) studies investigate the nature of the processes at play in compound retrieval. They agree that at some point one entry is apparently activating two separate forms.

Indeed, there must be different routes for a speaker to generate morphologically complex words, depending on the nature of the word. In their two-stage theory of lexical access Levelt, Roelofs and

Mayer (1999) distinguish three cases that may apply to compounds: (a) the single lemma-multiple-morpheme; (b) the single-concept-multiple-lemma; (c) the multiple-concept. These authors indicate frequently used compounds such as 'blackboard', 'sunshine', or 'hot-dog' as likely examples of the single-lemma-multiple-morpheme case. This theory, however, does not distinguish between transparent and opaque compounds. An opaque compound (like 'hot-dog') may be thought to be more economically processed as a single lemma-single morpheme unless there is evidence indicating an alternative account. Evidence from aphasia proves that composition also occurs for opaque compounds.

Two-stage models have, in fact, been challenged, and a model has been proposed that dispenses with the intermediate lemma stage, whereby morphemes are linked directly to distributed semantic representations and grammatical features (Caramazza, 1997). The way such a model would deal with compound words has not so far been made explicit. Some difficulties may, however, arise from aphasiological studies like those reported by Delazer and Semenza (1998) and Badecker (2001). As Badecker puts it, compounds require representational units that bind all the components of a form together into a single lexical item, along with specifying how these components must be combined. Since aphasic performance indicates that compounds are not stored as single morphemes, some other type of unit must bind these pieces together for the particular lexical meaning. It is at the level of this unit that substitutions leading to compound neologisms take place. This level must also be independent from the meaning itself because patients have otherwise intact semantics. In other words, aphasiological data on compound processing seem to support the idea of an intermediate form between the conceptual semantic representation and the phonological form.

The variable of semantic transparency in the processing of compounds has been specifically investigated by Libben *et al.* (1998). Libben's Automatic Progressive Parsing and Lexical excitation (APPLE) model of morphological parsing isolates constituent morphemes of a compound through a left to right recursive parsing procedure. It incorporates a check for the orthographic and the lexical status of both constituents of the parse. Within this model (see Jarema, this volume for a fuller description), semantic transparency is represented in two distinct ways. The first, on the lexical level, deals with the semantic relationship between the meaning of a morpheme within a compound and the independent meaning of that same morpheme. In addition, at the conceptual level, the model considers transparency associated with the compound as a whole. On the conceptual level, meaning components that are not transparent are actively inhibited, while the only meaning receiving activation is that of the whole compound. Libben's (1998) patient RS could distinguish existing from novel compounds, thus showing intact lexical representations. She tended, however, to interpret semantically opaque compounds in terms of a blend of constituent and whole-word meaning (e.g. for 'butterfly' she provided the description 'it is a pretty fly, it's yellow'). She thus revealed, according to an interpretation within the APPLE framework, activation of all possible representations at the conceptual level, in absence of the inhibitory processes that would select the right response. Deep dyslexic patient JO (McEwen *et al.*, 2001), although rarely reading compounds correctly, seemed to process the entire string. She preferred transparent constituents, often reading transparent components first in compounds that have an opaque component followed by a transparent component like 'strawberry'. She showed evidence for both constituents and whole-word access: for instance, in reading 'pancake', she produced 'cake, breakfast..., syrup': after reading the second constituent 'cake' correctly, she provided two semantic associates for the whole compound. According to McEwen *et al.*, JO's compound word reading results are consistent with a model of compound processing in which (a) both transparent and opaque compounds are linked to their constituents in the mental lexicon, (b) both constituents are obligatorily activated in visual word recognition and (c) semantic opacity creates incompatibilities that are normally resolved prior to output.

4.6 Gender assignment

The issue of gender in compounds has been addressed in two studies in Italian (Luzzatti and De Bleser, 1996; Mondini *et al.*, 1999), with respect to the distinction among rule-based, lexically based and semantically based assignment. In Italian all nouns belong to two gender classes, masculine and feminine, irrespective of the natural gender. For nouns referring to living beings, the grammatical gender often coincides with the natural one, which can be derived from underlying semantic knowledge. If the entity referred to has no natural gender, grammatical gender is then a purely lexical feature. Gender of nouns percolates to articles (Masc: *il*; Fem: *la*).

The following rules apply to most *simple nouns* that, in Italian, are inflected also in the citation form: the suffix *-o* is usually masculine singular (*il toro*, 'bull'; *il vaso*, 'vase') and the suffix *-a*, feminine singular (*la suora*, 'nun'; *la bocca*, 'mouth'). However, both natural and grammatical gender are not always reflected in these rules. Thus the suffix *-a* may apply to masculine singular (e.g. *il poeta*, 'male poet'; *il diploma*, 'diploma'); in the same way the suffix *-o* may apply to a few feminine words (e.g. *la mano*, 'hand'). In some other cases, the -a suffix prevails over the natural gender in determining grammatical form, as in the case for *la guardia*, 'policeman', or *la sentinella*, 'sentinel'. There is another singular suffix *-e*, whose gender is unpredictable (e.g. *il ponte*, 'bridge', is masculine, *la torre*, 'tower', is feminine). Therefore, here again, grammatical gender is a lexical feature.

In compound nouns, gender depends on the structure and position of the head. Noun-noun compounds take the gender of the head of the compound (e.g. for left-headed compounds, *la **casa** albergo*, 'boarding house' or *il **bagno**schiuma*, 'bubble bath', and for right-headed ones, *la ferro**via***, 'railway' or *il via**dotto***, 'viaduct'). Verb-noun compounds are exocentric and are generally masculine, irrespective of the noun component in the compound, which can be either masculine ending with *-o* or feminine ending with *-a* (e.g. *il segnalibro*, bookmark, or *il colapasta*, 'colander').

In derived nouns, the suffix determines the gender of the noun. Thus, for example, the suffixes *-aggine* and *-udine* indicate feminine gender (e.g. *la similitudine*, 'similitude'), the suffixes *-ore* and *-iere*, masculine gender (e.g. *il bollitore*, 'kettle').

Luzzatti and De Bleser (1996) described an agrammatic patient (DR) showing a dissociation between regular (preserved) and irregular (impaired) inflections. The patient was required to assign the correct article to a list of nouns as well as to nonwords made up of a non-existing stem and a real derivational suffix. DR correctly assigned the article to derived nouns, but failed with pseudoderived nonwords. Luzzatti and De Bleser interpreted these findings to be the result of a parsing defect rather than a morphological impairment. Thus, DR would not parse the derivational suffix, and therefore would not access gender information if the suffix was attached to a non-real stem. This result, however, did not support the findings obtained by Burani and Laudanna (1992) on lexical decision times of derived words and nonwords, showing that derivational suffixes also undergo standard morphological parsing analysis when they are bound to nonwords.

Mondini *et al.* (1999) replicated Luzzatti and De Bleser's (1996) study, administering the same items to their own patient MB, affected by Broca's aphasia and deep/phonological dyslexia. In the task, the subject has to assign the gender of nouns by adding the article. In the experimental materials, simple masculine and feminine nouns appeared with different endings (about half of the items had conceptually based natural gender, for example *suora*, 'nun', feminine, which matched the grammatical one, while the other items designated objects and carried a neutral gender, so that the grammatical gender could not be guessed from the meaning of the noun). Compounds were: noun-noun compounds (half right-headed and half left-headed) with constituents of different gender (masculine nouns ending in *-o* combined with feminine nouns ending in *-a*; feminine nouns ending in *-a* combined with masculine nouns ending in *-o*), and verb-noun compounds whose noun component was either feminine ending in *-a* or masculine ending in *-o*. In addition, nonwords were administered either as simple elements ending with -*o* or -*a*, or as pseudo-derived nonwords where the nominal derivational suffix (-*ore*, -*iere*, -*trice*, -*aggine*, -*udine*) modified a nonword. MB failed with items that had no natural gender and where the ending vowel (-*e*) does not contain morphological cues. He was, however, perfect in applying (and often generalizing) the major ending rule (Masc: -*o*; Fem: -*a*) to both words and nonwords. He was also flawless in gender assignment of pseudo-derived nonwords, where he made gender choice based on the derivational suffix (e.g. -*aggine* is feminine; -*iere* is masculine). The patient failed with compounds, where he decided mostly on the basis of the ending of the second noun. In particular, he also used this strategy with verb-noun compounds, assigning gender on the basis of the (right) nominal ending. He was therefore, accidentally, successful only with verb-noun compounds ending in -*o*.

MB's performance seemed to reflect a dissociation between correct semantically based and rule-based gender assignment (it remains difficult to establish how much of his success was due to the application of a strategy or to intact competence) and impaired lexically based gender assignment. MB's behavior differed to some extent from that observed in other agrammatics, and in particular from that of Luzzatti and De Bleser's (1996) patient DR. Like MB, this patient showed a dissociation between regular (preserved) and irregular (impaired) inflections. However, unlike MB, he failed with pseudo-derived nonwords. For this reason, as mentioned above, he was thought to have a parsing deficit preventing him from analyzing the pseudoword into each of its component parts and thus recognizing the derivational suffix.

4.6.1 *Agreement between components*

Processing compounds may require processing agreement between components. Luzzatti and De Bleser (1996) addressed this issue with respect to noun-noun and verb-noun compounds, while Mondini *et al.* (2002) studied the production of noun-adjective (NA) and adjective-noun (AN) compounds. Both these studies were conducted on Italian.

In Italian, the syntactic head of endocentric noun-noun compounds can be either the first or the second noun (*la casa/albergo*, 'boarding house', but *il via/dotto*, 'the viaduct'). The inflectional number affix can appear word-externally, like in most languages of the world (*il via/dotto*) or if the compound is left-headed, number inflection is word-internal (*le case/albergo*) or in some rare cases, it occurs both within and outside of the compound (*le case/madri*, the mother-house).

In exocentric verb-noun nominal compounds, neither the noun nor the verb stem is head of the compound. Internal inflection cannot take place since verb stems do not inflect for number. External number may occur, but only in cases where the masculine or feminine noun, entering the verb-noun compound as modifier, has a plural form ending with -*i*. In all other cases the plural form is identical to the singular.

Luzzatti and De Bleser (1996) described the performance of two patients, MG and DR, with verb-noun and noun-noun compounds intermixed with singular items. The patients' task was to produce the plural form. Both patients tended to treat all compounds alike, whether they were verb-noun or noun-noun, left-headed or right-headed, and they mainly pluralized the final noun. MG uniformly treated compounds as head-final. DR overgeneralized external number assignment. According to Luzzatti and De Bleser this was not necessarily due to an impairment of syntactic analysis as such. Another explanation is that DR had a preference for inflectional processes to take place externally. While this is obligatory in many languages, it is just one possible option in Italian. Alternatively, assuming that internal affixation is marked, DR may have simply exhibited reliance on the unmarked rule. The question remains as to whether this behavior was strategic or just an example of normal recruitment of morphological processes.

Italian NA or AN compounds can be written as one word (e.g. *terraferma*, 'main land'), or as two separate words (e.g. *febbre gialla*, 'yellow fever'). However, from a syntactic point of view, the latter are also considered atoms since they do not allow insertion of another adjective, movement of a constituent, or positional exchange between the noun and the adjective. In Italian, all nouns, even those referring to inanimate objects, feature a masculine or feminine grammatical gender marker. Most adjectives must be inflected accordingly. While nominal inflections -*o* and -*a* are transparent for grammatical gender (-*o* = masculine; -*a* = feminine) and can easily be copied onto the modifying adjectives, the inflectional suffix -*e* is gender opaque, being equally distributed in masculine and feminine nouns.

Mondini *et al.* (2002) required two aphasic patients with symptoms of agrammatism to produce NA or AN compounds both in isolation and in sentences. Each item was matched with a noun-adjective pair that does not have the status of a compound, holding the noun constant, while varying the adjective. The type of agreement was identical, for example the compound *sangue freddo*, 'cold blood', was matched with the noun phrase *sangue secco*, 'dry blood'.

The two aphasic patients were able to inflect adjectives embedded in a compound noun, but could not process gender agreement in a standard noun phrase. Moreover, the aphasics seemed to be sensitive to the order that is canonical in Italian (N-A) when processing non-compound pairs (i.e. they were better at producing *libro rotto*, 'broken book' (N-A) than *strana moda*, 'strange fashion' (A-N), which are both non-compounds), but they processed AN compounds (e.g. *alta moda*, 'haute couture') and NA compounds (e.g. *febbre gialla*, 'yellow fever') equally well.

According to Mondini *et al.* (2002), these findings suggest differential processing for NA and AN compounds and N-A and A-N noun phrases. While the latter require a standard morpho-syntactic operation that is often impaired in agrammatic patients, the former seem to be processed as whole words. This conclusion is intriguing given that, in other respects, compounds seem to be retrieved in a decomposed form. Decomposition, however, has been demonstrated to come into play in the case of free morphemes. Bound morphemes such as gender inflectional suffixes do not seem to necessarily undergo decomposition, but could be integrated within the whole-word phonological form.

4.7 The case of prepositional compounds

In Romance languages, like Italian and French (see also Nicoladis, this volume), noun modification may be realized by means of N-N composition, but the most productive solution is prepositional compounding, a type of compound where the modifying element is a prepositional phrase (e.g. [il [[mulino]N [a vento]PP]]NP, the windmill). The compound status of prepositional (PC) compounds is not unanimously accepted (see Dressler, this volume). In fact the N-Prep-N structure does not necessarily constitute a unitary lexical element: it may also express non-lexical syntactic relations like a specification adjunct (the Italian equivalent of the Latin or german genitive case: e.g. *la casa di Maria*, 'Mary's house'), or a locative adjunct, etc.

Strictly speaking, PC compounds may be viewed as constituting a system that looks more like lexicalization of syntax than like a specific, morphological compounding process (Di Sciullo and Williams, 1987; Spencer, 1991). However, at least in Italian (Dardano, 1978), PC compounds are most often opaque with respect to the choice of the linking preposition (a clear example is *film in bianco e nero*, 'black and white movie' [lit: movie/IN_{Prep}/black and white] vs. *film a colori*, 'color movie' [lit: movie/A_{Prep}/colors]) and the presence or absence of the definite article which is semantically unmotivated (e.g. *tiro a segno*, 'target-shooting' [lit: shoot/Prep/target] vs. *tiro al piattello*, 'clay-pigeon shooting' [lit: shoot/Prep+the/clay-pigeon]). Moreover, N-Prep-N phrases with a compound status do not allow the insertion of an adjective between the head noun and the modifying prepositional phrase. Therefore, when modifying the compound noun *sedia a rotelle* (wheelchair [lit: chair/A_{Prep}/wheels]) with the adjective *rotta*, 'broken$_{fem}$' the adjective has to be located at the end (*sedia a rotelle rotta*, 'chair/A_{Prep}/wheels/broken') and not after the head of the compound (*sedia rotta a rotelle**, [lit. chair/broken/A_{Prep}/wheels]). These are compelling reasons to consider at least these PC compounds as lexicalized items.

The intriguing peculiarities of PC compounds make them an interesting case in the study of lexical access in speech production.

PC compounds, indeed, are just one example that does not clearly fit into Levelt et al.'s (1999) classification. The same difficulties seen at the formal level remain when considering actual processing. The above-mentioned criteria (opaqueness of linking prepositions, impossibility of adjective insertion) would indicate a classification within the single lemma–single morpheme. On the other hand, if PC compounds are nothing other than lexicalized syntax, a simple concept–multiple lemma classification would be more appropriate. Processing of single concept–single lemma entails events that are different from those involved in processing single concept–multiple lemma ones. It may very well be, however, that in the case of PC compounds, these events overlap and both the single lemma and the lemmas corresponding to the single components are activated.

Mondini et al. (2005) studied the processing of PC compounds in several tasks: repetition, reading, writing, naming, and completion in a group of agrammatic patients and in an agrammatic, phonological dyslexic patient. A further task required the subject to state which preposition had to be inserted between the two main elements spoken aloud by the examiner. Patients showed difficulty in the production of the linking preposition in PC compounds. This happened even with fully lexicalized compound forms, where the linking preposition is syntactically and semantically opaque. The patients' performance was thought to reveal that these unitary forms are decomposed somewhere in the course of processing, where they apparently become sensitive to the patient's agrammatism. However, the opaqueness of the linking preposition makes a whole form representation necessary. Mondini et al. (2005) suggest that lexical retrieval of a PC implies the activation of both the whole form of the compound and of its separate components before accessing PC phonological representation. According to this hypothesis, the production of a PC would imply a dual route procedure: a single representation of the concept underlying the PC activates both one lemma corresponding to the whole PC and three independent lemmas bearing the syntactic aspects of each component of the compound. In a normal speaker, these alternative routes would interact when retrieving the phonology of a PC.

However, the retrieval of the form as a unitary lemma representation is the only effective alternative for the retrieval of prepositions in idiosyncratic fully lexicalized PCs (e.g. *film a colori*, [lit. movie with colors], 'color movie' vs. *film in bianco e nero*, [lit. movie in black and white], 'black and white movie'). The whole form is far less frequent than each single subcomponent and may be more at a disadvantage in a generically damaged system. Most types of aphasia are sensitive to word frequency effects in retrieval. Nevertheless, agrammatism, a condition where the processing of function words is impaired, would hinder the retrieval of the preposition along the decomposition route.

Agrammatism would thus damage the phonological realization of closed-class words even within completely lexicalized locutions.

4.8 Conclusions

Aphasiological research seems to have contributed to knowledge of the representation and processing of compound words on an equal footing with experimental psychology. Converging evidence from formal linguistic analyses, laboratory data, and clinical/experimental observations on brain-damaged patients is seldom so equally balanced and convincing as it has been on this particular topic.

The main contributions from neuropsychology provide evidence for:

(a) The independence of different types of lexical knowledge (phonological compound status, the order of constituents, word formation rules; see Badecker, 2001; Blanken, 2000; Hittmair-Delazer *et al.*, 1994; Semenza *et al.*, 1997).

(b) De/composition during processing, even for opaque compounds (Badecker, 2001; Mondini *et al.*, 2004; Semenza *et al.*, 1997).

(c) The independence and dissociability of mechanisms of gender assignment: based on meaning, rules, or lexical idiosyncrasies (Luzzatti and De Bleser, 1996; Mondini *et al.*, 1999).

(d) Simultaneous activation of the compound components in retrieval (Blanken, 2000; Delazer and Semenza, 1998).
(e) The activation of all meaningful representations, including both those associated with isolated components and those associated with whole words (Mondini *et al.*, 2005).

Several questions, however, especially those concerning processing events, are still open to speculation: this seems to be due to a lack of theoretical constructs rather than to a lack of empirical findings. Some of those reported in this review could indeed lead the way to significant theoretical progress.

5

Preschool Children's Acquisition of Compounds

ELENA NICOLADIS

When children initially use compound words such as *candlestick*, it is unlikely they know that they are using a word that can be decomposed into the constituents *candle* and *stick* (Berko, 1958; Clark and Berman, 1984). As children get older, they can learn the basic principles of noun-noun compounding, realizing that compounds are combinations of two parts, one a head, that is the superordinate category (*stick*), the other one a modifier (*candle*). This may be the point in development when children can start to create novel compound words.

Children's use of novel compounds can shed light on how they think about the world. For example, an English-speaking child called whiskers 'a nose beard' (Becker, 1994). A French-speaking boy called headlights that looked like eyes 'phares-yeux', 'headlights eyes' (see Nicoladis, 1999). One French–English bilingual boy pointed to a bar of blue soap and called it 'requin savon', 'shark soap' (Nicoladis, 1999). This last compound was composed of two French words but was in the wrong order for French. Children's novel forms and their errors in creating these forms allow us a window into the kinds of cues they use in acquiring the underlying structure.

In addition, acquisition provides one piece of evidence for how compounding morphology is best described relative to the rest of language. For example, if compounds are acquired like similar syntactic forms, then it can be argued that they share some properties with syntax (e.g. Baker, 1998), at least in children's minds. Alternatively, if children acquire compounds differently from similar syntactic forms, then it can be argued that morphology is best described as distinct from syntax (e.g. Selkirk, 1982).

The purpose of this chapter is to review some of the important findings in children's acquisition of compounds. To that end, we will first turn our attention to what children have to learn about compounds, and take a brief look at some important cross-linguistic variation in compounds.

5.1 What do children have to learn? Cross-linguistic variation in compounds

Compounds are often used to name things, rather than describe them (Downing, 1977). Compound words are, by definition, composed of at least two root words (Fabb, 1998). Apart from that defining feature, there are few cross-linguistic similarities in compound words in terms of semantics, special compounding phonology or morphology, and parts of speech that can be included in compounds (see Dressler, this volume, for further details). Perhaps the single most difficult problem facing children acquiring compounds is that there are no cross-linguistic universals for what can be described by compounds (see Jarema, this volume). For example, compare the following: English 'slippers', French 'pantoufles' or 'chaussons', Hebrew 'na'aley $^\wedge$ báyit' = 'shoes $^\wedge$ house' = house shoes. The English word 'slippers' and French 'chaussons' use derivations, the French 'pantoufles' is a non-decomposable word and the Hebrew term is a compound noun. Children have to learn what can be named with a compound in their language. When compounds exist, they often pick out a semantic subcategory, so a 'picture frame' is a kind of frame (Clark, Gelman, and Lane, 1985).

Languages also differ in terms of what compounds can refer to. For example, in English, compound nouns can rely on a variety of semantic connections between two nouns (Downing, 1977). A 'snow fort' refers to a fort made out of snow while a 'snow suit' refers to a suit worn in the snow and 'snowfall' refers to snow that has fallen (see Clark, 1981, for further examples). 'There are potentially infinitely many relations between modifiers and heads [in compound nouns]' (Clark et al., 1985, p. 84). In contrast, in languages like Estonian and Hungarian, compounds cannot have modifiers that refer to shape or appearance (Hiramatsu et al., 1999). In French, however, modifiers referring to shape or appearance are allowed in noun-noun compounds with no conjoining preposition; for example 'assiette-poisson', 'dish-fish' would probably be interpreted as a dish in the shape of a fish.

Compounds sometimes contain reversals of common word ordering.[1] For example, the English form object-verb-er (e.g. 'book binder') reverses the usual phrasal ordering of verbs and objects (e.g. 'a person binds books'). Baker (1998) argues that this form has preserved an older English word order. The French word 'malfaiteur' (literally 'evil-doer') is an unusual construction in French, also reversing the usual phrasal order of S-V-O. This word retained its original Latin word order in modern French. Some French adjective-noun compounds reverse their usual order in adjectival phrases. For example, many French adjectives go to the right of nouns in phrases and yet in 'chauve-souris' ('bald mouse' = bat), 'rouge-gorge' ('red throat' = robin), and 'blanc-bec' ('white beak' = a nasty young fellow) all have adjectives to the left of the nouns, following their original Latin word order. More recent additions to French also reverse the usual order of adjectival phrases, as in 'libre échange' ('free exchange' = free trade) and 'libre service' ('free service' = self-service); both of these compounds were adopted as translations from English. Children's input is presumably not marked for etymological information. They must somehow learn

---

[1] It is a controversial issue whether compound nouns have underlying argument structure, like syntax. For example, compare Selkirk's views (1982) and those of Lieber (1983) and Roeper and Siegel (1978). I have described deverbal compounds like *firefighter* as object-verb-er because this is how child language researchers have commonly described them.

the forms in the input, even when the forms do not correspond to usual word ordering.

A further complication for children is that surface form does not guarantee structure. For example, while a word in the form noun-verb-er might most commonly be object-verb-er, this is not necessarily the case. For example, a 'wedding singer' is someone who sings at weddings and not somebody who sings a wedding while arguably a 'blues singer' is someone who sings the blues. A toy called a 'power launcher' is made for launching racing cars while a 'rocket launcher' launches rockets.

In some languages, compounds are marked morphologically, in others phonologically. For example, in Hebrew, compounds are often marked by complex morphology (see Clark and Berman, 1984, for a review of Hebrew word formation devices). Swedish compound nouns are formed using phonological rules that do not occur in the independent form of the words, as well as intonational patterns that mark the compound as a whole (Mellenius, 1996). The most common construction for French compound nouns is two nouns conjoined with a preposition (e.g. 'cuiller à thé', 'spoon for tea' teaspoon), although they can also be formed by root + root nouns (Nicoladis, 1999). English compounds are often marked by distinctive stress patterns (Clark *et al.*, 1985).

Languages also differ in terms of morphology allowed within compounds. For example, Germanic languages generally do not allow regular plurals in non-head position while Romance languages do (see Lardiere, 1995, for a discussion). Hebrew also seems to allow regular plurals in non-head position of compound nouns (e.g. 'ótobus ^ nos'im' = 'bus ^ passengers' = passenger bus, Clark and Berman, 1987, p. 548). Nevertheless, even in Germanic languages, exceptions to this rule are allowed. For example, regular plurals can occur if the regular plural marks a different meaning than the singular form (e.g. honours student, parks commission; see Gordon, 1985). Another exception occurs when including a phrase with a differential meaning within a compound (e.g. a red rats eater is not the same thing as a red rat eater; Alegre and Gordon, 1996).

In sum, there are cross-linguistic differences in compounds in terms of what compounds can be used to describe, parts of speech that can appear in compounds, their frequency and productivity, word order, morphological and phonological distinctions from other forms, whether or not plurals can appear in non-head position. There may nevertheless be good reasons for looking exclusively at compounds in acquisition. First, traditional descriptions of language place compounds collectively 'below' syntax, suggesting that there may be some properties that compounds in all languages share (see Selkirk, 1982).

A second reason to focus exclusively on compounds is that, as will be discussed below, Clark and her colleagues have attempted to predict how children might acquire word formation devices that explain children's acquisition of compounds across languages. One point that can be briefly discussed here is the importance of children understanding pragmatic factors in the acquisition of compounds. Namely, children must understand that a novel compound must be transparent in meaning if it is to be understood by their interlocutors. 'Novel compound nouns are by nature CONTEXTUAL: to arrive at the intended interpretations of such compounds, addressees are typically dependent on pragmatic factors' (Clark and Berman, 1987, p. 550, emphasis in original). Clark and Berman (1987) further argue that only with time and repeated usage can compounds become opaque in meaning. If children understand the pragmatic factors underlying understandable usage of novel compounds, then they should use novel forms only when they have a lexical gap (Clark, 1981). In other words, '[...] both speakers and addressees assume that if there is a conventional term for x, speakers will use it' (Clark, 1998, p. 514).

Before further discussing possible explanations of the acquisition of compounds, it is important to review the available data on the acquisition of compounds. In spite of the wide variety of form and meaning of compounds across languages, most of the research has focused on children's ability to create novel noun-noun and object-verb-er compounds in English. By focusing on novel compounds, it is possible to verify that children actually understand the underlying principles of structuring their compounds. While the number of forms scrutinized remains small, it is nevertheless possible to distinguish potential patterns in acquisition on the basis of: frequency and productivity in the input; meaning; acquiring the meaning of compounds; order of elements within compounds; differences in comprehension and production; and the use of inflection and linking elements within compounds. Each of these topics will be discussed in turn.

5.2 Role of frequency and productivity in the acquisition of compounds

Children's language acquisition is remarkable in terms of creativity (see Clark, 1993); they are nonetheless limited in their creativity by properties of the input. Frequency and productivity in children's input play an important role in how early in development and how often they produce compounds. For example, compound nouns are frequent and highly productive in English and English-speaking children produce compound nouns around the age of two years (Clark, 1981; Clark et al., 1985). Conversely, compound nouns are infrequent and not very productive in French and five- and six-year old French-speaking children rarely choose to produce compounds in creating novel lexical structures (see Clark, 1998). Similarly, in reviewing the spontaneous production data of a French-speaking boy, Nicoladis (1999) found that he used only lexicalized compound nouns before the age of three years; novel compounds appeared after three years of age. In contrast to the monolingual child, one study of a French–English bilingual boy showed that he produced novel compounds in both languages before the age of three (Nicoladis, 1999; see also Nicoladis, 2002a). This finding suggests that exposure to a language in which compounds are frequent may change the frequency with which children produce compounds in a language in which they are infrequent.

Further evidence that frequency plays a role comes from a study of four Mandarin Chinese–English bilingual children between 1;9

and 3;3 (Nicoladis and Yin, 2002). Using data from the spontaneous conversations of these children with adults, the researchers noted that noun-noun compounds appeared in the younger children's productions in both languages, while Chinese verb-verb compounds appeared only in the productions of an older child whose Chinese was stronger than his English. The frequency of different kinds of compounds in the children's Chinese *input* was dependent on their proficiency in Chinese. That is, the children who spoke Chinese better than English heard more Chinese verb-verb compounds than the children who spoke English better than Chinese. This result suggests that the parents may have modified their input for the child's benefit. The same pattern did not hold true for English. The same rate of different kinds of compounds was observed in the input of all the children, regardless of their input. This lack of difference could have been due to the fact that the adults interacting with the children in English were less familiar than the adults who spoke Chinese. It could also be attributed to the fact that there are many more different kinds of compounds in Chinese than in English, at least in child-directed speech. In any case, the results point to the possibility that the frequency of different kinds of compounds in children's input can change as they get older and children's acquisition may change as a result.

Frequency differences alone seem to account for the differences in acquisition patterns in English (produced around 2 years of age) and French noun-noun compounds (produced around 3 years of age) since there is little difference between the complexity of the constructions in the two languages. English compounds are composed simply of two root nouns while French compounds are usually formed with a preposition between two root nouns or sometimes simply of two root nouns. However, there is some evidence to suggest that frequency may interact with morphological complexity in acquisition. The evidence for this interaction comes from studies of Hebrew-speaking children. Compounds in Hebrew can require stem changes, the addition of affixes or can simply be two roots (see Berman, 1987). Compounds are low frequency in input and considered a more literary form than in English. Hebrew-speaking children have been noted to use compounds spontaneously as young as 1;6 but it is not clear that children understand that the words are compounds (Berman, 1987). Spontaneous novel compounds are used by Hebrew-speaking children starting around four years, and then usually in narrative contexts (Berman, 1987). Some evidence suggests that late production is in part due to difficulty with morphology since comprehension of complex forms appears earlier than production. From four years on, Hebrew-speaking children understand all morphological forms tested in a task eliciting the meaning of compounds (Clark and Berman, 1987).

Clark (1998, p. 519) summed up the effects of frequency and productivity in acquisition: 'And in the coining of new words, they [children] consistently favour more productive forms over less productive forms'. In other words, one limit to children's linguistic creativity with regard to compounds is the productivity of forms in their input language.

5.3 Acquiring the meaning of compound nouns

One theme in research on children's acquisition of compounds is asking when they understand the subcategorization role of compounds. The answer to this question has been important in understanding when children can organize their concepts in hierarchies (see Clark *et al.*, 1985, for discussion). English-speaking children seem to understand the subcategorization role of compound nouns quite early in development. Clark *et al.* (1985) gave twenty novel compounds to sixty English-speaking children between the ages of 2;4 and 6;0. They were asked to locate the picture of the novel compound (e.g. 'apple knife') from a display of four pictures (e.g. knife, apple, apple tree, egg beater). If children understood that an 'apple knife' was a kind of knife, they should have no trouble picking out the picture of the knife from the display. The youngest children in this study did in fact find this task difficult, scoring only

49 percent correct. The biggest improvement on the task was between the youngest children and the three-year-old children, the latter scoring 84 percent correct. Clark *et al.* (1985) further examined children's semantic abilities in creating compounds to see if they knew that compounds should refer to objects with some intrinsic property rather than an accidental combination of objects (cf. Downing, 1977). They gave a subcategories task to thirty-six English-speaking children between the ages of two and three years. In this task, children were asked what to call objects that were (1) inherently related (e.g. a house made out of a pumpkin); (2) semi-inherently related (e.g. a block decorated with a decal of a banana); and (3) accidentally related (e.g. a chair with a spider on it). The children at all ages were more likely to call inherent and semi-inherent pictures by compounds than accidental pictures; overall: inherent = 47 percent compounds; semi-inherent = 38 percent compounds, accidental = 30 percent compounds. These results suggest that by the age of three years, English-speaking children understand the subcategorization role of compounds.

In terms of comprehension of novel noun-noun compounds, English-speaking children as young as three years seem to differentiate between two objects that are interacting and two objects that are next to each other (Nicoladis, 2003a). In that study, children were asked to pick out the referent of a compound like fish shoes from four pictures: the head alone (e.g. shoes), the modifier alone (e.g. fish), the two objects juxtaposed (e.g. fish next to shoes) and the two objects interacting (e.g. fish on shoes). The children's performance showed some signs of improvement with age. Four year olds were less likely than three year olds to choose juxtaposed objects as the possible meaning of compounds (Nicoladis, 2003a).

Similar results have been observed in Swedish-speaking children. Mellenius (1996) asked children to identify the correct object described by twenty-four novel noun-noun compounds (e.g. orm#glas 'snake glass'). The children had to pick the correct picture out of a display of four pictures (head noun [glass], modifier noun [snake], related to head item [cup], related to modifier item [fish]). Here again children were expected to pick out the head noun (i.e. glass in the above example). The children showed improvement with age between two and five years, with the biggest improvement between 2;4 and 3;0. These results suggest that Swedish-speaking, like English-speaking, children understand the subcategorization role of compounds by the age of three years.

Having to acquire both left-headed and right-headed compounds seems to pose little challenge to children's comprehension. In a study of twenty-five French–English bilingual children between the ages of three and four years, Nicoladis (2002a) showed that they were equally correct in both languages in their comprehension of noun-noun compounds. These results held even though these compounds are left-headed in French and right-headed in English. Furthermore, the bilingual children scored no differently from age-matched English-speaking monolingual children in their comprehension of noun-noun compounds (for further research on bilinguals' processing of compounds see Levy *et al.*, this volume).

Surprisingly enough, Hebrew-speaking children also show comprehension of novel compound nouns at around the age of three years. Recall that compounds are infrequent in Hebrew. Berman and Clark (1989) asked children to pick out something named by a novel compound from a display of four pictures. For example, they were asked to pick out a 'dog basket' and shown pictures of a basket with dogs, a basket with books, a basket, and a dog. Comprehension improved with age between the ages of two years and seven years, although their scores were near ceiling at three years. Note that this task does not require children to distinguish accidental arrangements of objects and interacting objects. It would be necessary to replicate this study with different distractors to be sure that Hebrew-speaking children can distinguish between these possible interpretations. Nevertheless, taking the results from English, Swedish, French, and Hebrew together, children seem to understand the meaning of novel compounds in terms of subcategorization by the age of three years.

Children's knowledge of compound nouns is not limited to subcategorization of concrete objects. Two studies by Gottfried (1997a, 1997b) have shown that English-speaking children can understand what she calls metaphoric compounds quite early in development. Gottfried (1997a) limits metaphoric compounds to those in which 'a known category label is intentionally mislabeled to show recognition of similarity' (p. 568). For example, an 'egg-ball' may be used intentionally to mark the similarity between an egg and an oval ball (example on p. 572). In one experiment, a group of three year olds and a group of five year olds were shown pictures of objects with both shape and color as metaphoric compounds as well as pictures of hybrid objects (e.g. a plate etched with features of a fish) to see how children would form literal compounds. Tommy (a puppet) called an object by an inappropriate label, for example called a cherry-ball 'a lemon-ball' and the children were asked to think of a better name for the object. The children produced more metaphoric compounds for shape (15–30 percent) than for color (5–30 percent). In another study, Gottfried (1997b) tested children's comprehension of metaphoric compounds. In one experiment, three year olds and five year olds were shown pictures of metaphoric compounds (metaphor based on both color and shape), representational items and simple stimuli. The children were first asked 'Where are the two pictures of bugs?', then 'Which one's the bug that looks kinda like a stick?' The five year olds were more likely to pick out appropriate pictures than the three year olds. Children's performance on the majority of the items showed they understood both category membership and the metaphoric nature of the target item. In another experiment (Gottfried, 1997b), one group of three year olds and one group of five year olds were shown a display of four pictures (e.g. lemon-ball, lemon next to a ball, composite of two objects unrelated to lemons or balls, complex item that could be labeled by a compound) and asked 'where is lemon-ball?'. The five year olds were more likely to select the appropriate picture than three year olds but both groups showed some confusion between the lemon-ball and the ball and the lemon: 'the data showed that neither three- nor five-year-old children were sure if a compound such as lemon-ball meant "lemon and ball" or "ball that looks like a lemon"' (p. 180). In sum, these two studies suggest that three- and five-year-old English-speaking children are starting to understand metaphoric compounds, at least when the metaphor is based on shape (see also Nicoladis, 2003a, for similar findings with literal compounds).

Children's errors may also reveal something about their knowledge of compounds. Some researchers have argued that children may systematically choose either the head or the modifier as the referent of a novel compound. For English compound nouns, when two- and three-year-old children were given a choice of four possible referents for novel compounds, they tended to choose the modifier noun alone when they did not choose the target (Clark, 1981; Clark et al., 1985). For example, when asked for the referent of *apple-knife*, two year olds often pointed to an apple. However, Nicoladis (2003a) reported that three-year olds did not show a preference for choosing the head noun or modifier noun. In Hebrew, Clark and Berman (1987) reported age differences in errors for describing a given novel compound. Three year olds described mostly the head only, while four year olds and older included something about both the head and the modifier. These results suggest that it is possible that even three-year-old children are not yet certain that compounds are more likely to refer to two objects inherently related rather than two objects accidentally together (see Clark et al., 1985). With such unsystematic findings across studies, it is difficult to make any conclusions about what children's errors reveal about their knowledge of the meaning of compounds at this point in time.

In sum, research to date suggests that children can have some understanding about the subcategorization function of compounds as young as two years of age. Children's understanding of the meaning of noun-noun compounds develops over the preschool years and into the school years. Preschool children's uncertainty of meaning may rest on the fact that the relationship between the two nouns in compounds can be so varied. For example, the word 'mountain' plays a different role relative to the head noun in *a mountain goat* and *a mountain bike*. It is possible that the variety of roles represented by noun-noun compounds makes children's acquisition of the meaning difficult. It should be noted that our understanding of acquisition is limited by researchers' use of distractors. Few studies have asked children to distinguish between referents of novel compounds that differed only by the order of the elements (cf. Nicoladis, 2002a). For example, to test children's understanding of the subcategorization role, researchers should ask children if a compound like 'clown-balloon' means a balloon with clowns on it or a clown holding balloons. Until more studies are done with these distractors, our conclusions must remain preliminary.

5.4 Acquiring the meaning of deverbal compounds

One way to see if children's acquisition is related to the transparency of the structure is to look at either kinds of compounds, some that include morphology that might help signal to children the meaning of the words (Clark, 2003). A number of studies have examined English-speaking children's ability to form compounds of the form object-verb-er, as in truck driver. This form is of particular interest because, as mentioned above, it does not follow the usual English order of verbs and objects in sentences: V-O (see Baker, 1998). Also, the suffix-er marks the verb for meaning. Object-verb-er compounds can also be used to name both agents (e.g. *house cleaner*) and instruments (e.g. *can opener*). Clark and Hecht (1982) found that three- and four-year-old children were better at using V-er to describe agents than instruments, but the difference disappeared in five year olds. Clark and Berman (1984) concluded that 'in languages where one device can conventionally be used for both agents and instruments, children should acquire agent uses before instrument ones. This is exactly the pattern of acquisition that has been observed [in Hebrew-speaking participants]' (p. 582).

Because object-verb-er compounds reverse the usual order of phrases, there has been some speculation that children might interpret the object in a deverbal compound as the subject. For example, they might understand a truck driver to mean a truck driving something. To test this possibility, Nicoladis (submitted) showed thirty-four English-speaking children between the ages of three and five years four pictures as possible referents for novel deverbal compounds (like *apple eater*). The children with lower vocabulary sizes were equally likely to pick the correct answer (e.g. someone eating an apple) and a picture with the object performing the action (an apple eating something). Only when children attained high vocabularies within this age group did they pick the correct answer more often than the distractor.

While it is tempting to interpret these results as support of the idea that children understand English deverbal compounds to have the same meaning as phrases, this possibility seems unlikely given the results from French. French deverbal compounds are in the order verb-object (e.g. chasse-moustiques 'chase-mosquitoes' meaning mosquito repellent), the same order as most phrases, SVO. Nicoladis (submitted) presented thirty-four French-speaking children of the same ages as the English-speaking children described above with four possible referents to novel verb-object compounds (like 'crève-bulles' 'pop-bubbles'). The French-speaking children with the lower vocabulary sizes were equally likely to pick the correct answer (e.g. something for popping bubbles) as the distractor with the object performing an action (e.g. bubbles popping something). Only children with high vocabulary sizes within this age group chose the correct answer more often than the distractor.

These results suggest that across languages children do not base the meaning of their deverbal compounds on phrases. Nicoladis (submitted) has suggested that children might attend instead to the meaning of other complex lexical items. For example, children might initially make little distinction in the meaning of words like 'playing cards', 'player piano' and 'baseball player'. They might base their constructions on words like 'playing cards' which are more frequent than object-verb-er compounds and thus interpret deverbal compounds as if they were verb-ing noun forms. This interpretation does not work very well for French, however, because there are no complex lexical items with the verb appearing regularly before the noun, other than deverbal compounds. Thus, a more adequate explanation of children's acquisition of the meaning of deverbal compounds is still needed.

5.5 Ordering the elements of compounds

As a general rule, children seem to have little trouble ordering noun-noun compounds. For example, Clark *et al.* (1985) reported virtually no order errors in English-speaking children's production of novel compound nouns (cf. Nicoladis, 2002a). Similar results were reported by Clark and Berman (1987) for Hebrew-speaking children. The lack of ordering errors has generally been interpreted as meaning that children understand that compound nouns serve a subcategorization role. One possible exception to this rule is compound nouns referring to hybrid objects (such as hand-chair meaning a chair in the shape of a hand or a fish-plate meaning a plate in the shape of a fish). Hiramatsu *et al.* (1999) reported that seven four-year old children had a higher rate of reversal in producing compounds describing hybrids rather than other kinds of objects. Similar results were reported by Gottfried (1997a) who found a high rate of reversals for hybrids relative to other kinds of objects. It is possible that three- to five-year-old children do not yet understand that English generally uses the function of the object (rather than shape or appearance) to identify the head. Children may have difficulty with hybrids because English rarely uses compounds to refer to hybrids (Hiramatsu *et al.*, 1999).

In contrast to the few ordering errors in monolingual children's noun-noun compounds, Nicoladis (2002a) found that three- and four-year-old French–English bilingual children were more likely to reverse compounds than age-matched English monolingual children. In this study, children were asked to form compounds for novel objects, all with a semi-inherent relationship (e.g. the target 'flower chairs' was three chairs with flowers on them). Objects such as these had posed no ordering problems for two- to three-year-old monolingual children in Clark *et al.* (1985). In the Nicoladis (2002a) study, however, the bilingual children were twice as likely to reverse compounds as the monolingual children. There were equal rates of reversals in both French and English compounds. While it is clear that these results must be attributed to the children's bilingualism, it is not clear exactly how exposure to two languages makes children reverse compounds. It is true that French compounds are left-headed and English compounds are right-headed. However, absolute ordering rules should be easy for bilingual children to acquire, as has been shown with other constructions (Müller, 1998). Nicoladis (2002a) argued that children may use cues from other constructions to guide their ordering of noun-noun compounds. For example, adjectives can appear both before and after nouns in French and have a similar meaning as non-head nouns inside compound nouns. It is possible that children order their compounds based on adjective-noun constructions (cf. Nicoladis, 2002c).

English-speaking children seem to have difficulty with the construction object-verb-er before the age of about five to six years (e.g. Clark *et al.*, 1986; cf. Gordon, 1985, who provided a template for the children to follow). Citing a private corpus, Clark *et al.* (1986) state that English compounds with a verb base are rarely used spontaneously before three years of age. When they are produced before this age, children often fall back on the canonical ordering of VO; for example, Clark (1981) reported that two-year-old children create verb-noun compounds (e.g. fix-man).

Children between the ages of three and six years were shown actions done by people and actions done with instruments and asked to name the picture (Clark *et al.*, 1986). Three and four year olds formed more compounds with agents than instruments; five and six year olds slightly more compounds with instruments than agents. The youngest children broke grammatical rules (e.g. 'breaker-bottle' for bottle breaker) while older children rarely did.

Similar results were obtained with a different experimental paradigm. Clark and Barron (1988) asked children between three and six years to tell a puppet how to say an object-verb-er compound correctly. The puppet used both grammatical and ungrammatical compounds. The ungrammatical compounds included: reversed noun-noun compounds (e.g. 'hat-snow' to refer to a hat for keeping warm in the snow), verbal compounds in reversed order (e.g. 'puller-wagon'), the -er on the wrong component (e.g. 'wagoner-pull'), and reversals and the -er on the wrong component (e.g. 'pull wagoner'). The older children accepted fewer ungrammatical compounds as grammatical than the younger children. All children were best at detecting ungrammaticality of reversed noun-noun compounds, then compounds of the type puller-wagon, then pull-wagoner and then wagoner-pull. When children were asked to repair the ungrammatical forms, most (93 percent) of their repairs resulted in compound nouns.

In both these experimental manipulations, Clark and her colleagues (Clark and Barron, 1988; Clark et al., 1986) have reported that a predictable series of stages in the formation of compound nouns emerges. Here is how a child in each stage might refer to someone who cuts grass:

(1) verb + noun (e.g. cut man)
(2) verb + object (e.g. cut grass), verb-ing + object (e.g. cutting grass), verb-er + object (e.g. cutter grass)
(3) object + verb-er (grass cutter).

They explain these stages by arguing that children first nominalize VP and then put it in canonical order (stage 2), just like noun-noun compounds: 'the verb base is treated as the head, just as it would be in a verb phrase: affixes used in compounds are attached to the verb, as in a *breaker-bottle* (a man who breaks bottles)' (Clark and Barron, 1988, p. 13). Then children have to learn that the object of the verb cannot fulfill the role of subcategorization, something they learn around four to five years. To reach the final stage, children have to unlearn the canonical ordering of verbs and objects in order to create correctly ordered compounds.

There are a number of reasons to doubt the interpretation put forth by Clark and her colleagues. First, the necessity of stage 2 has been challenged by Becker (1994) who examined one North American boy's lexical innovations between two and five years. The boy was observed at home in conversation with his parents; a total of 210 conversations were analyzed. The child used noun-noun compounds more frequently than agent or instrument compounds. The boy produced no examples of stage 2 above, otherwise the developmental order held up as predicted. On the basis of these results, Becker argues that not all children follow the same stages of development. Naturally, it is possible that the occurrence of novel compounds of any particular form are sufficiently rare to have been missed in the kind of observational data used by Becker.

Another reason to doubt the interpretation of Clark and her colleagues is that it is not clear that children base their stage 2 constructions on phrases (see, for example, the discussion of comprehension errors of deverbal compounds above). Stage 1 forms already reverse canonical phrasal ordering (e.g. in 'a cut man', 'man' would be the subject of 'cut'). Also, the rate of production of stage 2 forms has been shown to be dependent on frequency in the input. For example, French–English bilingual children have been shown to produce more verb-object forms (stage 2) in English than monolingual children (Nicoladis, 2003b). The bilingual children hear grammatical verb-object forms in French, which may affect their English production. Similarly, British English children have been shown to produce more verb-object forms (stage 2) than Canadian English children (Nicoladis and Murphy, 2002). British English allows some verb-object forms like *answer-phone* that are not allowed in Canadian English. These results suggest that children form their deverbal compounds by analogy to other lexical forms in their input even if these forms are in another language, rather than on phrases. Children may extend the structure of one form to another on the basis of analogy with already known forms (e.g. Krott and Nicoladis, 2003).

In sum, it is clear that ordering the elements of compounds can pose a challenge to children. Researchers are in fair agreement that the challenge must come from the fact that other linguistic structures are ordered differently in the language the children are learning. However, they do not yet agree on whether the distracting linguistic structures are limited to phrases or whether they might also include other lexical structures. Part of the difficulty in reaching a clear conclusion comes from a paucity of cross-linguistic studies on this issue.

5.6 Comprehension and production

A general rule about language acquisition is that comprehension precedes production. Some researchers have argued that compounds are no exception to that general rule. For example, Clark and Barron (1988, p. 16) conclude that 'acquisition proceeds in part by gradual coordination of production with comprehension'. A crucial test for this rule would be examining the same children's comprehension and production of compounds. Few studies have done so. For this reason, some of the discussion of the evidence for or against comprehension preceding production will occasionally be considered on the basis of the age of the children.

The clearest evidence of comprehension preceding production of compounds comes from studies of Hebrew-speaking children. Hebrew-speaking children rarely produce compounds before the age of four years (Berman and Clark, 1989). The one exception to this rule is when no stem changes are required to form a compound. Clark and Berman (1987) found that when no changes are required, even three year olds produced more than 90 percent of compounds correctly. In this same study, it was found that even five-year-old children made many errors in production when a stem change was required (see also Clark and Berman, 1984, for similar results). In contrast to the relatively late appearance of compounds in production, Berman and Clark (1989) found that Hebrew-speaking children's comprehension scores were near ceiling at three years. Clark and Berman (1987) report that complexity of morphological form had no effect on comprehension but did have an effect on production. Early comprehension and late production has been observed in derivational morphology in Hebrew in general; Ravid and Avidor (1998) argue that the late production of nominalization morphology in Hebrew-speaking children is due to the fact that these forms appear primarily in texts and cannot be acquired before children have sufficient familiarity with reading.

In English the evidence for comprehension preceding production is weaker. There are anecdotal reports of the production of novel compounds before the age of two years (see Clark, 1981). In experimental studies with compound nouns, children aged two to three years old produced compounds to subcategorize less than 50 percent of the time (Clark *et al.*, 1985). In the same study, but with different children, the biggest improvement on a comprehension task was just before the children were three years old and made little improvement after that age. Taken together, these results suggest that comprehension and production of compound nouns emerge close together in development (cf. Nicoladis, 2003a). As for compounds with a verbal base, Clark and Barron (1988) point out that the children in their study were able to judge a compound ungrammatical before they could make a grammatical repair. The latter finding could be due to the complex task demands of repairing a given form or could be due, as the authors argue, to comprehension preceding production.

In Swedish, the evidence for comprehension preceding production is the weakest of the three languages to be discussed. Swedish-speaking children produce novel compound nouns at an early age (Gustafsson, 1978 and Söderbergh, 1979, as cited in Berman and Clark, 1989), probably around the age of two years. Mellenius (1996) cited evidence that novel Swedish nouns were produced occasionally before two years of age (e.g. 'konstboll' 'art-ball', by a child who was 1;10). In contrast, recall that Swedish children's comprehension of the subcategorization role of compound nouns may be acquired a bit later, between 2;6 and 3 years (Mellenius, 1996). It is possible, therefore, that in Swedish, children's production of compounds to indicate subcategorization may precede full comprehension of the subcategorization role.

In sum, in Hebrew, children's production of compounds is late relative to their comprehension. The lag in production is undoubtedly due to the complex morphology and infrequency of compounds in spoken input. In English and Swedish, there is some evidence to suggest that while some comprehension may precede production, it is not clear that full comprehension precedes production. That is, it is possible that children have some understanding of the function of compounds before their initial production and their production helps their comprehension. Such a conclusion awaits further study, preferably of the same children in comprehension and production tasks.

5.7 Inflection and linking elements inside compounds

One property of compounds in some languages such as English (Gordon, 1985) and German (Clahsen, 1995) is that regular plurals are not allowed in the head position of compounds while irregular plurals are (cf. Seidenberg *et al.*, 1999). For example, Gordon argues that 'rats eater' is not permitted in English while 'mice eater' is. Gordon (1985) argued that the reason that regular plurals are not allowed is because of the use of level-ordering in the formation of compounds (cf. Selkirk, 1982). That is, regular plurals are applied to compounds only after the compounds have been formed, so it is not possible to form a compound with a regular plural in non-head position. Gordon (1985) further argued that level-ordering must precede morphological acquisition because children almost never hear irregular plurals in compounds and yet know that they are allowed (see also Clahsen, 1995). Gordon further argued that level-ordering could not be learned, because children's compound structure was constrained by rules they had only rarely heard (for example, children understand that irregular plurals are allowed in English compounds although most of the compounds they hear with the singular form, as in *toothbrush*). Evidence for this argument comes from a study (Gordon, 1985) in which children between three and five years were asked to create novel compounds with plural form + eater (e.g. mice + eater, rats + eater). The children avoided regular plurals in non-head position 98 percent of the time and allowed irregular plurals 90 percent of the time. Similar results were found by Clahsen (1995) for German-speaking children's lexicalized compounds. Furthermore, Alegre and Gordon (1996) found that English-speaking children did allow regular plurals in non-head position if a difference of meaning was marked. For example, the children in their study differentiated between 'red rats eater' (i.e. an eater of red rats) and 'red rat eater' (i.e. an eater of rats who is red). In sum, children's complex and near-perfect understanding of the rules about plurals in compounds supports the argument that level-ordering is in place before children learn to form compounds.

One difficulty with the argument that level-ordering is not learned is that not all languages avoid regular plurals in non-head position. Both Hebrew and Romance languages, for example, allow regular plurals in non-head position (see Lardiere, 1995; see also examples in Berman and Clark, 1989; Clark and Berman, 1987). Children must be prepared to learn a language that allows and does not allow plurals inside compounds. Furthermore, two-year-old monolingual children (Lardiere, 1995), three- and four-year-old French–English bilingual children (Nicoladis, 1999; Nicoladis, 2003c), and older second language learners (Lardiere, 1995; Murphy, 1997) have been shown to use plurals in non-head position of English compounds. Murphy (1997) and Nicoladis (2003c) further argue that speakers' consistency in use of level-ordering was related to their proficiency in English; that is, the less proficient in English the speakers were, the more likely they were to use regular plurals in non-head position of English compounds. These results suggest that bilingual children and second language learners must learn to avoid regular plurals in English and their ability to do so is directly related to their knowledge of English.

Further evidence against level-ordering constraining children's acquisition comes from the fact that English-speaking children allow regular plurals in their ungrammatical compounds (i.e. stage 2 compounds like verb-object forms). Nicoladis and Murphy (2004) showed that both British and Canadian children produced novel forms like a juggle-suns (with plural non-heads) to refer to a single machine juggling multiple suns. Level-ordering would predict that children would avoid regular plurals even in ungrammatical compounds because the constraint applies to compounds the children have heard only rarely or not at all (Gordon, 1985). Nicoladis and Murphy (2004) have argued that children learn to avoid regular plurals inside English compound nouns by analogy with already known compounds (see also Haskell *et al.*, 2003). According to this explanation, children must learn many compounds before they can learn to avoid plurals within novel compounds. Thus, bilinguals and second language learners may simply not know enough compounds to apply the general rule.

The preceding discussion shows that children learn to avoid inflection inside compounds. There is also evidence that children learn to include linking elements, that is linguistic elements between two parts of a compound word that often have no meaning within the compound. Mellenius (1996) showed that ten Swedish children between the ages of 3;5 and 6;8 often included the required linking element -s in elicited compounds. Nicoladis (2002b) has argued that French prepositions inside compounds of the form noun-preposition-noun bear some resemblance to linking elements. Three- and four-year-old French–English bilinguals produced prepositions more often than not when required, with the older children producing the same preposition used by adults more often than the younger children.

Languages differ as to the extent to which inflection is avoided and linking elements are required within compounds. Children seem to learn what their language requires in terms of avoidance or inclusion of small linguistic elements inside compounds in the preschool years.

5.8 Stress patterns

In English the stress pattern of compounds distinguishes them from other kinds of sentential constructions. There is surprisingly little study of children's production of stress patterns in compounds.

The little extant evidence suggests that stress is an early and near-perfect acquisition in young children. Clark (1981, p. 318) reported: 'In my own longitudinal and experimental data as well as in more casual observations of a larger number of children, I have found consistent use of the appropriate stress pattern on all noun + noun compounds'. Clark et al. (1985) also report virtually perfect production of stress on novel compound nouns by young English-speaking children. These reports are limited to English-speaking children's compound nouns. Further research on how and when children acquire appropriate stress patterns for compounds is clearly merited.

5.9 Explanations of children's compound acquisition

A number of different explanations for children's acquisition of compounds have been suggested. The single—and best described—explanation comes from Clark and her colleagues. They have attempted to devise an explanation of compounds in the context of explaining children's novel word formations in general (e.g. Clark, 1981). They argue that several principles are important in children's word formation, notably, principles of semantic transparency, simplicity, conventionality, and productivity (e.g. Clark and Berman, 1984; Clark et al., 1986). According to the principle of semantic transparency: 'Known elements with one-to-one matches of meaning to form are more transparent for constructing and interpreting new words than elements with one-many or many-one matches' (Clark and Berman, 1984, p. 547). According to the principle of simplicity of form: 'simpler forms are easier to acquire than more complex ones' (Clark et al., 1986, p. 9). '[S]implicity is measured by degree of change in a form. The less a word changes, the simpler it is' (Clark and Berman, 1984, p. 548). This principle explains why adding an affix like -er on noun-verb compounds makes them harder to learn than simple noun-noun compounds in English. In keeping with the principle of simplicity, children use the strategy of making as few changes as possible to an old word in order to form a new word (Clark *et al.*, 1986). According to the principle of conventionality, children's choice of words becomes more constrained by conventional grammatical usage as they get older. This principle is motivated largely by the assumption that children's novel word formations are used when children have a lexical gap (Clark, 1981). In other words: 'children don't limit themselves to talking about things for which they already have words. They try to talk about everything that interests them. They therefore need more words constructed just for the occasion than adults do' (Clark, 1998, p. 515). Finally, according to the principle of productivity: 'Those word formation devices used most often by adults in word innovations are preferred in the language for constructing new word forms' (Clark and Berman, 1984, p. 548; see also Berman, 1987). This principle explains why the highly productive English suffix -er is acquired before the less productive -ist (Clark and Berman, 1984).

Clark's explanation of novel word formation has proved a better explanation of compounding than others (e.g. see the discussion of Selkirk, 1982, in Clark *et al.*, 1986) and remains unchallenged in its entirety. Yet, some parts of her explanation remain untested or have been questioned recently (e.g. Becker, 1994). One principle that has been questioned is the principle of conventionality. Becker (1994) examined longitudinal data from one English-speaking child and found examples of him using both a conventional form and a novel form, sometimes in the same utterance. As Becker points out, these data suggest that children's novel word formation is not always due to lexical gaps and further explanations are needed to explain why and when children use novel forms. 'These findings appear to support the notion that innovations are more influenced by lexical knowledge that can form the basis of generalizations...than by lexical gaps that need to be filled in categories for which there is little knowledge' (Becker, 1994, p. 206).

As an alternative to Clark and her colleagues' attempt to explain children's acquisition of compounds, Nicoladis (1999) has suggested that children might acquire compounds by analogy with already-known compound words as well as similar-meaning structures in their input. For example, because the order of modifying words (i.e. both adjectives and modifying nouns in compounds) is universally consistent within languages, children might acquire their noun-noun compounds by analogy with adjectival phrases. She found evidence against this position when the three-year-old French–English bilingual boy in her study was significantly worse at ordering compounds compared to adjectival phrases in both French and English. Nicoladis concluded that children probably do not use adjectival phrases alone as templates for their compound nouns although they may use adjectival phrases as one cue to their understanding of compound nouns (see also Nicoladis, 2002c).

Surprisingly little attempt has been made to relate children's acquisition to research on adult processing of compounds. For example, Libben (1998) pointed out the importance of decomposition and semantic transparency in compound processing in adults, two variables which are thought to be important in acquisition (see Clark, 1981). According to Libben's (1998) APPLE model, parsing of compounds occurs from left-to-right. If this were also true in children's processing, then they might favour the left-most part of compounds in comprehension tasks. This has been found to be the case in English (Clark, 1981; Clark *et al.*, 1985) and Hebrew (Clark and Berman, 1987). While these errors may be related to the choices made available to children (see Gottfried, 1997a), it would nonetheless be interesting to make connections between children's acquisition and adult knowledge of compounds.

5.10 Conclusion

Children's ability to create novel forms in their target language is impressive and their ability to form novel compounds is no exception. Children can use novel compound nouns with a variety of meanings from early on, sometimes with meanings that they are unlikely to have heard before (see Hiramatsu *et al.*, 1999). The results of research on the acquisition of compounds differ somewhat depending on whether comprehension or production is measured. It has been hypothesized that comprehension of compounds precedes production (e.g. Clark and Barron, 1988). However, although empirical work thus far has suggested that comprehension precedes production in Hebrew, it is not so clear that this is true in English and Swedish (see Table 5.1). One possible explanation for the mismatch in comprehension and production is that different task requirements are tapped in the tasks. For example, if a child thought that compounds could be used to name two objects that were in his visual field at the same time but not necessarily interacting, then he might produce a novel compound when asked to name it, but show no difference in comprehension between a target form (with two interacting objects) and a distractor (with both objects visible). In other words, vague comprehension of novel compounds might precede production of novel compounds which might then lead to a more refined comprehension of novel compounds.

There are a number of factors that seem to play a role in children's acquisition of compounds. We know that frequency and productivity in the target language are important in children's acquisition of compounds. Table 5.1 summarizes children's approximate age of

TABLE 5.1. Approximate ages of acquisition of compounds relative to frequency

Language	Form	Frequent?	Production	Comprehension
English	noun-noun	Yes	2 years	2–3 years
English	object-verb-er	No	5–6 years	4–6 years
Swedish	noun-noun	Yes	2 years	2;6–3 years
Mandarin Chinese	noun-noun	Yes	2–3 years	?
Mandarin Chinese	verb-verb	Yes	3 years	?
Hebrew	noun-noun	No	3 years	3 years
Hebrew	various morphological variations	No	5 years +	3 years
French	noun-(preposition)-noun	No	3 years	3 years
French	verb-object	No	4–5 years	4–5 years

acquisition of different kinds of compounds in different languages. While there is a general tendency for highly frequent forms to be acquired earlier, children can acquire some low frequency forms fairly early (as in Hebrew and French noun-noun compounds). It would be interesting to have more sensitive measures of frequency, rather than simply classifying compound types as low or high frequency. Furthermore, it may be important to look at the frequency in individual children's input, as there has been some suggestion that the frequency in the input might change as children's proficiency changes (Nicoladis and Yin, 2002).

Frequency is clearly an important factor in acquisition, but it is not the only one. The fact that children make ordering errors in some compounds suggests that children are not attending exclusively to these forms in order to acquire them. For example, if children attended exclusively to the order of English object-verb-er compounds like *truck driver* and *bookbinder*, they would have no difficulty at all in ordering their novel object-verb-er compounds. And yet, between the ages of three and four years, English-speaking children misorder the elements of their deverbal compounds (Clark et al., 1986). Clark and her colleagues have attributed children's errors on these forms to canonical phrasal structure. I have argued that children might be patterning their deverbal compounds on more frequent complex lexical structures such as *playing cards* (Nicoladis, submitted). In any case, it is clear that children's acquisition does not always rely solely on the form of the compound alone (e.g. Clark and Barron, 1988). For example, the very fact that monolingual North American children create forms like break-bottle or breaker-bottle that do not exist in their input suggests that they base their compounds on something other than the object-verb-er compounds already in their vocabularies (like *dishwasher* and *firefighter*).

There is still much work to be done in understanding children's acquisition of compounds. Research to date has largely concentrated either on noun-noun compounds or on the English object-verb-er construction. For this reason, we know nothing about the acquisition of other kinds of compounds, such as adjective-noun compounds (e.g. 'the White House') or even the common construction in English of verb-particle (e.g. 'rundown', 'a run-around'). Future research would benefit by gathering more cross-linguistic evidence. To date most of the work on acquisition of compounds has been done in English. Yet the existing cross-linguistic evidence is a valuable test of proposed general principles (e.g. Berman and Clark, 1989). Research on children's acquisition has (understandably) focused on novel compounds and therefore, usually, on compounds with transparent meaning. For this reason, we do not know if opaque compounds pose any particular difficulty for children, as they seem to do in processing by adults (e.g. Libben, 1998) or if there is any difference in the acquisition of lexicalized compounds vs. novel compounds. These data are essential to complete the picture of children's acquisition of compounds. To date there have been few attempts at explaining compound acquisition and none of the extant explanations is unproblematic.

In closing, I would like to area out one area of agreement among researchers in compound acquisition. In contrast to syntactic acquisition (see Selkirk, 1982), where much of the theory has focused on unlearned aspects, the current research on the acquisition of compounds has emphasized the importance of learning in terms of attending to frequency of different kinds of compounds in the input, acquiring the meaning of compounds, ordering elements within compounds, and the use of derivation and inflection within compounds (cf. Gordon, 1985). While much work is still to be done in determining what kinds of cues children use to learn compounds, for the moment it remains unquestioned that these cues must be learned on the basis of what is in their input.

6

Doghouse/Chien-maison/Niche: Approaches to the understanding of compound processing in bilinguals

ERIKA S. LEVY, MIRA GORAL, AND LORAINE K. OBLER

At the age of five, the French–English bilingual niece of one of the authors pointed to a doghouse and asserted it was a 'chien-maison' (lit. 'dog house'). Although the actual word for 'doghouse' in French is 'niche', she had translated the English compound structure and constituents of 'doghouse' into French, thus creating a novel compound. Similarly, Nicoladis (1999 and this volume) described a French–English bilingual child calling blue soap 'requin savon', (lit. 'shark soap'), a novel compound composed of French lexical items, but English compound structure. While questions of how the bilingual lexicon is structured remain unresolved even for single morphemes, questions about how multimorphemic words—and compounds in particular—are stored, processed, produced, and translated have hardly been addressed.

This chapter explores relevant work in the fields of the bilingual lexicon and cross-linguistic compound variation, which should contribute to research investigating questions that surface at the interface of the two fields—that is, when bilinguals process compounds. We begin with an overview of what is known about the bilingual lexicon from psycholinguistic studies of monomorphemic words, in order to provide concepts useful for discussions of compounding. We will then discuss compounds and particular characteristics of compounds that vary crosslinguistically, thereby raising questions about how such differences might affect the way bilinguals process compounds. These questions lead us to several hypotheses; we review the small number of experiments that provide data relevant to these hypotheses, and we suggest directions for future studies to better understand the mental representation of compound words and morphological processing within the bilingual lexicon.

6.1 Overview of the bilingual lexicon

A central question in the literature on the representation of languages in the bilingual monomorphemic lexicon involves the relationship between a bilingual's two linguistic systems. At base, the question of interest is whether the two systems share a common representation or whether information for each language is stored separately (e.g. Albert and Obler, 1978; de Groot and Kroll, 1997; Harris, 1992; Kroll and Dijkstra, 2002; Schreuder and Weltens, 1993). Since Weinreich (1953) posited three types of lexical memory stores for bilinguals (compound, coordinate, and subordinate), distinguishing 'meaning unit' and 'word', researchers have incorporated such notions into models of bilinguals' mental lexicons. Indeed, de Bot *et al.* (1995), for example, stressed that discussions of interdependence versus independence of languages must specify the levels of representation in question. Psycholinguists have distinguished at least two levels of representation in the mental lexicon: the conceptual level and the lexical level (e.g. de Groot and Kroll, 1997). Others have added an intermediate level, the lexical–syntactic level, such as Levelt's (1989) 'lemma' level.

6.1.1 Concepts, lemmas, and lexemes

Meaning and real-world knowledge are thought to be managed at a conceptual/semantic level, a level generally believed to be shared by a bilingual's languages (Potter, 1979; Snodgrass, 1984). Evidence for a shared conceptual system comes, in part, from cross-language semantic priming, categorization tasks, and code-switching phenomena. If both languages of a proficient bilingual share a conceptual representation, then semantic priming (i.e. facilitatory or inhibitory effects due to the activation of shared semantic information) is expected to occur across languages. Indeed, cross-language studies have observed semantic priming when the prime was presented unmasked, at least in proficient bilinguals. For example, de Groot and Nas (1991) found that translation equivalents yielded significant priming effects (e.g. participants responded faster to the Dutch word 'jongen' when it was presented within a second after its English translation equivalent, 'boy', than when it was presented within a second after an unrelated English word). Moreover, the rapid rates with which proficient bilinguals are able to switch from one language to another, even within a phrase, and perform cross-language categorization tasks generally support the conclusion that a bilingual's languages are mediated by a common conceptual system (e.g. Caramazza and Brones, 1980; Potter *et al.*, 1984; Shanon, 1982).

An intermediate level of representation, the lemma level, has been proposed to manage certain syntactic functions for each language (Levelt, 1989). The lemma specifies each lexical item's syntactic properties, such as its grammatical gender, its syntactic category, whether it has an overt plural marker, and whether it is a count noun. Whereas several studies have demonstrated the usefulness of such an intermediate level of representation (e.g. Bock and Griffin, 2000; Dell *et al.*, 1997), the need for a lemma level has been controversial (e.g. Caramazza, 1997). (For a discussion of lemmas in aphasiological research, see Semenza and Mondini, this volume.) Lemmas are thought to be language-specific (Garrett, 1990b; de Bot *et al.*, 1995).

Finally, the lexical level in bilingual processing is generally thought to consist of relatively independent but interconnected forms for each language. The degree to which lexemes, that is the phonological or orthographic forms of words in each language, are interconnected may depend on the age at which the second language (L2) was acquired and on the degree of similarity between the two languages. For example, when two languages are learned simultaneously, they are more likely to share representations than when they are learned at different periods of an individual's life.

Various models have been proposed in the psycholinguistic literature to explain the relationship of bilinguals' two lexicons at the conceptual, lexical, and lemma levels. For recent reviews, see for example, Gollan and Kroll (2001) and Kroll and Dijkstra (2002). In addition, individuals' relative levels of proficiency in the two languages have been shown to factor into the relationships between their languages at the three representation levels.

6.2 Proficiency

Kroll and Curley (1988) and Chen and Leung (1989) showed that individuals just beginning to learn an L2 translated into their second language more quickly than they named pictures in that language, suggesting stronger associations between L2 words and their equivalent L1 words than between L2 words and conceptual representations. The more proficient the participants became in the L2, however, the more similar the latencies became in picture naming and translation, suggesting a shift away from lexical mediation toward conceptual mediation with increased proficiency. Further support for a lexical link, that is a link between translation equivalents in a bilingual's languages, that is stronger in less proficient bilinguals than in more proficient bilinguals comes from studies in the translation of cognates and cross-language Stroop tests (e.g. Chen and Ho, 1986; Tzelgov et al., 1990) as well as the translation of concrete and abstract words (de Groot, 1992; de Groot and Hoeks, 1995).

Most studies in bilingual lexical representation employ single words as stimuli. Clearly, research design requires consideration of stimulus characteristics such as concreteness, cognate status, and translation equivalence. While variables such as concreteness level and cognate status mentioned above have been considered, we do not find mention of whether the translation equivalents include compounds in one language or both languages. By compounds, we refer to grammatical lexical combinations that form words (see Dressler, this volume).

Compounds may not be expected to differ from single words at the concept level, although this has yet to be tested in studies of the bilingual lexicon. However, differences between single words and compounds may be expected at the lemma level, the level at which morphological information is assumed to be accessed, as well as at the lexeme level, the level at which language-specific form characteristics are accessed.

6.3 Methods for studying compounds in bilinguals

An obvious way to begin investigating questions of bilingual processing of compounds is to consider research techniques that have been used in studies of monolinguals. Among the methods used to study monolingual compound-processing are off-line and on-line lexical decision tasks, constituent priming, constituent identification, and compound parsing. These methods can be used in bilingual contexts, such as cross-language priming (i.e. the prime is presented in one language and the target in the other language) and mixed-language presentation (i.e. the list of compounds used in any given task includes items from both languages). In addition, various tasks that include translation from one language to another may be used.

Transfer errors, that is, errors made in L2 that clearly reflect structures or features of the speaker's L1, can be taken as evidence for close relations among lexical items of the two languages (Krashen, 1981). Based on the models of the bilingual lexicon (e.g. de Groot and Kroll, 1997; Kroll and Dijkstra, 2002; Kroll and Stewart,

1994), we make the following assumptions: when individuals learn a second language, compounds, as other lexical items from L2, will be closely associated with their translation equivalents in L1. Evidence for shared representations, including transfer errors in the production and comprehension of compounds in L2, is expected. Compounds are, at least sometimes, composed on-line (see Libben, this volume), and bilinguals are expected to transfer the structures and rules of one language onto the other.

We can assume that a bilingual's lexicon specifies the template of compounds in each language, possibly at the lemma level. The notion of a template is consistent with Semenza and Mondini's (this volume) description of aphasics' awareness that their target word is a compound, but inability to access the compound's constituents. There is now preliminary evidence suggesting that bilinguals are sensitive to the morphological structure of translation equivalents in their languages, that is, whether a compound in one language is also a compound in their other language or not. Blekher (2004) and Goral *et al.* (in preparation) found that translation equivalents that shared their morphological structure were more easily judged as equivalent items than translation pairs that were a compound in one language and a single word in the other.

Further, whether representations of compounds in the two languages are shared (rather than separate) may depend upon the degree to which the compounds share the characteristics mentioned above. Predictable errors in processing L2 compounds might occur if compound structure differs between languages. Bilinguals whose L1 has, for example, right-headed compounds and whose L2 has left-headed compounds, might be expected to make errors of constituent misordering and produce right-headed L2 compounds. As individuals become more proficient in L2, such transfer errors are less likely to occur, because the concepts will exert more influence on compound production than will language-specific lemmas and/ or lexical forms. Below we discuss evidence for the influence of specific compound characteristics on bilingual processing of compound-compound translation equivalents.

6.4 Cross-linguistic variations in compound structure: Consequences for compound processing in bilinguals

An unresolved question in the literature in morphological processing revolves around the degree to which multimorphemic strings are decomposed as opposed to being processed as whole words. Studies of compounds with monolingual speakers have demonstrated that various factors play a role in the representation and processing of compounds (e.g. Sandra, 1990; Libben, 1998; Kehayia *et al.*, 1999; Dressler, this volume; Libben, this volume; Nicoladis, this volume). These include the semantic transparency of constituents, morphological headedness, the position of individual constituents in the string, productivity and frequency of compounds in the language, compound-internal characteristics, and phonological and orthographic features of compounds. These characteristics, of course, differ from language to language, as discussed in greater detail by Jarema (this volume). In studies of bilingual processing, questions arise regarding how bilinguals decompose, compose, and translate multimorphemic items with characteristics that differ across their languages. In this section we will consider the influence these variables might have on bilingual compound representation and processing. Additional variables to consider include formal and structural similarities between languages and an individual's language history.

6.4.1 *Semantic transparency and morphological headedness*

Research studies of the mental lexicon have focused on how semantic transparency and morphological headedness affect the processing of multimorphemic words. Sandra (1990) studied the role of semantic transparency of compound constituents in compound processing in English. He found that primes that were semantic associates of compound constituents facilitated response times to semantically transparent compounds but not to semantically opaque compounds. Sandra concluded that morphological decomposition occurred with semantically transparent compounds, but not with compounds containing an opaque constituent. In contrast, a study on English compounds by Libben *et al.* (2003) found priming effects from both constituents to compounds of varying degrees of opacity. In other words, facilitation occurred for compounds that were transparent (as in each component of 'doorbell') or opaque (as in each component of 'humbug'), as well as opaque/transparent and transparent/opaque compounds, such as 'strawberry' and 'jailbird'. This indicated some decomposition even in compounds with one opaque constituent. However, reaction times overall were longest for compounds in which the head (the second constituent in English) was opaque, suggesting that compound transparency is related to the transparency of the constituents as well as their position in the string.

Because English compounds are always right-headed, it was unclear whether priming was due to morphological headedness or position in the compound. As reported in Jarema (this volume), Jarema *et al.* (1999) investigated the processing of compounds in French and Bulgarian in a study in which semantic transparency was varied employing Libben *et al.*'s (2003) four-way classification. Constituent priming was found throughout in both French and Bulgarian (with the exception of opaque-opaque constructions in Bulgarian), suggesting that processing of compounds involves the interaction of semantic transparency, position in string, and morphological headedness.

Based on the study by Sandra (1990), as well as on the finding by Libben *et al.* (2003) that reaction time was greatest for compounds with opaque heads, and on the lack of constituent priming found in fully opaque Bulgarian compounds (Jarema *et al.*, 1999), it appears that semantic transparency plays a role in lexical retrieval, in that compound recognition relies more on decomposition when constituents are transparent, and more on whole-word representation when compounds are opaque. Compounds with at least one opaque element (e.g. 'butterfly') are likely to be accessed as a whole unit, because their meaning cannot be derived from their constituents alone. It should be noted that when transparent compounds are of low frequency (e.g. 'lemon picker'), retrieval is probably heavily reliant upon decomposition, because such words are unlikely to have achieved whole-word status in most individuals' lexicons.

Of interest, then, is how the bilingual lexicon handles lexical items that are transparent in one language but not in the other. We have presumed thus far that lexical items in one language have translation equivalents in another language. That is, a French–English bilingual's lexicon is expected to include a lexical entry for 'fromage' and a parallel one for 'cheese'. This assumption is challenged when compounds are introduced. For example, bilinguals may have the word 'niche' ('doghouse') in their French lexicon, but the translation equivalent, the transparent compound 'doghouse' might, according to some of the literature discussed above, be expected to be stored predominantly in decomposed form. (See also Gagné and Spalding, this volume, for a discussion of decomposition of compounds.) Thus some would claim that the English translation equivalent 'doghouse' is stored in its constituent parts, 'dog' and 'house', until on-line composition of the compound is required. How, then, is the English counterpart of 'niche' represented in the bilingual lexicon? Is there an 'empty slot' where the translation equivalent would normally be—perhaps a lemma waiting to be filled with its constituents? Or, in some as yet undefined form of transfer of structural characteristics, does 'doghouse' have the status of a single word for proficient French–English bilingual adults, but not for English-speaking monolingual adults?

Further questions arise for more opaque compounds such as 'butterfly'. If opaque compounds are stored primarily as whole units and are less likely to be generated on-line, translation of opaque compounds might be more efficient than translation of transparent compounds, because compounds with at least one opaque constituent (e.g. 'butterfly') will have a parallel whole-word counterpart ('papillon'), rather than an 'empty slot'. Or conversely, as *'chien-maison' (for doghouse, instead of 'niche') suggests, perhaps translating a compound would lead the L2 learner automatically to expect that the translation equivalent would also be a compound, and a compound made up of the translation equivalents of the constituents (e.g. *'beurre-mouche'—literally, 'butterfly'). When, contrary to expectation, the translation equivalent turns out to be a monomorphemic word, the lexical search for a compound will have cost processing time and will potentially result in transfer errors.

A dual approach, as described by Libben (this volume), in which a compound is represented both as a whole word and as its ordered constituents, might help to explain bilinguals' compound representation and processing, although bilinguals' sequencing of compound constituents may prove to be prone to error. An investigation tapping into several of these questions might involve having participants perform translation tasks and noting any words that come to their minds en route to the translation. Similarly, studies employing reaction time measures may provide information on the impact of semantic transparency on bilingual processing.

6.4.2 Structural features

In her study of bilingual children's compound production, Nicoladis (1999) analyzed the compounds her French–English bilingual son Jason (aged 2;9–3;3) spontaneously produced. Although he did say 'brush-teeth' for 'toothbrush', he used right-headed compounds when he spoke English more often than when he spoke French (a generally left-headed language), suggesting that, even at this early age, bilingual children are sensitive to structural differences of compounds in their two languages.

If a language contains compounds that are generally left-headed, transfer might occur, in that the same order might reveal itself in a bilingual's L2, even if compounds in that language are generally right-headed. This was the case for one of the authors, whose L1 is Hebrew (a language with left-headed compounds), who used to refer to her car key in English as *'key car' or ask for a bagel with *'cheese cream'. The converse transfer of English right-headed compounding to compound production in French was revealed in the previously discussed example of 'chien-maison' (for 'doghouse'), a French–English bilingual produced a right-headed compound in a language in which compounds are generally left-headed. These transfer errors in ordering may be taken as evidence for on-line composition of target compounds from their constituents.

That transfer errors do occur between two languages that share only part of their structural restrictions of compound construction was demonstrated in a recent study by Nicoladis (2003b), in which she compared production of English deverbal compounds in French–English bilingual children and in monolingual English-speaking children. She found that the bilingual children produced more verb-object compounds (which are grammatical in French but ungrammatical in English) than did the monolingual English-speaking children.

Researchers might further investigate morpheme-ordering strategies in bilinguals by measuring response times in a lexical decision task. Evidence for bilingual activation during presumably monolingual tasks has been reported in recent studies of bilinguals (e.g. de Groot *et al.*, 2000; Dijkstra *et al.*, 2000). Crucial to such studies would not only be which constituent was the head of the compound, but also which was visually (or auditorily) the first constituent in the string. As described in Jarema (this volume), Kehayia and her colleagues (1999) investigated constituent activation in Greek and Polish compounds. Results of a visual lexical decision task showed activation of both components during priming. The first component was found to have an advantage, despite the fact that the compounds were right-headed. Thus, for bilingual studies involving morphological headedness, it is important to consider the positional advantage that has been demonstrated for first constituents in compounds (Libben *et al.*, 2003; Jarema *et al.*, 1999).

6.4.3 *Syntactic categories*

Syntactic categories of constituents permitted within compounds vary across languages, as do the categories of words that result. Constituents in English compounds are often two nouns, whereas such sequences are less common in French (see Dressler, this volume, for types of compounds, and Jarema, this volume, for cross-language differences in compound structure). Controversy remains regarding what structures qualify as compounds in certain languages, as, for example, in Italian (Luzzatti and de Bleser, 1996) and Hebrew (Borer, 1988). Finnish has some 'semi-compounds' that have features of compounds (e.g. compound stress, lexicalization, conceptual unity), as well as markings of adverbs (Mäkisalo, 2000). We may also expect the transfer of possible syntactic forms from L1 to L2. A French–English bilingual, for example, might tend to use more noun-noun compounds than a monolingual French-speaker, and an English–Finnish bilingual may produce fewer 'semi-compounds' in Finnish than a native Finnish speaker. Similarly, bilinguals may misinterpret certain compounds if one of their languages allows a structure that the other one does not. For example, a Hebrew–English bilingual may have more trouble processing the word 'spoon feed' as a verb than will a German–English bilingual because noun-verb compounds are virtually nonexistent in Hebrew.

6.4.4 Productivity and frequency

Two interrelated characteristics of compounds that vary cross-linguistically are their productivity and frequency within a language. German, for example, in which compounding is highly productive, yields a vocabulary rich in compounds (as also shown in Dressler, this volume). To mention just a few examples, 'glove' is 'Handschuh' (lit. 'hand-shoe'), 'thimble' is 'Fingerhut' (lit. 'finger-hat'), and 'skunk' is 'Stinktier' (lit. 'stink-animal'). It is reasonable to hypothesize that German-speakers with English as their L2 might 'over-compound', creating compounds in English when the target English word is monomorphemic.

In the bilingual language-acquisition literature, among the most cited sources is Leopold's (1949) chronicle of his bilingual daughter Hildegard's linguistic development. Hildegard, who was exposed to German and English, produced numerous novel compounds in both languages. In German, these included 'Spielfreude' (lit. 'play-pleasure') and 'Einreibzeug' (lit. 'rub-in-stuff', meaning 'salve'). English words she produced included 'washday', a compound not used in her home, for the day on which laundry was done. Hildegard tended to create novel compounds in German more frequently than in English. Other studies have confirmed that English-speakers start using compounds earlier in acquisition than French-speakers, probably due to the relative frequency and productivity of compounds in English (Nicoladis, 1999). Indeed, Nicoladis and Murphy (2002) demonstrated that the input children received from their environment influenced their compound production. These observations suggest that part of knowing a language is recognizing the degree to which it is appropriate to construct compounds. In bilingual speakers, these judgments of appropriateness may depend upon the relative frequency and productivity of compounds in each of their languages.

It should be noted that for all suggested studies, it is prudent for researchers to consider not only the frequency of compounds in each language, but also the frequency of the particular compound and its constituents in each language. Responses will inevitably depend, in part, on how frequently particular words and perhaps their constituents and the translation equivalents of constituents, are used in the language (Caramazza *et al.*, 1985; Libben *et al.*, 1999). Indeed, as discussed in Dressler (this volume), Jarema (this volume), and Semenza and Mondini (this volume), the effects of compound frequency as well as of constituent frequency have been assessed in a number of studies with monolinguals, yielding mixed results (e.g. Andrews, 1986; Blanken, 2000; van Jaarsveld and Rattink, 1988; Zhou and Marslen-Wilson, 1994). Another major factor that will influence reaction times and errors in such a task is the semantic transparency of the compounds (discussed above) and the systematicity with which constituents are used in compounds (e.g. 'twenty' in 'twenty-one', 'twenty-two', etc. is systematic). Error analysis should help tease apart the various interacting influences on reaction times and transfer errors in the translation tasks.

6.4.5 Pluralization

Compound-internal variables are also likely to reveal aspects of the nature of the bilingual lexicon. Rules for pluralizing compounds, for example, differ cross-linguistically. Errors in compound pluralization by children and L2-learners have been discussed in the linguistics and language acquisition literatures as both arguments for and against access to morphological level-ordering in Universal Grammar (UG). An innate predisposition to permitting irregular plurals—but not regular plurals—within compounds has been discussed by Clahsen (1995), Clahsen et al., (1992), and Gordon (1985). Lardiere (1995), in contrast, presented data that demonstrated that a restriction on plurals in compounds was freely violated by L2 learners, and that the constraints violated depended upon the participants' L1. Thus, according to Lardiere, a Spanish–English bilingual's production of *'eater-flies' in English was a reflection of Spanish compound structure rather than of UG. That is, in Spanish, compounds may consist of a verb followed by a pluralized noun, as in a 'lavaplatos' (lit. a 'wash-plates', meaning 'dishwasher'). Thus, the structure of *'eater-flies' would be permissible in Spanish, and bilingual speakers might transfer this construction onto their second language, thereby revealing information about their first language, and not necessarily about UG.

For the purposes of understanding the status of compounds in the bilingual lexicon, we might ask what transfer errors tell us about processing in bilinguals. In German, for example, the first element of a compound may be pluralized if the plural is irregular, so, for instance, in the German word 'Kindergarten', the first element is pluralized because 'Kind' ('child') takes the irregular -er plural suffix, whereas *'Autosberg' ('car heap') is not a permissible form because the plural suffix -s for Auto is regular (Clahsen, 1995). In contrast, in English, the first constituent of a compound is usually not pluralized. Thus if compounds are formed on-line, and transfer of pluralization rules occurs, a German speaker might pluralize the first element of an English compound (e.g. *'micetrap') if the plural of the first element in English is irregular, but not if it is regular (e.g. 'bedroom').

A further research question involves orthographic differences in marking plurals. In French orthography, for example, a high percentage of compounds do not have plural markers (whereas a silent orthographic 's' marks most other plural morphemes in French). Thus the plural form 'porte-monnaie' ('purses') is orthographically as well as phonologically identical to the singular form 'porte-monnaie'. If French-speaking individuals fail to pluralize compounds in their L2 English orthography or speech, this could be an indication of transfer from L1.

6.4.6 *Phonology*

In the psycholinguistic literature, researchers have investigated the mechanisms of morphological processing by observing participants' parsing of ambiguous compounds. In studies of prelexical parsing of ambiguous novel compounds (e.g. 'clamprod'), Libben (1994) and Libben *et al.* (1999) suggest that parsing of such compounds generates several possible representations, which are then evaluated, resulting in the most appropriate parse. Additional issues arise for bilinguals: given an ambiguous novel compound without being told which language it is in, according to the constraints of which language will a bilingual evaluate the possible parsing candidates? That is, does a French–English bilingual have separate 'evaluators' for French and for English? Is one of them more active than the other, and how can this be determined? A closer look at phonological parsing of compounds would be one approach to addressing these questions.

Other phonological features that may be studied include compound stress. In Finnish, as in English, stress is a salient indicator of compounding—the main stress of a compound is in the first syllable only, whereas noun phrases may have two main stresses (Mäkisalo, 2000). Would Finnish speakers transfer the stress rules of Finnish when producing French compounds, for example (in which the first syllable of a compound is unlikely to be stressed), or is Finnish speakers' production of stress in French dependent on their general 'prosodic' accent in L2, with compounds treated prosodically as any other type of French word? This question could be addressed by having native French speakers rate Finnish speakers' degree of accent in French, and specifically their degree of accent in compound production. Of course, this study could also be performed via acoustic analysis of the intonational contour of Finnish speakers' production of French compounds within discourse in French.

6.4.7 Etymology and orthography

Etymologically, languages may be closely related (e.g. Italian and Spanish), resulting in phonological, lexical, morphological, and syntactic similarities. Alternatively, they may be genetically unrelated but may have been spoken in close proximity or by a bilingual population (e.g. Arabic and Persian) and therefore have many lexical similarities but fewer formal similarities. And, of course, languages may be altogether unrelated (as with Hebrew and Chinese), resulting in few similarities.

Pairs of languages may share an alphabet or use different scripts (e.g. Hebrew script versus the Roman alphabet) and may differ in their grapheme–phoneme correspondence. As mentioned above, cross-language priming effects have been found for cognates, that is words with similar form and meaning. Priming even occurs for words with identical spelling but different pronunciations and meanings in two languages. For example, Beauvillain and Grainger (1987) found a priming effect for 'homographic noncognates' such as French 'four' (pronounced [fuR], 'oven') and English 'four', an effect largely dependent on the frequency of the meaning of the priming letter string within the target language (e.g. the number 'four' in English). Thus, creation of stimuli for any study of words in two languages must take into account how closely words in the two languages resemble each other, both orthographically and in speech.

Studies involving compounds might reveal priming or interference in bilinguals' lexicons for constituents that are homographic noncognates (e.g. the morpheme 'pain' in English and French 'pain', meaning 'bread' when presented with English 'back pain', for example), homographic cognates or non-homographic cognates, as pointed out by Jarema (2003, personal communication).

Compounds in languages that share the same orthography are likely to have more links in mental representation than compounds from languages that use different orthographies. Furthermore, compounds can be written as single words, as hyphenated words, and as two monomorphemic words; in some languages (e.g. English), all three variations may be found. Processes of compound recognition and constituent identification may depend on the visual presentation of the word(s) (e.g. de Jong *et al.*, 2002). Compounds that are overtly marked as morphologically complex forms, for example, with a graphemic change (e.g. hyphenation in French compounds, letter substitutions or omissions within feminine or plural Hebrew compounds) may be processed differently from compounds that cannot be easily distinguished from monomorphemic words. Transfer of the orthographic conventions of one language into the other may be expected for languages that differ in their orthographic and/or morphosyntactic features.

6.5 Neurolinguistic evidence of compound processing: Compounds in polyglot aphasia

Several methods have been mentioned thus far for research into compound processing in bilinguals: lexical decision, cross-linguistic priming, parsing patterns, examination of transfer errors, translation tasks, reaction times, accentedness rating, and acoustical analysis. Studies of polyglot aphasics (bilingual or multilingual individuals who have experienced damage to the language areas of their brain due to stroke or injury) are likely to provide further information about brain regions involved in processing compounds in healthy brains. Semenza and Mondini (this volume) review studies in monolingual aphasia focusing on compound processing. Study of aphasic bilinguals' translation and paraphrasing may similarly provide evidence for pre-morbid representation of compounds.

Previous work on affixation and morphological deficits in various languages has provided information on crosslinguistic patterns in morphological processing (e.g. Tyler *et al.*, 1990; Miceli *et al.*, 1992; Friederici and Frazier, 1992; Menn and Obler, 1990). Results from studies of morphological processing in healthy bilingual brains provide evidence both for (e.g. Nicoladis, 2003b) and against (e.g. Unsworth, 2000) morphological transfer between a bilingual's languages.

Cases of polyglot aphasia have shown that, following a stroke in the language areas of the brain, bilinguals may reveal parallel patterns of linguistic deficits in both languages or, less often, one language may be more affected than the other. For the cases of parallel deficits, one might predict equal difficulty in both languages for producing compounds, unless compounding is more frequent in one language than in the other. The cases of differential recovery pose an interesting question: if selective deficits occur, with one language remaining largely unimpaired, does the processing of compounds show the same selective deficit (i.e. impaired only in one language but intact in the other)? Fabbro *et al.* (1997) report case studies of one Italian–English bilingual and two Friulian–Italian bilingual patients with tumors or ischemic brain lesions in the thalamus. Neurolinguistic testing revealed primarily morphosyntactic deficits, which were more severe in their second language than in their first, possibly pointing to separate morphological processors for each language that would, then, potentially treat compounds differently.

Data on compound-processing, as well as processing of other types of morphemes, from bilingual patients with deficits similar to those described in the studies above, may begin to answer questions about brain regions responsible for morphological processing in bilinguals. Brain-imaging studies using techniques such as fMRI and PET scans and ERP, would complement aphasia studies by pointing to regions and temporal processes (in neurologically-intact bilinguals) that are involved in the production of compounds.

6.6 Language histories

Last, but perhaps most importantly, participants' language histories and current proficiency must be considered for any studies of bilingual language processing. As suggested in various studies (e.g. de Groot and Kroll, 1997), age of acquisition and current proficiency are two of the predominant factors that will determine routes of lexical processing. Other factors that have been found to influence an individual's linguistic 'status' include whether bilinguals learned their languages simultaneously or consecutively, whether both languages were consistently used over time, the setting in which languages were learned (e.g. Weinreich, 1953; Hyltenstam and Obler, 1989; Bialystok and Hakuta, 1994), in which modality languages were learned (i.e. written or oral) (Albert and Obler, 1978), and what other languages have been spoken in the environment (e.g. Tees and Werker, 1984). All of these factors will likely enter into how compounds are represented and processed in the bilingual's lexicon.

6.7 Conclusion and future directions

From language to language, compounds may vary along virtually every possible linguistic dimension. When two languages are stored within a single brain, questions arise as to how the two systems are represented and processed. Researchers may begin to answer such questions by learning the properties of complex structures such as compounds in two languages, noting the time required for bilinguals to process them during various carefully-designed tasks, and observing how the compounds emerge after processing. Well-informed analysis of reaction times and transfer errors requires consideration of the prevalence and productivity of compounds within a language, semantic transparency, morphological headedness, position of constituents in a string, morphological constraints, phonotactics, permissible syntactic categories, orthography, etymological relatedness of languages, and individuals' language histories.

Careful consideration of tasks and modalities selected is also crucial, as visual and auditory lexical processing may call for different theoretical models. Analyses that take these factors into account should permit further understanding of the representation and processing mechanisms of compounds and of the bilingual brain.

Further documentation of bilinguals' transfer errors involving the structure and lexical content of compounds is expected to reveal active links between L1 and L2 lexemes and/or lemmas in on-line processing. Ultimately, investigations of the nature and implications of compound representation and processing in bilinguals may be extended to study the mechanisms of trilingual and multilingual processing.

Acknowledgments

The authors wish to thank Ray Jackendoff and two anonymous reviewers, as well as the editors of this volume, Gary Libben and Gonia Jarema, for their suggestions for this chapter.

7

Conceptual Combination: Implications for the mental lexicon

CHRISTINA L. GAGNÉ
AND THOMAS L. SPALDING

Compounding is a common word formation process in all languages. Of particular relevance to the current chapter are compounds that are formed by combining two or more words. Although such compounds can take many forms including verb-noun, verb-verb, adjective-adjective, and noun-noun there is a general preference for noun-noun compounds in most languages (see Dressler, this volume). Because compounding is so prevalent, understanding both the process of compounding and the access and use of familiar compound words is critical to understanding the mental lexicon as a whole. In this chapter, we will demonstrate how research on conceptual combination can provide insight into the structure and content of the mental lexicon. In particular, we will provide evidence that relations are important for the representation and use of compound words. Previous chapters in this volume (e.g. Libben; Jarema) have discussed why understanding compounds is important for understanding the lexicon. The current chapter tackles the issue of how novel compounds are processed. This issue is relevant because a major assumption in the literature is that compound words start out as novel compounds and then become lexicalized at some point in their history (see the chapters by Jarema, Dressler, and Libben, this volume).

Let us begin with a simple example. The compound word *teapot* is formed by combining *tea* and *pot*. In general, compounds denote contrasts between subcategories and provide labels that distinguish among members of a single category (Berman and Clark, 1989). For example, the terms *teapot* and *coffeepot* distinguish two types of *pots*. In this case, the modifiers *tea* and *coffee* indicate the type of substance for which the pot is designed. Thus, the main distinguishing characteristic between these two types of pots is that one is used for tea and the other is used for coffee. Notice that the head noun *pot* could be modified in ways other than just its function, as evidenced in the combinations *plastic pot* and *office pot*, where the material and location of the pot are used to create the subcategory.

In these examples, it is clear that the modifier and head noun are not merely linked to each other. Instead, there is a relation that denotes the manner in which the head noun should be modified. Thus, *teapot* and *coffeepot* are formed using a relation such as *head noun FOR modifier*, *plastic pot* is formed using the relation *head noun MADE OF modifier*, and *office pot* is formed using the relation *head noun LOCATED modifier*. The relation that is used to link the constituents of a compound heavily influences the meaning of the compound. Indeed, the relation is critical to the very purpose of creating the compound: the relation determines, to a large extent, the contrast that is relevant for the compound. A pot made of plastic contrasts with pots made of other materials, rather than with pots that have a particular location or contain a particular substance.

Thus, it appears that relational information is an important aspect of a compound's representation and meaning. However, this type of information has not been incorporated into current theories of compounds and there has been little research investigating whether relations affect the processing of familiar compounds. Instead, much of the research on compounding has focused on the nature of the representation of compounds in the mental lexicon (Andrews, 1986; Monsell, 1985; Sandra, 1990; Zwitserlood, 1994). In particular, a main issue is whether compound words are represented as whole words or as their constituents. This issue is strongly related to the issue of relation use, in the sense that if the compound word is stored, accessed, and used as a single unit, it is not clear what role the relation could play. Whereas some researchers have argued that decomposition does not occur for compound words (Butterworth, 1983), others have found evidence of decomposition (Libben, 1998; Libben *et al.*, 2003; Zwitserlood, 1994). This discrepancy about whether a compound is represented as a whole word or in terms of its constituents appears to be related to semantic transparency (see also Jarema, this volume).

There is growing evidence that semantic transparency plays an important role in the processing of multimorphemic compounds (Libben, 1998; Libben *et al.*, 2003; Zwitserlood, 1994). In particular, semantic transparency appears to determine whether a compound's constituents are linked to the whole word. The distinction between a lexical and conceptual level has been useful for explaining the processing of transparent and opaque compounds (Libben, 1998; also see Libben, this volume, for a discussion of the issue of transparency). Only constituents that are semantically related to the meaning of the compound as a whole are linked to the compound word in the lexicon. For example, the word form for the compound *blueberry* is linked to *blue*, *berry*, and *blueberry* at the lexical level. The lexical entry *blueberry* is transparent for both the first and second constituents and, thus, Libben (1998) proposed that this entry is linked to the concepts *blue*, *berry*, and *blueberry* at the conceptual level. In contrast, the compound *strawberry* is only transparent in terms of its second constituent. Consequently, the lexical entry for *strawberry* is linked to the concepts *berry* and *strawberry* at the conceptual level. It is not linked to the concept *straw*. In both examples, the compound's lexical entry is connected to its respective conceptual representation. Notice that the conceptual level plays a large role in representing semantic opacity.

Although theories such as the ones proposed by Libben (1998; see also Zwitserlood, 1994) suggest that the lexical representations of semantically transparent compounds are linked to their constituents, relational information has not yet been incorporated into these views. That is, even though there is evidence to suggest that semantically transparent compounds (such as *snowball*) are represented in the lexicon in terms of their constituents as well as in terms of the whole word, relational information is not used to link the constituents to each other at either the lexical or conceptual level. Thus, what is missing from this analysis is information about the content of the conceptual representation. In addition, these theories focus on existing compounds (i.e. ones that have representations in the lexicon). Consequently, they do not provide information about how conceptual representations for novel compounds are formed. However, because the parsing procedure represented in these theories is based on the assumption that the lexical and conceptual levels are involved in the interpretation and processing of compound words, it becomes necessary to examine the conceptual system in general and conceptual combination in particular. Novel compounds (e.g. *pieberry*) do not yet have a representation at either the lexical or conceptual level and, thus, the meaning of these items must be computed by other means. It is possible that the method used to understand novel compounds might also affect the processing of familiar compounds because all compounds start out as novel combinations. In fact, the creation of noun compounds is so productive that linguists such as Downing (1977) have suggested that, in English, nominal compounding provides a 'back door' into the mental lexicon. Although some compounds (e.g. *funeral train, apple juice seat*) are short-lived, others (e.g. *typewriter, snowflake, computer chip*) have entered the language. Therefore, it seems likely that a better understanding of how modifier-noun combinations are formed and interpreted will help us understand how complex words are processed and represented in the mind.

Given that all familiar semantically transparent compounds start out as novel phrases, it seems that the processing of novel phrases and familiar compounds might be similar. In particular, it seems a natural question whether the relations that are so important when the compounds are first formed maintain that importance when the compounds become more familiar. To better understand how relations might affect the processing of familiar compounds, we will examine a body of research in which relations have been shown to play a large role—namely the conceptual combination literature.

The process in which two or more concepts are combined to form new concepts is called conceptual combination. The conceptual combination literature is highly relevant to the study of compound words because compound words (e.g. *snowball*) represent combined concepts in the conceptual system. That is, the conceptual representation of *snowball* is formed from the concepts *snow* and *ball*. Researchers studying the problem of conceptual combination are trying to identify both the underlying conceptual structures that allow this process to occur and the on-line processing that occurs during conceptual combination. Recognizing that compound words (in the language system) are connected to combined concepts (in the conceptual system) provides a new perspective and raises some important questions about how compounds are represented and accessed.

A major assumption in the area of conceptual combination is that understanding a combined concept involves creating a new concept because a combined concept is more than a hybrid of its parts. For example, a *peeled apple* is no longer just an apple—its features are not entirely identical to those of an apple. A peeled apple is white, not red, and a peeled apple is likely to be used in a pie, and so on. In short, the concept of the head noun is modified in some way by the addition of the modifier. Although one might think that this modification would be a simple process of adding the meaning of the modifier to that of the head noun, this has not turned out to be the case (Medin and Shoben, 1988; Murphy, 1988, 1990). Instead, the interpretation of combined concepts involves an interaction between the two constituents, rather than an additive process. For example, the fact that peeled apples are white is not part of the meaning of peeled, but is inferred, based on the interpretation of the entire phrase (see Gagné and Murphy, 1996; Springer and Murphy, 1992). Peeled oranges are not white, are not likely to be used in a pie, and so on. Thus, *peeled* cannot be adding the same feature to apple and orange. Because a modifier-noun phrase denotes a new concept, theories of conceptual combination have focused on understanding how the new concept is formed.

Theories of conceptual combination have adopted one of two approaches. Some theories such as the schema-modification theory

(Murphy, 1988, 1990) have taken a schema-based approach. Others, such as the Competition-Among-Relations-in-Nominals (CARIN) theory (Gagné, 2001; Gagné and Shoben, 2002) have taken a relation-based approach. These theories offer competing views about how conceptual combination might occur. Thus, before discussing how the notion of conceptual combination can be applied to lexicalized compounds, it is first necessary to discuss the nature of these theories.

Murphy's (1988; 1990) schema modification theory suggests that conceptual combination is based on the transfer of information from the modifier to the head noun, and the head noun is proposed to play the dominant role during conceptual combination. Proponents of these theories (Murphy, 1988, 1990; Wisniewski, 1996) propose that the head noun (e.g. spoon) is represented as a structured set of slots (e.g. MATERIAL) and fillers (e.g. wood, metal, and plastic). During conceptual combination, a specific dimension within the head noun's representation is selected and its value is changed to match the value present in the modifier. For example, the value in the MATERIAL dimension is changed to *wood* for the combination *wood spoon*. The more available a slot, the easier it is to interpret the combination. Consequently, these theories predict that interpreting a combined concept should take longer if the required dimension is not part of the head noun schema. For example, the combination *cold garbage* should be more difficult to interpret than *cold beer* because the schema for *garbage* does not include a dimension for temperature.

The schema modification theory uses world knowledge to explain how the various slots within the schema are altered during conceptual combination. World knowledge is used in two ways. First, it is used to identify which slots should be affected by the modifier. Second, it is used to elaborate the combined concept by altering slots within the head noun schema that were not directly altered by the modifier. For example, in the case of *apartment dog*, the modifier *apartment* is placed in the *habitat* slot within the schema for dog. Then, world knowledge is used to revise other relevant slots such as *size*. Due to the use of world knowledge, this theory allows for the alteration of dimensions other than the one(s) denoted by the modifier.

Although the schema modification theory proposes that world knowledge plays a large role in conceptual combination, the way in which it exerts an influence is not clearly defined. As Murphy (1988, p. 554) points out, the schema modification model 'refers to people's world knowledge in a rather unconstrained manner'.

The CARIN theory was developed based on the notion that specific aspects of world knowledge directly influence conceptual combination (Gagné, 2000, 2001; Gagné and Shoben, 1997). This theory uses a relation-based approach. A key assumption of the CARIN theory is that conceptual combination involves the selection of a relation that links the constituents. This theory is based on the claim that one aspect of world knowledge that is particularly relevant to conceptual combination is relational information about how objects, people, and so on interact. This information is used to select a relation that links two constituent concepts during the formation of a new combined concept. For example, *chocolate bee* is formed using the relation *noun MADE OF modifier* to link *chocolate* and *bee*. However, *honey bee* is formed by using the relation *noun MAKES modifier*. This theory is consistent with emerging evidence that relational information plays a vital role in the organization of the conceptual system (see Medin, 1998) as well as with early linguistic theories of nominal compounding (Gleitman and Gleitman, 1970; Kay and Zimmer, 1976; Levi, 1978). For example, Levi (1978) developed a taxonomy of general thematic relations that can be used to classify noun compounds. Other linguists (Downing, 1977; Kay and Zimmer, 1976; Warren, 1978) have also proposed that noun combinations embody a relation between two (or more) constituent concepts, but they disagree about the exact number and nature of these relations.

According to CARIN, the selection of this relation is heavily influenced by how the modifier has been used in previous combinations. In other words, just as people know that the concept *dog* has members that range in typicality, they know that *mountain*, when used as a modifier, typically denotes a locative relation, but can, in some cases, denote an *about* relation (as in *mountain magazine*). This information about how a concept can be used to modify other concepts heavily influences the ease with which concepts can be combined. The claim that relation selection is influenced primarily by the modifier rather than the head noun is derived from the structure of the combined concept. Combinations consist of a modifier and a head noun, and the roles played by these constituents differ. The modifier implies a contrast among members of the head noun category and indicates that the head noun must be altered (Gelman and Markman, 1985; Markman, 1989). For example, the modifier *chocolate* in the combination *chocolate bee* indicates that the primary difference between this particular bee and most bees is that this bee is made of chocolate. Put another way, the modifier indicates the relevant contrast set, whereas the head noun provides the category name (Markman, 1989). For these reasons, it seems reasonable to assume that a modifier's past usage with various relations would more strongly influence relation selection than would a head noun's past usage.

These two proposals are key elements of the CARIN theory (Gagné and Shoben, 1997; Gagné, 2001). According to this theory, relations compete with one another such that strongly activated relations are more likely to be selected than are less activated relations. A second claim is that the modifier's past usage with various relations strongly affects the likelihood that a relation will be selected. To represent knowledge about how concepts can be used to modify other concepts, the CARIN theory assumes that relations have different strengths for various concepts. For example, the *noun MADE OF modifier* relation is stronger for *chocolate* than is the *noun DERIVED FROM modifier* relation. Knowledge about the modifier's past usage with various relations is called the modifier's relational distribution and this distribution is used to determine which relations should be considered during the conceptual combination process. The difficulty of creating a combined concept is a function of the relative strength of the required relation. Gagné and Shoben (1997) proposed that the frequency of a relation for a particular concept is a reasonable index of strength. Thus, the

CARIN theory posits that, other things being equal, it is easier to combine two concepts when the required relation is highly frequent for the modifier than when it is not frequent. For example, the locative relation (noun LOCATED modifier) is a highly frequent relation for the concept *mountain,* in that approximately 80 percent of phrases of the form *mountain*-X in the Gagné and Shoben corpus used this relation. Therefore, it should be easier to interpret *mountain bird* (a bird in the mountains) than to interpret *mountain magazine* (a magazine about mountains).

However, absolute frequency is not the only factor that affects the ease with which concepts can be combined. The strength of the other relations in the modifier's relational distribution also plays a role. To illustrate, the three most frequently used relations for *headache* are CAUSES (33 percent), ABOUT (33 percent), and FOR (21 percent). The three most frequently used relations for *juvenile* are FOR (33 percent), HAS (20 percent), and ABOUT (15 percent). Thus, the most frequently used relation for the modifiers *juvenile* and *headache* are equivalent. This implies that the ease of selecting the most frequently used relation for combinations using these two modifiers would be equivalent. However, relations compete for selection and it is more difficult to select the most frequent relation for *headache* than for *juvenile* because the frequency of the next most frequent relation is higher for *headache* (33 percent vs. 33 percent) than for *juvenile* (33 percent vs. 20 percent).

The selected relation provides a framework around which the semantic representation of a combination is constructed. As argued in Gagné and Murphy (1996), the relation might determine which features are initially added to the representation of a combined concept. For example, the feature *white* might become part of the representation for *peeled apple* because the combination is interpreted as 'an apple that is peeled' and the act of peeling reveals the inside of the apple. However, the feature *round* is not readily available because the interpretation 'an apple that is peeled' has no strong consequences for the apple's shape. Gagné and Shoben (1997) make a similar argument when they claim that the properties of *mountain bird* are a consequence of the relation used to interpret the combination. For example, because it is a bird that lives in the mountains, a mountain bird is likely to be better able to withstand cold than the typical bird. This is not to say that features that are true of all birds (i.e. features not unique to mountain birds) are never added to the representation of *mountain bird*. Instead, it appears that such features become available after features that are particularly relevant to the combination (Gagné and Spalding, 2004b; Gagné and Murphy, 1996; Springer and Murphy, 1992). In this way, the relation is used to specify properties of the entire phrase.

An objection to the use of relations is the assertion that meaning is often more specific than that depicted by a general relation. However, the fact that meanings can be further specified does not provide strong evidence against the use of relations in the processing of compounds. These relations are categorical and, like other categorical structures, relations have subcategories. Consider the category *bird*. Knowing that an object is a *bird* provides a lot of information even though the actual object can be further specified as a *robin* or, even more specifically, *the robin in my backyard*. Indeed, one of the fundamental facts in the category literature is that categorical information is not always used at the most specific possible level (see, for example, Rosch *et al.*, 1976). In much the same way, *picture book* and *student book* belong to the same relation category: *noun HAS modifier*. However, it is possible to further specify the meaning of these items; *picture book* depicts a HAS-PART relation whereas *student book* depicts a HAS-OWNERSHIP (see Levi, 1978). Again, this subcategory structure allows for the further refinement of a particular meaning, but at the same time does not entail that knowledge about more general relations is ignored during processing. Knowing that a compound uses a HAS relation rather than a CAUSES relation (for example) provides a lot of information, just as knowing that an object is a member of the category *bird* provides a lot of information.

Also note that this view does not assume that the relation between constituents in compounds is unambiguous. On the contrary, this view claims that during interpretation multiple relations compete for selection and this aspect allows (in fact, nearly compels) compounds to be potentially ambiguous. For a given situation, however, the compound is likely to be viewed as unambiguous by the comprehender because, in most cases, he/she must converge on a single meaning to integrate the conceptual representation for the compound with the rest of the sentence and, if provided, discourse. By allowing the meaning of compounds, even lexicalized compounds, to be constructed rather than retrieved, this approach allows for all levels of representation (lexical, conceptual, and discourse) to play a role in comprehension and ambiguity resolution.

7.1 Empirical findings and their implications for the CARIN theory and schema-based theories

Before discussing how research on conceptual combination can help researchers understand compound words, we will first address the question: which theory of conceptual combination is the most promising? To date, there has been more empirical support for the CARIN theory than for the schema modification theory. There is a growing body of evidence to suggest that the availability of particular relations affects the processing of novel noun-noun compounds (Gagné, 2000, 2001, 2002; Gagné and Shoben, 1997). Relation availability can be viewed in two ways. First, it can refer to the frequency with which a modifier has been used with a particular relation (Gagné, 2001; Gagné and Shoben, 1997). For example, when *mountain* is used as the first word of a noun-noun phrase (e.g. *mountain cabin*), the relation that is most often used to interpret the phrase is a locative one (i.e. *head noun LOCATED modifier*).

This prediction has been tested in a number of experiments (Gagné and Shoben, 1997; Gagné 2001). Prior to conducting their experiments, Gagné and Shoben (1997) created a corpus of novel noun-noun combinations by crossing ninety-one modifiers with ninety-one head nouns. This set of possible two-word combinations was examined and 3,239 of these items were determined to have a sensible, literal interpretation. Each item was then classified according to the relation required to link the constituent concepts. The categories were based on Levi's (1978) relational categories. This information was used to determine the frequency with which various modifiers and head nouns are used with each of these relations. For example, the modifier 'plastic' appeared in forty-one combinations in the corpus. Of these, twenty-eight used the *noun MADE OF modifier* relation, seven used the *noun ABOUT modifier* relation, two used *the noun DERIVED FROM modifier* relation, and one used the *modifier CAUSES noun* relation. After calculating this information for each modifier and head noun in the corpus, each relation was categorized as high or low frequency for each modifier and each head noun. This categorization was carried out as follows: the most frequent relation was selected for a particular modifier or head noun. If this relation was used with 60 percent or more of the combinations for that word, then the relation was the sole high frequency relation for that word. If not, the next highest frequency relation was selected until the combined frequency for all selected relations accounted for 60 percent of the combinations using a particular word. All other relations were considered low frequency relations. For example, the modifier juvenile was used in forty-nine combinations. The most frequently used relation for this modifier (*noun FOR modifier*) was used in 34 percent of the combinations. Therefore, the next most frequent relation for juvenile (*noun HAS modifier*) was selected. Together, these relations accounted for 61 percent of all combinations using juvenile and, therefore, these relations were deemed 'high frequency relations' for the purpose of the experiments.

This corpus was used to select items for each of three experimental conditions. The HH condition contained combinations for which the required relation was highly frequent for both the modifier and head noun. For example, *mountain bird* can be interpreted using the relation *noun LOCATED modifier* and this relation is highly frequent for both *mountain* and *bird*. The HL condition contained combinations for which the required relation was highly frequent for the modifier, but not for the head noun. The LH condition contained combinations for which the relation was highly frequent for the head noun, but not for the modifier.

Participants viewed the combinations one at a time on a computer screen and indicated whether they had a sensible literal interpretation. A set of nonsense filler items was included in the stimulus set. The primary variable of interest was the response time for the sense–nonsense judgment. As predicted by the CARIN theory, responses to the HH and HL combinations were faster than responses to the LH combinations, indicating that it was easier to select a relation when it was highly frequent for the modifier than when it was not frequent. The difference between the HH and HL conditions was not statistically significant, indicating that the frequency of the relation for the head noun constituent did not strongly affect relation selection. Thus, the data from these experiments indicate that the availability of a relation for the modifier (as defined by the modifier's past usage in other combinations) affects the ease of interpreting a novel combination.

To further test the CARIN theory, the sense–nonsense response times were fitted using a strength ratio as an index of the availability of a particular relation based on the modifier's relational distribution. The strength ratio is the mathematical instantiation of the theory (see Gagné and Shoben, 1997, for details). If the assumptions of the CARIN theory are valid, then the strength ratio should be a good predictor of the ease with which a combined concept can be interpreted. To illustrate how a strength index was computed for each combination, consider the concepts *mountain bird* and *mountain magazine*. For *mountain*, the locative interpretation was used for 82 percent of all combinations using *mountain* as the modifier. The next most frequently used relation for this concept was *noun ABOUT modifier*, *noun USES modifier*, and *noun MADE OF modifier* which, in order, were used for 10 percent, 2 percent, and 1 percent of the combinations using mountain as the modifier. The combination *mountain bird* requires the locative relation, thus, the ratio would be based on $.82 / (.82 + .10 + .02 + .01)$. The strength ratio for *mountain bird* would be quite high. In contrast, the strength ratio for *mountain magazine* would be much lower. The ratio is $.10 / (.10 + .82 + .02 + .01)$. Notice that, in this example, the modifier has a highly dominant relation and that this dominance is reflected in the strength ratio. For modifiers that do not have a highly dominant relation, the difference between the strength ratios for the most and second most frequent relations is not as dramatic. For example, the proportions of the four most frequent relations for juvenile are .34, .20, .15, and .10. Thus, the ratio for a combination using the most frequent relation is .34 / (.34 + .20 + .15 + .10), whereas the ratio for the combination using the second most frequent relation is .20 / (.20 + .34 + .15 + .10). A stepwise regression using the strength ratio along with word frequency and word length for both the modifier and head noun yielded a multiple R of . 54 and .64 for Experiments 1 and 3 in Gagné and Shoben (1997), respectively. The fits are comparable to models in similar areas such as Holyoak's (1978) reference point model, Chumbley's (1986) model of category membership verification, and Shoben et al.'s (1983) subtraction point model.

A second way to view relation availability is in terms of recent usage. Relations that have been used recently should be more available than relations that have not been used recently. Thus, the goal of more recent research has been to determine whether relational availability is affected by recent exposure to combinations with similar modifiers and head nouns. In the experiments reported in Gagné (2001), novel modifier-noun combinations (e.g. student vote) were preceded by one of several prime combinations. The primes were manipulated such that the prime shared either the same modifier or head noun. In addition, the primes used either the same relation as the target combination (e.g. student accusation and employee vote) or a different relation (e.g. student car and reform vote). A neutral prime that used a different head noun and modifier as the target, but used the same relation was included.

Participants made sense–nonsense judgments to two-word combinations. A set of nonsense filler items was included. For the experimental items, the prime combination immediately preceded the target combination. Participants responded to both the prime and target combination and there was nothing in the procedure to differentiate prime and target trials. The influence of the prime combination on relation availability was determined by comparing the same relation prime to the different relation prime. For example, if recent exposure to a combination using the same modifier and relation as the target combination increases relation availability, then responses to the target *student vote* should be faster when preceded by the prime *student accusation* (same relation) than when preceded by the prime *student car* (different relation). Primes containing the same head noun as the target were also used to further test the CARIN theory's prediction that relational information is not associated with the head noun. That is, CARIN predicts that responses to the target combination should be unaffected by whether the prime combination used the same relation (e.g. employee vote) or a different relation (e.g. reform vote) when the head noun is repeated. The data are consistent with the CARIN theory. Relation priming was obtained only when the modifier constituent was in common. More recent evidence indicates that the modifier need not be identical for relation priming to occur; the same pattern of results are obtained when the modifier constituent of the prime combination is semantically similar to the target combination's modifier (Gagné, 2002).

It is worth noting that relation availability is based on the modifier's past usage, not on that of the head noun (Gagné, 2001; Gagné and Shoben, 1997). Although one might be tempted to attribute this finding to the fact that the modifier is the first constituent of English compounds, the finding that relation availability is connected to the modifier appears to be robust and has been replicated in studies involving Indonesian compounds (Storms and Wisniewski, in press) and French compounds (Turco, 2000). In both of these studies, the modifier was the second constituent. Storms and Wisniewski examine general relation usage. They had native speakers of Indonesian generate familiar noun-noun combinations given either the modifier or head noun. They classified these responses into relation categories and then derived relation frequencies for each modifier and head noun by counting the number of items in each relation category. Following the procedure of Gagné and Shoben (1997), a separate group of participants performed sense–nonsense judgments on items that had been classified as HH, HL, and LH. Only the effect of modifier relation frequency was reliable; responses were faster when the item used a relation that was highly frequent for the modifier. Response time was not affected by head noun relation frequency.

It might seem counterintuitive that the modifier's relational history has a greater effect on ease of comprehension than does the head noun's relational history. After all, the syntactic, semantic, and morphological properties of the entire compound are usually determined by the head noun (see Dressler, this volume). However, recall that the modifier and head noun play different roles. The head noun denotes the category (e.g. *teacup* is a type of *cup*) whereas the modifier is used to denote a subcategory within the head noun's category (e.g. the modifier *tea* distinguishes *teacups* from *cups* in general). Thus, the modifier is essential for constructing a structure that maps onto a subcategory. Put another way, if a speaker/writer wants to refer to the head noun category, s/he can just use the head noun by itself. It is only when s/he wants to refer to a particular subgroup within that category that a modifier is needed. Given the vital role that the modifier plays in denoting subcategories of the head noun, it is not so surprising that that knowledge about how the modifier has been used to modify other concepts (i.e. the modifier's relational history) has a larger effect than does knowledge about how the head noun tends to be modified. The head noun might exert an influence in other aspects of the conceptual combination process. For example, the head noun might be involved in determining whether the relation suggested by the modifier (in conjunction with the preceding context) is plausible (see Gagné and Shoben, 1997).

This advantage of the modifier information over head noun information has also been observed in the access of compound words. Jarema (this volume) discusses research in several languages that demonstrate that the first constituent has an advantage over the second constituent in terms of its ability to prime the compound. Although these studies do not examine the role of relational information, they do provide evidence of another situation in which the first constituent has a larger effect on the processing of the compound than does the second constituent.

To summarize, four main findings have emerged and all are consistent with the basic assumptions of the CARIN theory. First, relational information is used during the interpretation of novel modifier-noun combinations. Second, the frequency with which a relation has been used with a particular modifier influences the ease of interpreting a novel combination using that modifier. Third, the frequency with which a relation has been used with a particular head noun does not influence the ease of interpreting a combination. Fourth, recency of a modifier-relation pairing also plays a role. The availability of a relation is affected by recent exposure to combinations with identical or semantically similar modifiers.

Schema-based theories (Murphy 1988, 1990; Wisniewski, 1996) have difficulty accounting for the empirical findings discussed in the preceding paragraphs. The first problem with these theories is that they do not use a relation to link the modifier and head noun concepts. Instead, the theories claim that conceptual combination involves filling a slot within the head noun's schema and suggest that the head noun plays a dominant role in determining the ease of conceptual combination. This claim is inconsistent with the finding that ease of combining concepts is affected by the availability of the required relation for the modifier rather than by the availability of a slot in the head noun. The finding that a recent combination using the same head noun as the target combination does not influence comprehension time is deeply problematic because schema-based theories predict that a head noun prime using the same relation as the target combination should increase the availability of the relevant slot in the head noun schema and this increase in availability should decrease response time to the target combination.

A second problem is that schema-based theories suggest that recent exposure to a combination containing the same modifier as a subsequent combination should not influence the comprehension of the subsequent combination because there is no mechanism whereby the representation of the modifier is altered by the combination process. Although existing dimensions within the head noun schema are altered by placing the modifier in the appropriate dimension, according to schema-based theories, the modifier concept is unaffected. Thus, schema-based theories have difficulty explaining why it is easier to select a relation when it has been recently paired with the modifier because the schema supposedly being altered in the target combination (e.g. student vote) is not the same as the schema in the prime combination (e.g. student accusation).

To summarize, the empirical evidence strongly supports the CARIN theory of conceptual combination. Now we will turn our attention back to the issue of lexicalized compounds. As discussed previously, semantically transparent compounds also appear to be based on relations. A *teapot* is *a pot for tea* whereas a *plastic pot* is *a pot made of plastic*. Can the CARIN theory be applied to familiar compounds, as well? If so, what are the implications of this theory for understanding the core issues in compound representation and processing?

7.2 Applying the CARIN theory to lexicalized compounds

The explanation that has been put forth to account for relation priming in experiments involving novel compounds can be applied directly to compound words. Recall that the CARIN theory claims that during the processing of novel compounds, relations become activated and these relations compete for selection. The more available a relation, the more successfully it can compete. According to this view, it is easier to respond to the target following the same relation prime relative to the different relation prime because the required relation is more highly available following the same relation prime. This increase in relation availability results in decreased processing time for the target compound.

By this explanation, stored compounds are actively processed in much the same way that novel compounds are processed. That is, these compounds are decomposed and then re-composed using a relation to link the constituents. In other words, an important aspect of the processing of familiar compounds is establishing the relation that forms the basis for the representation of the whole word. To illustrate, the compound *teapot* is constructed using the relation *noun FOR modifier* to link the constituents *tea* and *pot*. The resulting representation denotes a subcategory of *pot*; one that is used for tea. This process of selecting a relation and constructing a unified representation is obligatory for novel compounds (e.g. *beach beverage*) because the compound is not part of the lexicon. We argue that this process is also obligatory for familiar compounds and propose that accessing familiar compounds involves exactly the same processing as computing the meaning of completely novel compounds, despite the widely-accepted notion that familiar compounds are stored in the mental lexicon but novel compounds are not.

The aphasiological evidence discussed by Jarema (this volume, see also Libben, 1998) is consistent with the proposal that various meanings compete for selection even for known compounds. It appears that the mixed aphasic in the study was unable to inhibit conceptual representations during the processing of compound words. For example, the person paraphrased *blueprint* as 'a print that is blue'. Note that, in this case, the compound is being processed as though it were a novel compound and that the relation *noun IS modifier* is highly frequent for the modifier *blue*. We suggest that this combination process always occurs during the processing of compounds, even for non-aphasics, but that the conventional (i.e. lexicalized) meaning is more strongly activated and, thus, can effectively compete with other alternative meanings.

Another reason to suggest that the interpretation of familiar compounds might involve an obligatory conceptual combination process, comes from data recently published by Gagné, Spalding, and Gorrie (2005). One aim of this study was to determine whether the ability to interpret familiar phrases (e.g. *bug spray*) was affected by recent exposure to an alternative, innovative meaning. For example, participants viewed the phrase as part of a sentence that was consistent with the established meaning (e.g. *Because it was a bad season for mosquitoes, Debbie made sure that every time she went outside, she wore plenty of bug spray*) or with the innovative meaning (e.g. *As a defense mechanism against predators, the Alaskan beetle can release a deadly bug spray*). Immediately after viewing this prime sentence, the participants viewed the target phrase (bug spray) with either the established definition (e.g. a spray for bugs) or the innovative meaning (e.g. spray by bugs) and indicated whether the definition was plausible. They were told that the definition did not have to be the best definition, but that they should indicate 'yes' if the definition was plausible. Filler items that did not have plausible definitions were included in the studies. Of most interest is the effect of the prime sentence on the percentage of plausibility judgments. When the sentence used the established meaning, the established definition was judged plausible 89 percent of the time. However, when the sentence used the innovative meaning, the established definition judged plausible only 64 percent of the time. In terms of response time, participants took longer to indicate that the established definition was plausible when the sentence supported the innovative meaning than when it supported the conventional meaning. Taken together, these findings suggest that the established meaning was competing with the innovative meaning constructed in the previous sentence and this competition decreased the availability of the established meaning.

Thus, there is some reason to believe that a process much like that described by CARIN is, in fact, occurring even with highly familiar phrases. This model has clear implications for core issues in compound representation and processing and leads to a very clear set of predictions about compound processing. If compounds are accessed by retrieving a unitary stored form, then there is no need to invoke a relation to construct a unified representation. Thus, we should find no effect of relation availability. However, if compounds are processed in a manner that is similar to the processing of novel compounds, as suggested by our model, then relation availability should affect the ease of accessing a familiar compound. That is, if *snowball* is accessed by decomposing it into *snow* and *ball* and selecting the noun MADE OF modifier relation to form a unified representation, then increasing the availability of this relation should decrease the time required to complete this process. Thus, the first implication of this view is that the effect demonstrated with novel compounds should also occur for lexicalized compounds.

To test this prediction, we manipulated relation availability by presenting target combinations after a prime combination containing the same modifier. The same relation prime (e.g. snowfort) used the same relation as the target (e.g. snowball) and the different relation prime (e.g. snowshovel) used a different relation. Participants performed a sense–nonsense judgment task for both the primes and the targets. We found that it took less time to respond to the target compound when preceded by the same relation compound than by the different relation compound. We obtained the same result when a lexical decision task was used (Gagné and Spalding, 2004b). These results are consistent with those found using novel combinations. According to the model outlined above, relation priming occurs because recent exposure to a compound facilitates the selection of that relation.

One could argue that these findings are also consistent with a storage-based model in which compounds in the mental lexicon are arranged into relation-based families based on the first constituent. If so, then retrieval of the prime compound might activate other compounds sharing the same relation. This activation might make it easier to respond to the target compound when the compound uses the same relation as the prime relative to when the prime uses a different relation. Thus, having just seen a prime with the same modifier and relation leads to faster processing than having just seen a prime with the same modifier, but a different relation.

Although this explanation appears promising, there are several challenges to this approach. In the case of novel compounds, Gagné (2002) found that even primes with semantically similar (rather than identical) modifiers lead to relation priming. If such effects are to be explained by the way in which familiar compounds are represented in the mental lexicon, then they must be organized in such a way that a semantically similar modifier with the same relation influences performance in a way that seems to be more profound than the same first constituent with a different relation.

Second, precisely how is priming to work in this view? For stored compounds, the prime would be in the lexicon and highly activated. So, when the target is accessed, the prime compound could directly affect the processing of the target. However, this would not be possible for novel compounds. In this case, the prime combination would (presumably) not yet be part of the mental lexicon, and thus not available to directly affect the processing of the target item. Yet, it is clear priming occurs for novel combinations even though these combinations do not have stored representations in the lexicon. In another study, we have also demonstrated that relation priming can be obtained in cases where the primes are novel (nonlexicalized) compounds and the target compounds are familiar (Gagné and Spalding, 2003). The activation of stored family members cannot account for this effect because the primes are not part of the mental lexicon and must be computed based on information in the language and conceptual systems.

A second implication of our model is that there is a strong link between the lexical item in the language system and the corresponding combined concept in the conceptual system. Current theories (e.g. Libben, 1998; Zwitserlood, 1994) represent compound words in the conceptual system as a single unit. That is, the compound word is linked to the concept. Although both the modifier and head noun representations are linked to the compound, this form of representation fails to include relational information about how the two constituent concepts are joined. The model that we propose and our recent data (Gagné and Spalding, 2003, 2004a, 2004b) suggest that the conceptual representation of *snowball* includes not just the knowledge that it is made up of *snow* and *ball*, but also the relation used to form the combined concept (*noun MADE OF modifier*).

A third implication of the model is that modifiers and head nouns should play different roles during the processing of compound words. In terms of contributing to the meaning of the compound, the head noun denotes the category (e.g. pot), whereas the modifier is used to form a subcategory (e.g. a teapot is just one of many kinds of pots). According to our model, the modifier is more influential in the initial selection of a relation than is the head noun. The head noun appears to evaluate plausibility. For example, consider the novel compound *mountain planet*. Even though the *head noun LOCATED modifier* relation is initially selected on the basis of the modifier's relational distribution, this relation is not plausible because planets are too large to be in the mountains. Thus, another relation must be selected. The primacy of the modifier in terms of relation selection has been clearly demonstrated with novel compounds, as discussed earlier. The same pattern should hold for familiar compounds.

A fourth implication is more speculative. Recent work has investigated the parsing strategies used to decode compounds. If our model of compound access is correct, then relational information might also be involved in parsing. Two interesting possibilities come to mind. First, parsing decisions could be influenced by the availability of a good relation to link the constituents of the compound. As an example, consider a compound like 'clamprod', which can be parsed as either clam-prod or clamp-rod (Libben *et al.*, 1999). One factor that could affect which decomposition is selected as the final output might be the ease of interpretation. Thus, a decomposition that results in a pair where the two constituents are easily linked by a relation might be preferred over a decomposition that results in a pair of constituents that are difficult to link. Second, if relations are involved, then we should expect the same modifier-head noun asymmetry in which the availability of a relation for the modifier has a greater effect than the availability with the head noun.

A final implication is more general. If the model of compound processing that we are proposing is correct, then theories that focus primarily on the structure of the mental lexicon need major revision. Our proposal is primarily about the processing that occurs, and as we mentioned above, a structural account faces serious challenges in attempting to account for the effects discovered so far. Focusing on the processing (rather than strictly on representation) involved in the mental lexicon in general might be more profitable. Indeed, this approach has already been fruitful in the conceptual combination literature.

7.3 Conclusions

Our aim in this chapter has been to describe some recent research on conceptual combination to draw out the implications that this work has for the study of the mental lexicon. In particular, we argue that the interpretation of lexicalized and novel compounds might involve the same kind of processing. Although the research extending the CARIN theory to the processing of compound words is new and somewhat preliminary, we believe that the evidence thus far clearly suggests far more similarity between novel and familiar compounds than would be expected by most theories of the mental lexicon.

8

Processing Chinese Compounds: A survey of the literature

JAMES MYERS

Chinese is the poster child of compounding, the language to cite for an example of morphology without much affixation. This alone should make Chinese worthy of its own chapter in a book on compound processing, but another point in its favor is its notoriously unusual writing system; orthography, as we will see, plays a crucial role in how compounds are processed in Chinese. The literature on Chinese compound processing is rich and ever-growing (indeed, some of it is also described in the chapters in this book by Jarema, Nicoladis, and Levy *et al.*). This chapter attempts to provide a general overview of this literature, the goal being not to argue for or review particular models, but rather to organize the key findings from a variety of sources in a way that highlights the universal and language-specific properties of Chinese compound processing (a very helpful earlier review by Taft *et al.*, 1999, describes only reading studies within a multilevel interactive-activation framework).

The chapter begins with overviews of Chinese, its orthography, and its morphology. The themes that organize the remainder of the chapter overlap with those addressed by other authors in this book. As with other languages, the Chinese literature consists primarily of reading experiments, but spoken word recognition and aphasiology have also been studied. The hope is that this review will not only introduce Chinese compounding to readers more familiar with other languages, but will also inspire them to build on paradigms or notions found in the Chinese literature but as yet unexplored elsewhere.

8.1 Linguistic background

For all its fame, Chinese seems to be subject to some common misconceptions among psycholinguists who do not work on it. To begin with, the term 'Chinese' is itself ambiguous, since it can refer either to a particular language or to an entire language family (Sinitic). As a particular language, 'Chinese' refers to Mandarin (also known as Standard Chinese or Putonghua). Chinese orthography is essentially nonphonetic, making it usable (with some adjustments) for all Sinitic languages. For language teaching and dictionaries, Mandarin can also be written with various supplementary phonetic systems; Mandarin romanizations in this paper use Hanyu Pinyin, the official phonetic orthography of the PRC and Singapore. For typographical convenience, Chinese examples in the text are only given in their Pinyin transcriptions (suppressing the tone diacritics), but all examples are given in characters in the appendix.

As noted in the introduction, it is important to say a bit more about Chinese orthography. It is, of course, nonalphabetic, and it is sometimes implied that an alphabetic system would not work for Chinese due to the large number of homophones; there are, for example, about thirty distinct characters all pronounced in Mandarin as *yi* with a high level tone (Ho, 1976). Such comments, of course, neglect the fact that spoken Chinese is understood without difficulty, a mundane but important observation to be returned to later.

The basic orthographic unit is the character, although often it is itself composed of elements that recur in other characters, often one part that gives some clue to the pronunciation and another part that roughly categorizes the meaning (the semantic radical); we will mostly ignore this 'subcharacter morphology' here (but see Taft *et al.*, 1999). A character virtually always represents one syllable and also almost always one morpheme, but belying the reputation of Chinese as an 'isolating' language, most words are not monomorphemic; Zhou and Marslen-Wilson (1995) estimate the proportion of disyllabic (two-character) words in Chinese as about 74 percent by type and 34 percent by token. As an example, the complex word *xiguazhi* (watermelon juice) is composed of the monosyllabic one-character morphemes *xi* (west), *gua* (melon), and *zhi* (juice); *xigua* itself means 'watermelon'. There are, however, some disyllabic morphemes, written with characters that share a semantic radical and which are virtually never used independently of each other (called binding characters by Taft and Zhu, 1995). An example is *putao* (grape); both of its characters are topped by the semantic radical for plants and neither appears in any other word. Recent borrowings of polysyllabic morphemes tend to be written with existing characters, chosen for their pronunciation; for example, *shafa* (easy chair), adapted from English *sofa*, is written with the semantically irrelevant characters *sha* (sand) and *fa* (send out), making it apparently monomorphemic in Chinese as well. It should also be noted that even aside from these types of words, characters are not identical to morphemes, since they often shift arbitrarily in pronunciation, meaning, or both, from context to context. Thus the first morpheme in *xingren* (pedestrian, lit. 'walk-person') and the second morpheme in *yinhang* (bank, lit. 'silver-store') are written with the same character.

Familiarity with Chinese orthography has a profound influence on native speakers' understanding of the notion 'word', which is often translated as *zi* (character). The more linguistically sophisticated prefer the term *ci*, but there is confusion about its precise meaning (historically it referred to a style of poetry). Spaces are never used to separate words in written text, making characters obvious but words much more abstract. Characters, even binding characters, are usually given separate entries in dictionaries and the distinction between word and phrase is much more unclear than it is in languages like English, even for linguists. Some, like Chao (1968), have even declared that whether or not Chinese 'words' (in the

English sense) exist at all is an empirical question, not one to be decided by universalist fiat. For example, Bates *et al.* (1993) argue that *chifan* (eat, lit. 'eat-rice') is a word, not a phrase, because it is semantically idiosyncratic, describing eating in general, even eating noodles. Yet its components can be separated syntactically (e.g. *chi-le-fan* 'ate', lit. 'eat-completive.aspect-rice'). Duanmu (1998), Packard (2000), and Xue (2001) give more reliable wordhood tests, but such academic exercises have yet to influence the intuitions of ordinary Chinese readers. In experimental studies of the Chinese 'wordhood' question, both Hoosain (1992) and Tsai *et al.* (1998) asked readers to draw slashes between word boundaries; results showed much disagreement, suggesting that what for some readers was a word, was for others a phrase.

Assuming for the moment that Chinese does indeed have words, we turn now to word structure. It is often implied that Chinese morphology consists entirely of compounding, but this is not quite correct. First, modern Chinese has a number of productive affixational processes, including derivational affixation, inflectional affixation (cf. the misleading title of Li *et al.*, 1993), and reduplication; overviews of Chinese morphology can be found in Li and Thompson (1981) and Packard (2000). An example of a productive derivational affix is *zhe*, roughly corresponding to agentive *-er* in English; thus 'author' is *zuozhe* (lit. 'maker'). An example of inflection is the completive aspect marker *le*, as in *zuo-le* (made). Reduplication can be found, for example, in *ganganjingjing* (very clean), derived from *ganjing* (clean).

Second, by the common definition by which compounds must be composed of free words (see, e.g., Bloomfield, 1933; Fromkin and Rodman, 1998, and review in Dressler, this volume), a large proportion of Chinese compounds are not genuine compounds, since the morphemes that compose them are not free words; the proportion of bound characters in the Academia Sinica Balanced Corpus of Modern Chinese (Chen *et al.*, 1996) is around 36 percent. Compounds composed of bound morphemes even include many fully transparent ones, like *xiaozhang* (school president). This state of affairs has led to two opposite reactions among linguists, with some (e.g. Sproat and Shih, 1996; Packard, 2000) arguing that boundedness has no effect on the analysis of a word as a compound, while others (e.g. Dai, 1992; Starosta et al., 1998) disagree. In favor of the latter position, Starosta et al. (1998) suggest that semantically opaque compounds like *dongxi* (thing, but literally 'east-west') should be considered monomorphemic, and that some bound morphemes should be reanalyzed as suffixes (e.g. *hao*, meaning 'good' in true compounds, merely marks successful completion in so-called resultative verbs like *xiehao* 'finished writing').

Third, compounding itself is a two-way operation, since consistent with word-based morphology (e.g. Anderson, 1992), a Chinese compound defines its component morphemes as much as they define it. As Libben (this volume) points out, the top-down element in compound semantics is a universal, but Chinese may take it to an unusual extreme, since new morphemes are readily created in Chinese by having individual characters inherit some aspect of compound meaning. Packard (2000) catalogs several examples of this, and it is easy to find more. For example, *feiji* (airplane) is literally 'fly-machine', but in compounds such as *jichang* (airport, where *chang* is 'lot'), *ji* has inherited the meaning of *feiji* as a whole. This process can even affect apparently monomorphemic words; thus the *tai* (lit. 'tower') of *Taiwan* (historically derived by metonymy from an Austronesian toponymic) has been reanalyzed as itself meaning 'Taiwan', as in *Taibei* (Taipei, literally 'Taiwan-north') and *laitai* (come to Taiwan).

In spite of all this, however, the impression that compounding is the primary morphological operation in Chinese is basically correct. Nominal compounds include the canonical endocentric modifier-noun type, several examples of which have already been cited (e.g. *xiaozhang* 'school president' [NN], *feiji* 'airplane' [VN]). Exocentric nominal compounds include those of the usual semantically opaque (or translucent) type, such as *dongxi* (thing, cited above) or *huasheng* (peanut, lit. 'flower-birth'), but also of the more interesting coordinative type, constructed productively from morphemes that contribute equally to the word meaning (e.g. *fumu* 'parents', lit. 'father-mother', and *zici* '*zi* and *ci*', seen in the title of Zhang,

1997). Chinese orthography also allows for the existence of oxymoronic 'monomorphemic compounds', both binding words (e.g. *putao* 'grape') or phonetic borrowings composed of nonbinding characters (e.g. *shafa* 'easy chair'). Beyond these types, most psycholinguistic research has yet to explore systematically very far, so this chapter will not have much to say about verbal compounds (e.g. *qiuzheng* 'seek proof' [VN], *yanzheng* 'test and verify' [VV]), adjectival compounds like *ganjing* (clean, lit. 'dry-clean'), and so on, although compounds of these types do appear occasionally in experimental materials.

This overview should suggest some predictions for processing. Since characters give readers a great deal of help in identifying morphemes (although not perfect, due to shifts in pronunciation and/or meaning), the most fundamental processing question is not the usual 'How are morphologically complex words decomposed?', but rather 'How are morphemes composed to form complex words?'. Indeed, in the spirit of Chao (1968), we should first ask whether words play any role in Chinese reading at all. Nor is the word the only notion open to question; as we have seen, Chinese orthography also gives rise to similar vagueness in the concepts 'morpheme' (as opposed to character) and 'compound' (as opposed to morpheme and affixed word).

Listeners are faced with quite a different situation from readers, of course. As pointed out by Packard (1999), the rampant homophony of Chinese morphemes makes it implausible to suppose that listeners access word representations by first activating morpheme representations. However, they do not seem to simply access words as whole phonological forms either, given evidence that access is syllable-based; for example, in a phoneme-detection task, Tseng *et al.* (1996) found that it was the lexicality of syllables that made the difference, not that of disyllables. Nevertheless, morpheme identification is expected to be much more difficult for listeners than for readers, perhaps delaying the time morphemes become activated during compound processing.

In addition to its unusual characteristics, Chinese also shares many morphological properties with other languages. These include right-headed nominal compounds, a gradient distinction between transparent and opaque compounds, and compounds built hierarchically from other compounds (e.g. *xiguazhi* 'watermelon juice'). With regard to these, we expect Chinese to behave essentially the same as has been found with other languages.

The following review is thus organized into four major subsections. First, we review evidence relating to the psychological reality of the word in Chinese compound processing. Next, we describe studies investigating the activation of morphemes, looking at evidence from distributional patterns, semantic transparency, and aphasia. Finally, we examine the role of compound structure in processing. These themes fit neatly into those discussed elsewhere in this book, but as we will see, there will be some surprising twists along the way.

8.2 Evidence for the reality of a word level

The vagueness of the concept 'word' in Chinese has practical consequences for psycholinguistic methodology. As pointed out by Hung *et al.* (1999), the use of that old workhorse, the lexical decision task, is problematic in Chinese, since we cannot expect naive participants to give consistent *ci* judgments when they are not sure what a *ci* is. Nevertheless, results from lexical decision tasks converge with those from other tasks on the same conclusion: although characters do have a quasi-wordlike status for Chinese readers, compounds in Chinese are indeed treated as lexical units at some level of processing, just as they are in other languages.

The first relevant piece of evidence comes from comparing *ci* judgments with *zi* judgments. Taft (2003) describes an experiment in which readers were asked to make lexical decisions about characters presented in isolation, some free and some bound. The participants who were asked to perform a character/pseudocharacter decision task (i.e. make *zi* judgments) showed no differences between free and bound characters, but those who had to make *ci* judgments on the same one-character items correctly gave more 'yes' responses to free than bound morphemes. Nevertheless, participants in the word-decision task still found it harder to reject bound but nonbinding characters than binding characters, although neither are free words. While these results confirm that Chinese readers do have a tendency to view characters as wordlike, the fact that boundedness affects *ci* judgments at all, while not affecting *zi* judgments, shows that the *ci* vs. *zi* distinction is a real factor in the judgment process.

The word superiority paradigm provides even stronger evidence for the reality of Chinese word units. In a word superiority effect, components are more readily recognized or identified in real lexical items than in nonwords (e.g. letters in English words; Reicher, 1969). Studies on Chinese have consistently found that lexical status at the *ci* level affects recognition at the *zi* level. Thus, in separate studies, Cheng (1981) and Mattingly and Xu (1994) showed participants two-character strings that were either real words or pseudowords (two real characters in a nonsense string), and asked them to detect a given character. Both studies found a word superiority effect: participants performed better with real words. The effect appears to be rather automatic; Chen (1999) found a word superiority effect even when the characters had to be detected in sentences, regardless of sentential context. Hung *et al.* (1999) were concerned that character detection is not identical to letter detection in English, since characters themselves are meaningful, and thus they had participants identify character components (e.g. radicals) rather than whole characters. Even with this variation in methodology, a word superiority effect was found. Liu (1988) also found a word superiority effect in the naming of characters in two-character strings, but no such effect for characters appearing in the second and third position of three-character strings. This may possibly relate to the predominance of two-character words in Chinese; the default parsing strategy for three-character strings may be to break them up, and in fact, Yin *et al.* (2004) have recently found evidence for just such a parsing strategy (discussed below).

Even when we turn to the *ci* decision studies that form the bulk of the research on morphological processing in Chinese, we find that they also provide evidence for the reality of the lexical status of the Chinese word: in all studies where word frequency is an experimental variable, it always has a facilitative effect on lexical decision time, separately from character, syllable, or morpheme frequency. We will note examples of this explicitly only when relevant, since word frequency effects are just as ubiquitous in Chinese as they are in other languages.

8.3 Character frequency

Researchers interested in morphology can hardly be satisfied with the discovery that Chinese has words; they want to know about morphemes. In this section we consider one commonly recognized diagnostic of the activation of compound components arising from a distributional property: morpheme frequency effects. It is very difficult to calculate morpheme frequency in Chinese, however. Clearly *xing* in *xingren* (pedestrian) and *hang* in *yinhang* (bank) should be considered distinct morphemes despite being written with the same character, but it is less clear what to do with characters showing no change in pronunciation across contexts and subtler semantic shifts: the character *kuai* means 'happy' in *kuaile* (happy) but 'fast' in *kuaisu* (speed), *jia* means 'family' in *jiaren* (family member) but 'house' in *jiashi* (housework), and so on. In practice, therefore, in all studies manipulating the frequencies of compound components, what is actually manipulated is character frequency, and we will make this explicit in our summaries.

Taft *et al.* (1994) is a typical study. They gave participants a visual lexical decision task with two-character words varying in the frequency of the first and second characters, but with word frequency controlled. Similar to some studies in other languages (e.g. Taft and Forster, 1976), compounds with two high-frequency characters (HH, e.g. *chengguan* 'near the city gate', lit. 'city-close') were responded to more quickly than words containing a low-frequency characters (HL, e.g. *jiajuan* 'wife and children', lit. 'family-concern'; LH, e.g. *anshu* 'eucalyptus', lit. 'eucalyptus-tree'). This facilitative (positive) effect of character frequency implies that word recognition does involve access of the component characters, as one would expect of Chinese reading. Interestingly, however, the effect was not completely consistent: LL words (e.g. *chouchang* 'disconsolate', lit. 'regretful-disappointed') were not accessed more slowly than HH words. Taft *et al.* (1994) suspected that the binding words in their set of LL words were responsible (e.g. *meigui* 'rose'), because their orthographic cohesiveness may have given them an advantage in ease of access. We return to this suggestion, and how it may be understood more formally, in the next section.

The role of character frequency in spoken word access is, as one would expect, quite different. Zhou and Marslen-Wilson (1994), also mentioned in Jarema (this volume), performed a complex set of nonprimed lexical decision experiments on spoken semantically transparent disyllabic Mandarin compounds, systematically varying syllable frequency, morpheme (character) frequency, and word frequency. Only one robust finding emerged: positive word frequency effects. There was no effect of character frequency, although negative syllable frequency effects were found for the first syllable of nonwords and for that of real words when word and morpheme frequency were controlled, suggesting cohort competition. As noted by Packard (1999) in a commentary on this study, the results seem to imply that the lexical representations for spoken compounds are processed at some point as morphological wholes, although other paradigms, described below, have also provided evidence for morpheme activation in spoken compounds (e.g. Zhou and Marslen-Wilson, 1995).

8.4 Transition probability and family size

Recall that Taft *et al.* (1994) found, to their surprise, that written words composed of high-frequency characters were recognized no faster than words composed of low-frequency characters. While they specifically blamed binding words for these results, they also made a more general observation. Namely, for low-frequency initial characters, there are fewer character types that may follow it than for high-frequency initial characters, as they confirmed with an off-line guess-the-next-character task. This higher transition probability for low-frequency characters means greater predictability of one character from the other. High character frequency thus exerts two conflicting forces on word recognition, both easing the activation of words and making it harder to narrow the choice down to just one of these words. Transition probability is related to family size (Schreuder and Baayen, 1997), which counts the number of word types containing a given morpheme; words containing morphemes from larger families will necessarily have lower morpheme transition probabilities, and vice versa. No matter how it is modeled, binding words will be predicted to be easier to access than nonbinding words; binding characters only appear in one word, making the character transition probability higher and character family size smaller. Indeed, like Taft *et al.* (1994), experiments by Lü (1996), Tsai (1998), and Hsiao (2004) have all found that binding words are recognized more quickly than nonbinding words, even fully opaque ones.

The cohesiveness of binding words can also be demonstrated in tasks involving isolated characters, as in Taft and Zhu (1995). A timed naming task found that first-position binding characters (e.g. *qiu* of *qiuyin* 'earthworm') were named faster than second-position binding characters (e.g. *yin*), suggesting that the pronunciation of binding words must be accessed as a whole. However, a timed real/pseudo-character decision task found no difference in reaction times due to binding character position, nor was there a positional effect in the naming of nonbinding but bound characters that always appear in the same position in different words (e.g. *xun* 'die for a cause' only appears in first position, *lü* 'companion' only appears in second position). Thus it appears that only some properties of binding characters, such as their pronunciation, are stored as part of a whole word, whereas all properties of nonbinding characters are stored independently. Mattingly and Hsiao (1997) confirmed this latter conclusion, finding no differences between bound (but not binding) characters and free characters in both an off-line radical identification task and a timed real/pseudo-character decision task. However, Taft and Zhu (1997) failed to find a difference between two-character binding and nonbinding words in a primed naming task; for both types of words, first-character naming latency was sped up by prior presentation of the second character, which seems to imply that even the pronunciations of nonbinding words may be stored as wholes.

When the transition probability or family size is manipulated in written nonbinding words, the above effects are not found, and instead the more familiar positive character frequency effects return. In a study that investigated this systematically, Lü (1996) pitted words like *qiushi* (embarrassing thing, lit. 'dry ration-thing') against words like *shanshi* (good deeds, lit. 'good-thing'); both words are matched in frequency and share the same second character, but the first character in *qiushi* appears virtually only in this one word, while the first character in *shanshi* also appears in several other words. Lü found that words with larger families, like *shanshi*, were recognized more quickly, and the same effect (i.e. positive character frequency) also appeared when the manipulated character was in second position.

If negative character frequency effects occur under certain circumstances in reading, what do we expect with spoken compounds? Since Liu *et al.* (1996) have found that for readers, character frequency has its greatest effect on the early stages of processing, we do not expect a direct effect of character frequency itself in spoken word access. Thus, for listeners, the positive effects of high transition probability and small family size may be revealed more clearly. Myers and Gong (2002) examined this possibility in a small-scale partial replication of Zhou and Marslen-Wilson (1994). Transparent disyllabic Mandarin compounds were controlled for syllable frequency and cohort size; word frequency and character frequency were varied separately. Participants in a nonprimed auditory lexical decision experiment showed the usual positive word frequency effects, but also significant character frequency effects (the authors claim that the null results of Zhou and Marslen-Wilson, 1994, were due to their use of a smaller frequency range). In contrast to what is found with written transparent compounds, the character frequency effects were negative: words with higher-frequency characters (e.g. *benneng* 'instinct') were responded to more slowly than words with lower-frequency characters (e.g. *banzou* 'accompaniment').

Surprisingly, precisely the same result is found even when the characters are not morphemic at all. Reconfirming the earlier findings of Tsai (1998), Myers and Lai (2002) found in an auditory lexical decision task that (monomorphemic) binding words like *putao* (grape) were recognized more quickly than monomorphemic nonbinding words like *shafa* (easy chair), matched for word frequency, syllable frequency, syllable transition probability, first-syllable cohort size, and acoustic duration. The hypothesis that participants activated orthographic representations of the words, and made their decisions on these, was ruled out by the lack of an effect when the same items were presented visually (thus failing to replicate the findings of Lü, 1996). Thus, again, it appears that in processing spoken compounds, transition probability or family size plays a role without character frequency affecting responses directly. Clearly, more work needs to be done to reconfirm this effect and explore its possible causes, but in the meantime it presents a cautionary message: even when working with spoken words, be aware of the possible interference of orthography.

8.5 Semantic transparency

Transparency is in principle independent of distributional properties, but it may covary inversely with them, since transparency is related to productivity and hence to lower transition probability and larger families. This leads to conflicting forces again. As we saw, compounds may be recognized faster if they are more 'cohesive' or have smaller families, but such compounds tend to be semantically more opaque (as is certainly the case for binding words). By contrast, if characters are automatically activated during reading, opacity should hurt word access (as pointed out by Libben, this volume), since activation of semantically irrelevant components will result in competition with the word. Perhaps given such conflicts, fully consistent effects of semantic transparency on compound access have proven difficult to demonstrate; for example, Jarema *et al.* (1999) found that transparent compounds were recognized more quickly than opaque compounds in French, but more slowly in Bulgarian. The delicate nature of semantic effects can be seen in Chinese studies as well. Some (e.g. Tsai, 1994; Myers *et al.*, 2004a) find that semantically transparent compounds like *huayuan* (garden, lit. 'flower-yard') are responded to more quickly than semantically idiosyncratic or opaque compounds like *huasheng* (peanut, lit. 'flower-birth'), while others find the reverse pattern (e.g. Su, 2000; Liang, 1992; Lee, 1995), or no difference at all (Chen, 1993; Myers *et al.*, 2004b).

In an attempt to clarify the role of semantic transparency, some studies also take component frequency into account. Peng *et al.* (1999) first held semantic transparency constant and varied word and character frequency in a visual lexical decision experiment, and like Taft *et al.* (1994), found a positive frequency effect for both words and characters. When they held word frequency constant and crossed character frequency with semantic transparency, however, character frequency effects were found to depend on transparency: for transparent words the character frequency effect was positive, but for opaque words the effect was negative (i.e. higher character frequency meant slower word responses). Peng *et al.* (1999) suggest that activation at the compound level was inhibited for opaque compounds due to activation of the competing semantics of the component characters. This certainly makes sense, but when Liang (1992) and Lee (1995) performed similar experiments, they found only positive character frequency effects for transparent compounds; there was no effect for opaque compounds.

A variation on the usual visual lexical decision task may help to shed more light. Chen (1993), Tsai (1994), and Lee (1995) varied stimulus-onset asynchrony (SOA) between the appearance of the first and second character of a two-character compound. While the details of their results varied, the general finding was that character frequency effects depending both on transparency (positive for transparent compounds, negative or absent for opaque compounds) and on SOA; at the longest SOAs (200–600 ms), Chen (1993) found negative character frequency effects regardless of transparency. The effect of SOA implies that at least in this paradigm, negative character frequency effects can be caused by competition between the whole word and the component characters, consistent with Libben's proposal.

Myers *et al.* (2004b) addressed the nature of semantic transparency by using another novel variant on the visual lexical decision task. Opaque and transparent compounds were presented in separate blocks, with block order counterbalanced across participants. When transparent compounds were presented first, reaction times were the same for both types of compounds, but when opaque compounds were presented first, reaction times for the transparent compounds dropped off significantly over the course of the block. At the very least, this suggests that activation of character semantics is not obligatory, since otherwise such a context-dependent shift would not have been found: transparent compounds should always have been easier to recognize.

8.6 Priming

If the component morphemes of a complex word are activated during lexical access, the morphemes should be capable of priming or being primed. However, one must be cautious when designing and interpreting morphological studies (as often emphasized in the literature, e.g. Zhou and Marslen-Wilson, 2000), because the priming may actually be due to form similarity (e.g. a character in the prime may prime itself in the target) or word-level semantics (particularly if the prime and/or target are transparent). There are a number of techniques that can be used to deal with these problems, but overall the morphological priming literature is not altogether satisfying; too many poorly-understood variables are in play at the same time. For Chinese, one of the most important is modality, and so this is how we arrange the review, looking first at visual-visual priming, then auditory-auditory priming, and finally cross-modal priming.

Visual-visual priming is the most commonly used in Chinese, and in almost all such studies, the primes and targets are both two-character strings. One of the experiments in Peng *et al.* (1999) employed a paradigm of this type, where the manipulation involved whether the first characters of prime and target were identical or entirely unrelated. In order to ensure that any priming effects could not be due to whole-word semantic priming, the word meanings of primes and targets were unrelated. Note, however, that this requirement means that in the identical-character condition, the character could not contribute the same meaning to prime and target. This was the case both for transparent primes (e.g. prime *anning* 'quiet', lit. 'peace-peace', begins with the same character as target *anzhuang* 'install') and opaque primes (e.g. prime *kuaihuo* 'happy', lit. 'happy/fast-life', begins with the same character as target *kuaisu* 'speed'). Facilitative priming was found, but it was not a simple case of form priming, since the effect was found only with transparent primes. This is consistent with the hypothesis that readers activate the components of transparent compounds, but it does not seem quite right to say that what was activated here were morphemes, due to the meaning mismatch across prime and target. As Taft *et al.* (1999) recognize in their analysis of these results, we must acknowledge a role for characters even in morphological processing.

One technique for distinguishing form priming from morpheme priming is to use a paradigm in which a prime component is related to the meaning of the whole target compound, so that prime and target do not share any characters. In an unpublished conference paper (Liu and Peng, 1995) summarized in Taft *et al.* (1999), an experiment of this type is described, and again effects were only found for semantically transparent primes, not opaque primes. Again the experimenters were careful to make sure that their results could not be due to word-level semantic priming, since semantic primes, as wholes, were not related to their targets (e.g. transparent *beipan* 'betray', lit. 'back-rebel', primed *fugai* 'cover', semantically related to *bei*, but opaque *mashang* 'immediately', lit. 'horse-on', did not prime *mianyang* 'sheep').

Liu and Peng (1997) found another way to circumvent possible objections, using two-character primes that were opaque (e.g. *caoshuai* 'sloppy', lit. 'grass-command'), but paired with two-character targets to which they were either semantically related as wholes (e.g. *mahu* 'careless', lit. 'horse-tiger', related to *caoshuai*), only via the prime's first character (e.g. *shumu* 'tree', lit. 'tree-wood', related to *cao*), or only via the prime's second character (e.g. *lingdao* 'lead', lit. 'lead-guide', related to *shuai*). At the shortest SOA (43 ms), priming only occurred in the whole-word condition, as might be expected of semantically opaque primes. However, at a longer SOA (143 ms), priming was found in all three conditions, revealing activation of whole words and both of their constituent morphemes. Another experiment compared transparent and opaque primes with an intermediate SOA of 86 ms, and morpheme priming was found only with transparent compounds. The morphemes in opaque compounds thus do not reveal their activation until late.

Zhou *et al.* (1999) further examined the time course of visual compound processing in a complex series of primed visual lexical decision experiments, using two-character primes and targets (apparently at least somewhat transparent) put into two SOA conditions (57 ms, 200 ms) or masked priming. For each target (e.g. *huagui* 'luxurious', lit. 'splendid-valuable'), the prime either shared the same morpheme written with the same character (e.g. *huali* 'magnificent', lit. 'splendid-beautiful'), shared a character used with a different meaning (e.g. *huaqiao* 'overseas Chinese', lit. 'China-bridge'), or shared a homophone (including same tone) written with different characters (e.g. *huaxiang* 'glide', lit. 'slide-soar'). Importantly, primes and targets were pretested to ensure that they were matched in degree of whole-word semantic relatedness across prime types. The positions of the key characters were also varied (both first character, both second character, or second in prime and first in target). The results showed that the morpheme priming effect was consistently greater than character priming, and there was no homophone priming at all. The position of the key characters did not make much difference, except that masked morpheme priming was markedly reduced if the position differed across prime and target. These results are again consistent with previous evidence for component activation when reading Chinese compounds. However, the fact that spatial overlap was relevant for masked morpheme priming and that mere character matching also caused some priming, even at the late SOA of 200 ms (in the second-position and mixed-position conditions), shows again that the character also plays a crucial role in Chinese compound processing. This observation is strengthened by another of their experiments, which found facilitated lexical decisions for monomorphemic nonbinding words (e.g. *shafa* 'easy chair') from masked transparent primes beginning with the same character (e.g. *shatan* 'sandy beach').

Finally, Zhou *et al.* (1999) compared morpheme priming with word-level semantic priming head on, using for each target (e.g. *yisheng* 'doctor', where *yi* means 'cure') either a prime sharing the same first morpheme (e.g. *yiyuan* 'hospital') or a prime matched for word-level semantic relationship but without any morphological, orthographic, or phonological overlap at the character level (e.g. *hushi* 'nurse'). With masked primes, morphological priming added a facilitative effect on top of that for whole-word priming. However, this effect has proven difficult to replicate (Chen, 2002).

Yet another way to deal with concerns over word-level semantic confounds is to use a long-term priming paradigm, in which earlier items in a list of single-stimulus trials act as primes for later items. Research on other languages has suggested that semantic priming disappears in such a paradigm, while morphological priming does not (see Feldman, 2003, for a review). The only Chinese study employing this paradigm so far (Zhou and Marslen-Wilson, 1995) used spoken stimuli. Recall that the homophony of Chinese morphemes makes it unlikely that spoken compounds are activated via prior activation of their morphemes (Packard, 1999), and that Zhou and Marslen-Wilson (1994) had failed to find character frequency effects in auditory lexical decision. The negative character frequency effects found by Myers and Gong (2002) and Myers and Lai (2002), however, suggest that characters (or morphemes) are indeed activated at some later stage. Thus long-term priming should be a particularly useful way of revealing morpheme activation in spoken compounds.

Zhou and Marslen-Wilson (1995) ran a complex set of long-term priming experiments with lexical decision tasks, using auditory Mandarin disyllabic primes and targets. The material design was the basis of Zhou *et al.* (1999), just described, and so it involved the same four prime-target relations (identical, morpheme, character, homophone) and the same three positions of the relevant characters in primes and targets (both first, both second, second in prime and first in target). SOA was also varied, but across a larger time scale, with immediate priming, a short lag (one or two intervening items), a long lag (forty or more intervening items), and a medium lag somewhere in between. Results showed similar patterns for both character and homophone primes, presumably because character primes were also homophones. These form priming effects were weak, variable, and sometimes inhibitory (in first position, implying cohort competition), but morpheme priming was always positive. Its effects also lasted longer than character and homophone priming, suggesting both that it differed from them and that it could not be due to semantic relatedness. Thus the morphemes in spoken compounds do appear to become activated in the course of lexical access.

One final technique for ruling out form-based explanations for morpheme priming effects is to use primes and targets of different modalities (e.g. Marslen-Wilson *et al.* 1994). For some reason, however, in Chinese this method only seems to have been used in two unpublished master's theses. In one of the experiments in Lee (1995), auditory disyllabic Mandarin primes were used with two-character visual targets, revealing facilitatory priming when the prime was transparent and it shared an initial morpheme (same character, meaning, and pronunciation) with the target (e.g. prime *caiyi* 'suspicion', target *caimi* 'solve riddles', where *cai* means 'guess'). The cross-modal primed lexical decision experiment in Tsai (1998) used auditory disyllabic primes (e.g. *shudian* 'bookstore') and single character targets representing either the same first character (e.g. *shu* 'book') or a homophone of it (e.g. *shu* 'sparse'). Homophone priming was not found, but facilitatory character priming was found not only with transparent primes (e.g. *shudian*), but also with opaque (e.g. *huasheng* 'peanut', lit. 'flower-birth') and monomorphemic nonbinding primes (e.g. *jita* 'guitar', lit. 'lucky-third person'). Further work seems to be needed to explore the cross-modal paradigm, or indeed priming paradigms generally, to accommodate the many conflicting findings within a single coherent model.

8.7 Aphasiological evidence

We end this review of evidence for component activation in Chinese compound processing with intriguing, if somewhat controversial, evidence from aphasia. Morphologists are particularly interested in errors by aphasics that reveal knowledge of word-internal structure (see Semenza and Mondini, this volume). For example, it is found that Italian Broca's aphasics, who tend to have difficulty with verbs as free words, also have difficulty producing verbal morphemes in nominal compounds (Semenza *et al.*, 1997). Precisely the same pattern has been reported in (Mandarin) Chinese by Bates *et al.* (1991) and Chen and Bates (1998). Just as in Italian, picture-naming tasks reveal that Chinese Broca's aphasics have greater difficulty correctly producing verbs than nouns, and just as in Italian, this difficulty is also found with the verbal morpheme in verb-noun compounds, such as *chifan* (eat, lit. 'eat-rice'). Even more interesting, there appears to be a complementary pattern of errors for Wernicke's aphasics, who both make more errors when producing free nouns and when producing the nominal morpheme in such verb-noun compounds.

The problem in interpreting such results, however, as Zhou *et al.* (1993) point out in a critique of Bates *et al.* (1991), is that it is hard to be certain that it is truly a sublexical phenomenon, since in a verb-noun construction the noun is the object of the verb, just as in a standard Chinese verb phrase. Bates *et al.* (1993) admit that they do not have a very good response given the stimuli that they used. Chen and Bates (1998) provide new data from a study that crossed syntactic category at both the word and morpheme level. Their test items thus included not only verbal verb-noun compounds like *chifan*, but also nominal verb-noun compounds like *feiji* (airplane, lit. 'fly-machine'). The results for verbal verb-noun compounds were replicated, but for the morphemes in nominal verb-noun compounds, both Broca's and Wernicke's aphasics made more errors with the verbal morpheme. They ascribed this unexpected symmetry to the atypicality of nominal verb-noun compounds, which, unlike the situation in Italian, are marked in Chinese compared with nominal noun-noun compounds. Lee *et al.* (2005) have recently provided additional evidence showing that aphasics do indeed retain awareness of the differences in typicality across compound types.

8.8 The role of compound structure

The discussion of the differential processing of verbal and nominal verb-noun compounds raises the more general question of the processing effect of compound structure. This question has been little investigated so far in Chinese, just as is unfortunately the case for other languages (see Libben, this volume), but relevant studies do exist.

The earliest study to look at compound structure in terms of headedness appears to be Zhang and Peng (1992). In a series of nonprimed visual lexical decision experiments, participants were presented with nominal coordinative compounds (e.g. *fuxiong* 'father and elder brothers') and nominal modifier-noun compounds (e.g. *muxiao* 'alma mater', lit. 'mother-school'). For coordinative compounds, positive character frequency effects were found for both positions, indicating equal importance, whereas for modifier-noun compounds, a positive character frequency effect was only found for the first position. In a later study, Zhang (1997) used a primed (visual-visual) lexical decision task to examine modifier-noun and coordinative compounds, with two-character primes and targets that either matched in the first or second character. Priming effects were reversed for the two structures: coordinative prime-target pairs resulted in faster responses if the second character matched, while modifier-noun prime-target pairs resulted in faster responses if the first character matched. This result partly fits the findings of Zhang and Peng (1992), in that there appeared to be activation of the first morpheme in modifier-noun compounds and the second morpheme in coordinative compounds.

However, the activation of the nonhead (first position morpheme) in modifier-noun compounds seems to conflict with the suggestions made by Libben (this volume), according to which the head (the second morpheme) should be more prominent. One possible way of accommodating the results is suggested by a nonprimed visual lexical decision task experiment described in Zhang (1997) that found that coordinative compounds were responded to more slowly than modifier-noun compounds of matching word frequency. This makes sense, given that coordinative compounds, though productive, appear to be marked in Chinese relative to modifier-noun compounds. Perhaps, then, access of the more typical type of nominal compound (modifier-noun) involves left-to-right processing, producing more prominent activation of the first component, while coordinative compounds require more active processing of both components. Before we speculate too far, however, it should be noted that speed-accuracy trade-offs in the Zhang and Peng (1992) study have made their results controversial, and they were not replicated by Taft *et al.* (1994) in a reanalysis of their own results.

Recently the head/nonhead issue has been investigated in a series of visual-visual primed lexical decision experiments by Ji and Gagné (2004) that used modifier-noun compounds as both primes and targets and varied the semantic relations between modifiers and heads. For example, for the target *shudian* 'bookstore', the prime *shujia* 'bookcase' matches in modifier and has the same semantic relation between modifier and head as the target, while prime *shuhao* 'book number' also matches in modifier but encodes a different modifier-head relation; *bingdian* 'cookie store' and *ridian* 'day store' represent a similar contrast in head-matched primes. Faster responses were found for prime-target pairs with the same relation, both for modifiers and for heads. However, the advantage of having the same modifier relation was lost when target heads appeared 350 ms before the whole compound was shown, whereas the advantage for having the same head relation was not lost when target modifiers were delayed. These results can be interpreted as supporting a stronger role for heads in the processing of modifier-noun compounds.

Other types of morphological structures were investigated by Hsu et al. (2004), who examined the role of morpheme syntactic category in compound processing in unimpaired adults. Asked to judge the syntactic category of nominal and verbal compounds containing nominal and verbal components, readers showed faster response times for nominal noun-noun compounds than for nominal verb-verb compounds, and the opposite was found with verbal compounds. Even if this pattern is due less to conflicts between the component and word level than to typicality effects (noun-noun compounds are usually nominal, verb-verb compounds usually verbal), it still suggests that morphological structure is available during compound processing.

The simplest aspect of compound structure is bare morpheme order. We would expect compound components to be processed left to right, at least in the initial stages, and this is just what the evidence seems to show for a variety of European languages (see Jarema, this volume). The same seems to hold for Chinese. We have already seen the special status accorded the first morpheme in modifier-noun compounds (Zhang and Peng, 1992; Zhang, 1997), and other studies provide further support. For example, using a task in which participants were asked to freely associate to compound targets, Huang (1979) found that participants tended to begin by listing words that shared the first character with the target, and only later moved to the second. Mattingly and Xu (1994) found that first-position characters showed a greater (positive) frequency effect on character detection times in two-character pseudowords. However, there was no such effect for real words, which they interpreted as implying that characters in real words are processed in parallel (although of course it is always risky to make much of null results). Recently, Wong and Chen (2002) employed eyetracking to study the influence of the semantic ambiguity of compound components on reading. They found longer eye fixations on the second character for compounds beginning with ambiguous characters used with a nondominant meaning (e.g. *bangzhu* 'gang master', where *bang* usually means 'help', not 'gang') than for those whose first characters were unambiguous (e.g. *wuzhu* 'house master').

The left-to-right nature of compound parsing is made particularly clear if one examines compounds longer than those that have attracted virtually all of the field's attention. Yin *et al.* (2004) recently did just this, using a variety of tasks requiring readers to parse three-character compounds, both lexical and novel. It was found that even for monomorphemic nonbinding words (e.g. the phonetic loan *maikefeng* 'microphone'), which presumably have an entirely flat structure, the preferred parse was left-branching, that is [[XY]Z]. This preference is also found in Dutch and German (Baayen *et al.*, 2002), suggesting that it may be due to a universal parsing strategy related to the 'late closure' strategy of syntax (Frazier, 1987).

Myers (2004a) and Myers (2004b) tried to pin down the time course of position-in-the-string effects by using variants on the visual lexical decision task. Following Libben *et al.* (2003), they reasoned that position-dependent processing may be revealed by varying the location of semantic transparency in a compound. Thus their compound materials were pretested as being transparent (T) in both positions (TT, e.g. *baise* 'white', lit. 'white-color'), opaque (O) in both (OO, e.g. *shenjing* 'nerve', lit. 'god-ways'), or a mixture (OT, e.g. *huoche* 'train', lit. 'fire-vehicle'; TO, e.g. *shiguang* 'time', lit. 'time-bright'). In both studies, OO and OT compounds were recognized the most slowly (precisely this same pattern has been found independently by Hsiao, 2004, using a different paradigm and different materials). This not only provides more evidence for the special role of the first position, but also supports the explanation proposed by Libben (this volume) for transparency effects as being due to inhibition by opaque components.

Myers *et al.* also reasoned that if position-in-the-string effects are due to early processing stages, the first-component effect should tend to play a more important role early on in access. In one experiment in Myers *et al.* (2004a) examining this hypothesis, isolated characters were used as primes and compounds containing these characters (in first or second positions) as targets, and in a complementary experiment, primes were compounds and targets were isolated characters. The expectation was that the compound processing stages probed in each experiment would relate to the length of time between display of the compound and onset of response (i.e. earlier stages for character-compound priming, later stages for compound-character priming). This predicted that responses to compound targets should be facilitated by first character primes, while responses to character targets would not be affected by character position in the compound primes. This is precisely what was found. Semantic transparency of the first component was also found to play an early role: in character-compound priming, TO compounds showed the greatest sensitivity to character position, being responded to much faster if its first character was prime, while for compound-character priming there were no prime type by target type interactions. Myers *et al.* (2004b) probed time course in a different way, by placing the prime within the compound targets themselves. That is, the first or second character, normally black, briefly (50 ms) flashed bright red, either early (0 ms SOA) or late (200 ms SOA) during presentation of the four types of compounds. Again, when the flashing occurred early, the effect was greatest for first-position characters, and there was an interaction with transparency: opaque-initial compounds (OO, OT) were slowed, while others (TO, TT) were relatively unaffected.

8.9 Conclusions

A number of general conclusions emerge from this survey of Chinese compound processing. The most fundamental of these is the difficulty of defining the Chinese word, a problem closely related to the nature of Chinese orthography. Researchers who come to Chinese merely to fit data from yet another language into a universal theory of morphological processing should take this issue seriously.

In fact, the experiments with visual stimuli make it quite clear that characters have a great influence on the reading of words, and there is some evidence that they influence the access of spoken words as well. In spite of this, however, we can also safely conclude that words are also treated as units at some point during lexical access in Chinese.

Another safe conclusion is that the degree to which the components of a compound are activated, and when, depends greatly on properties such as semantic transparency, modality (spoken vs. written), and distributional properties of the component characters (e.g. their mutual predictability and whether or not they are binding characters). The precise way in which these factors influence word access is not always clear, but in general one can say that activation of characters is essentially obligatory in the reading of compounds, and that activation of these components occurs from left to right. When accessing spoken compounds, however, rampant homophony greatly affects the role of compound components. None of these findings are particularly unusual when seen in a cross-linguistic perspective, giving us increased confidence in universal principles of compound processing.

Nevertheless, the firmest conclusion that can be drawn from this survey is that much work remains to be done. In particular, the various possible explanations for negative component frequency effects (e.g. those based on transition probability vs. those based on family size) need to be sorted out, priming effects require further study, and the special challenges posed by spoken Chinese deserve far more attention than they have hitherto received. More research is also needed on compound processing by Chinese aphasics (see Packard, 1993), the acquisition of compounds (see Hsieh, 1989, for Mandarin, and Tsay *et al.*, 1999, for another Sinitic language), and the production of compounds by nonimpaired adults (e.g. Chen and Chen, in press, make the surprising claim that morphemes play at best a minimal role in spoken compound production; but cf. Zhou *et al.*, 2002). For a quick tour through several understudied topics in Chinese compound research, see Lu *et al.* (2001), who used regression analyses to investigate not only semantic transparency and frequency, but also word structure, syntactic category, sentential context, and the relationship between spoken word recognition and production.

It is also unknown how the processing of compounds fits into a more general picture of morphological processing. In particular, are there separate processing modes for compounding and affixation? The first study to look at this question in Chinese (Wang and Myers, 2004) employed two diagnostics: first-morpheme frequency effects should be less context sensitive for compounds than for suffixed words (Andrews, 1986), and compounds sharing the first morpheme should prime each other cross-modally while suffixed words should not (Marslen-Wilson *et al.*, 1994). Results did point in the direction of there being two distinct processing modes for compounding and affixation, even in Chinese, despite its fuzzy boundaries between morphological operations. However, as there has been little attention to this question in the morphological processing literature in general, we cannot be sure that the right diagnostics were chosen, or even that reliable diagnostics truly exist.

This chapter is thus far from complete; countless new studies on Chinese compound processing still wait to be done.

Acknowledgments

For help in finding references and for helpful suggestions, my thanks to Gary Libben and Gonia Jarema, the three Oxford reviewers, Marcus Taft, Hsuan-Chih Chen, Shuping Gong, Tingyu Huang, Hongbo Ji, Ching-yuan Lin, Huichuan Liu, Cui-xia Weng, Peiwen Tsai, and Jane Tsay. Naturally, all errors in description or interpretation are my own responsibility: caveat emptor! The author may be contacted at the Graduate Institute of Linguistics, National Chung Cheng University, Min-Hsiung, Chia-Yi 621, Taiwan, or by email at Lngmyers@ccu.edu.tw.

Appendix

TABLE 8.A1. Chinese examples cited in the text*

Pinyin	Characters	Pinyin	Characters	Pinyin	Characters
anning	安寧	huaqiao	華僑	qiuzheng	求證
anshu	桉樹	huasheng	花生	ridian	日店
anzhuang	安裝	huaxiang	滑翔	shafa	沙發
baise	白色	huayuan	花園	shanshi	善事
bangzhu	幫主	huoche	火車	shenjing	神經
banzou	伴奏	hushi	護士	shiguang	時光
beipan	背叛	jiajuan	家眷	shudian	書店
benneng	本能	jiaren	家人	shuhao	書號
bingdian	餅店	jiashi	家事	shujia	書架
caimi	猜謎	jichang	機場	shumu	樹木
caiyi	猜疑	jita	吉他	Taibei	台北
caoshuai	草率	kuaihuo	快活	Taiwan	台灣
chengguan	城關	kuaile	快樂	wuzhu	屋主
chifan	吃飯	kuaisu	快速	xiaozhang	校長
chi-le-fan	吃了飯	laitai	來台	xiehao	寫好
chouchang	惆悵	lingdao	領導	xiguazhi	西瓜汁
ci	詞	lü	侶	xingren	行人
dongxi	東西	mahu	馬虎	xun	殉
feiji	飛機	maikefeng	麥克風	yanzheng	驗證
fugai	覆蓋	mashang	馬上	yinhang	銀行
fumu	父母	meigui	玫瑰	yisheng	醫生
fuxiong	父兄	mianyang	綿羊	yiyuan	醫院
ganjing	乾淨	muxiao	母校	zi	字
ganganjingjing	乾乾淨淨	putao	葡萄	zici	字詞
huagui	華貴	qiushi	糗事	zuo-le	做了
huali	華麗	qiuyin	蚯蚓	zuozhe	作者

* Tone marks are suppressed in the Pinyin transcriptions. Characters are in the traditional form used in Taiwan, even though some of the experiments cited were conducted using the simplified characters standard in the PRC; these differences do not affect the points made in the text.

References

ACKEMA, P. (1999) 'The nonuniform structure of Dutch N-V compounds', *Yearbook of Morphology 1998*. Dordrecht: Kluwer, 127–8.

AHRENS, R. (1977) 'Wortfindungsstörungen für zusammengesetzte Worte (Nomina composita) bei Aphasien' [Word-finding Impairments for Compound Words (Nomina Composita) in Aphasias], *Archiv fur Psychiatrie und Nervenkrankheiten* 224: 73–87.

ALBERT, M., and OBLER, L. K. (1978) *The Bilingual Brain: Neuropsychological and Neurolinguistic Aspects of Bilingualism*. New York: Academic Press.

ALEGRE, M. A., and GORDON, P. (1996) 'Red rats eater exposes recursion in children's word formation', *Cognition* 60: 65–82.

ANDERSON, S. R. (1992) *A-Morphous Morphology*. Cambridge: Cambridge University Press.

ANDREWS, S. (1986) 'Morphological influences on lexical access: Lexical or nonlexical effects?', *Journal of Memory and Language* 25: 726–40.

ARONOFF, M. (1976) *Word Formation in Generative Grammar*. Cambridge: MIT Press.

ASHER, R. (ed.) (1994) *Dictionary of Language and Linguistics*. Oxford: Pergamon Press.

BAAYEN, R. H., and SCHREUDER, R. (eds) (2003) *Morphological Structure in Language Processing*. Berlin: Mouton de Gruyter.

——, KROTT, A., DRESSLER, W. U., JAREMA, G., and LIBBEN, G. (2002) 'Interfixes as boundary markers in compounds', paper presented at the Third International Conference on the Mental Lexicon, Banff, Alberta, Canada, October.

BADECKER, W. (2001) 'Lexical composition and the production of compounds: Evidence from errors in naming', *Language and Cognitive Processes* 16: 337–66.

BAKER, M. (1988) *Incorporation: A Theory of Grammatical Function*. Chicago: Chicago University Press.

—— (1998) 'Comments on the paper by Sadock', in S. G. Lapointe, D. K. Brentari, and P. M. Farrell (eds), *Morphology and its Relation to*

Phonology and Syntax. Stanford, CA: Center for the Study of Language and Information, 188–212.

BATES, E., CHEN, S., TZENG, O., LI, P., and OPIE, M. (1991) 'The noun-verb problem in Chinese aphasia', *Brain and Language* 41: 203–33.

BATES, E., CHEN, S., LI, P., OPIE, M., and TZENG, O. (1993) 'Where is the boundary between compounds and phrases in Chinese? A reply to Zhou et al.', *Brain and Language* 45: 94–107.

BAUER, L. (1978) *The Grammar of Nominal Compounding with Special Reference to Danish, English and French.* Odense: Odense University Press.

—— (1983) *English Word-Formation.* Cambridge: Cambridge University Press.

—— (1998) 'Is there a class of neoclassical compounds, and if so is it productive?', *Linguistics* 36: 403–22.

—— (2001) *Morphological Productivity.* Cambridge: Cambridge University Press.

—— (2005) 'The borderline between derivation and compounding', in W. U. Dressler, D. Kastovsky, O. Pfeiffer, and F. Rainer (eds), *Morphology and its Demarcations.* Amsterdam: Benjamins.

BEARD, R. (1995) *Lexeme-Morpheme Base Morphology.* Albany, NY: State University of New York Press.

BEAUVILLAIN, C., and GRAINGER, J. (1987) 'Accessing interlexical homographs: Some limitations of a language-selective access', *Journal of Memory and Language* 26: 658–72.

BECKER, J. A. (1994) ' "Sneak-Shoes", "Sworders" and "Nose-Beards": A case study of lexical innovation', *First Language* 14: 195–211.

BECKER, T. (1992) 'Compounding in German', *Rivista di Linguistica* 4: 5–36.

BERKO, S. (1958) 'The child's learning of English morphology', *Word* 14: 150–77.

BERMAN, R. A. (1987) 'A developmental route: Learning about the form and use of complex nominals in Hebrew', *Linguistics* 25: 1057–85.

—— and CLARK, E. V. (1989) 'Learning to use compounds for contrast: Data from Hebrew', *First Language* 9: 247–70.

BIALYSTOK, E., and HAKUTA, K. (1994) *In Other Words: The Science and Psychology of Second-Language Acquisition.* New York: Harper Collins.

BICKERTON, D. (1990) *Language and Species.* Chicago: Chicago University Press.

BISETTO, A., and SCALISE, S. (1999) 'Compounding: Morphology and/or syntax?', in L. Mereu (ed.), *Boundaries of Morphology and Syntax*. Amsterdam: John Benjamins, 31–48.

BLANKEN, G. (1997) 'Simpliza-Ja! Komposita-Nein! Aphasische Fehler bei der Produktion von Nomina Komposita. Eine Einzelfallstudie' Simplices-Yes! Compounds-No! Aphasic errors in producing Compound nouns. A single case study., in G. Rickheit (ed.), *Studien zur Klinischen Linguistik. Modelle, Methoden, Intervention*. Opladen: Westdeutscher Verlag.

—— (2000) 'The production of nominal compounds in aphasia', *Brain and Language* 74: 84–102.

BLEKHER, M. (2004) 'Derivational affixation and translation recognition in bilinguals', poster presented at the Fourth International Conference on the Mental Lexicon, Windsor, Ontario, Canada.

BLOOMER, R. K. (1996) 'Die pleonastischen Zusammensetzungen der deutschen Gegenwartssprache' Pleonastic compounds in current German, *American Journal of Germanic Linguistics and Literatures* 8: 69–90.

BLOOMFIELD, L. (1933) *Language*. New York: Holt, Rinehart and Winston.

BOCK, K., and GRIFFIN, Z. M. (2000) 'Producing words: How mind meets mouth', in L. Wheeldon (ed.), *Aspects of Language Production*. Psychology Press. Hove, 7–48.

BOOIJ, G. (1992) 'Compounding in Dutch', *Rivista di Linguistica* 4: 37–59.

—— (2003) 'Periphrastic word formation', in G. Booij *et al.* (eds), *Topics in Morphology*. Barcelona: Institut Universitari de Lingüística Aplicada, Universitat Pompeu Fabra, 15–27.

—— (2005a) *The Grammar of Words: An Introduction to Linguistic morphology*. Oxford: Oxford University Press.

—— (2005b) 'Compounding and derivation: Evidence for construction grammar', in W. U. Dressler, D. Kastovsky, O. Pfeiffer, and F. Rainer (eds), *Morphology and its Demarcations*. Amsterdam: John Benjamins.

——, LEHMANN, C., and MUGDAN, J. (eds) (2000) *Morphology. An International Handbook on Inflection and Word Formation*. Berlin: Mouton de Gruyter.

BORER, H. (1988) 'On the morphological parallelism between compounds and constructs', in Booij, Gert and van Marle, Jaap (eds), *Morphology Yearbook* 1, 45–65. Dordrecht: Foris.

BREKLE, H. (1984) 'Les composés ad hoc en allemand contemporain: Reflexions pragmatico-sémantiques' Ad hoc compounds in contemptorary German: Pragmato-Semantic reflections:, *DRLAV* 31: 97–106.

—— (1986) 'The production and interpretation of ad hoc nominal compounds in German: A realistic approach', *Acta Linguistica Hungarica* 36: 39–52.

BURANI, C., and LAUDANNA, A. (1992) 'Units of representation for derivedwords in the lexicon', in L. Katz, R. Frost (eds), *Orthography, phonology, morphology, and meaning*. Oxford, England: North-Holland, 361–78.

BUTTERWORTH, B. (1983) 'Lexical representation', in B. Butterworth (ed.), *Language Production* (Vol. 2, pp. 257–94). San Diego, CA: Academic Press.

CAPLAN, D., KELLAR, L., and LOCK, J. (1972) 'Inflection of neologisms in aphasia', *Brain* 95: 169–72.

CARAMAZZA, A. (1997) 'How many levels of processing are there in lexical access?', *Cognitive Neuropsychology* 14: 177–208.

—— and BRONES, I. (1980) 'Semantic classification by bilinguals', *Canadian Journal of Psychology*, 34: 77–81.

—— MICELI, G., SILVERI, M. C., and LAUDANNA, A. (1985) 'Reading mechanisms and the organization of the lexicon: Evidence from acquired dyslexia', *Cognitive Neuropsychology* 2: 81–114.

CHAO, Y.-R. (1968) *A Grammar of Spoken Chinese*. Berkeley: University of California Press.

CHEN, H.-C. and HO, C. (1986) 'Development of Stroop interference in Chinese-English bilinguals', *Journal of Experimental Psychology: Learning, Memory, and Cognition* 12: 397–401.

CHEN, H.-C. and LEUNG, Y.-S. (1989) 'Patterns of lexical processing in a nonnative language', *Journal of Experimental Psychology: Learning, Memory, and Cognition* 15: 316–25.

CHEN, J.-Y. (1999) 'Word recognition during the reading of Chinese sentences: Evidence from studying the word superiority effect', in J. Wang, A. W. Inhoff, and H.-C. Chen (eds), *Reading Chinese Script: A Cognitive Analysis*. Mahwah, NJ: Lawrence Erlbaum Associates, 239–56.

CHEN, K.-J., HUANG, C.-R., CHANG, L.-P., and HSU, H.-L. (1996) 'SINICA CORPUS: Design methodology for balanced corpora', *Language, Information and Computation* 11: 167–76.

CHEN, S., and BATES, E. (1998) 'The dissociation between nouns and verbs in Broca's and Wernicke's aphasia: Findings from Chinese', *Aphasiology* 12: 5–36.

CHEN, S.-C. (2002) 'Morphological processing and semantic processing in reading Chinese compound words', paper presented at the Tenth International Conference on the Cognitive Processing of Chinese and Other Related Asian Languages, Taipei, December.

CHEN, S.-T. (1993) 'Hanyu gouci zai yuedu licheng zhong dui yuyi chufa xiaogai de yingxiang' [The influence of semantic activation effects on Chinese morphology during reading], unpublished master's thesis, National Chung Cheng University, Chia-Yi, Taiwan.

CHEN, T.-M., & CHEN, J.-Y. (in press). Morphological encoding in the production of compound words in Mandarin Chinese.

CHENG, C.-M. (1981) 'Hanzi renzhi de licheng' [Perception of Chinese characters], *Acta Psychologica Taiwanica* 23: 137–53.

CHOMSKY, N. (1988) *Language and Problems of Knowledge*. Cambridge, MA: MIT Press.

CHUMBLEY, J. (1986) 'The role of typicality, instance, dominance, and category dominance in verifying category membership', *Journal of Experimental Psychology: Learning, Memory, and Cognition* 12: 257–67.

CLAHSEN, H. (1995) 'German plurals in adult second language development: Evidence for a dual mechanism model of inflection', in L. Eubank, L. Selinker, and M. Sharwood Smith (eds), *The Current State of Interlanguage*. Amsterdam: John Benjamins, 123–37.

—— (1999) 'Lexical entries and rules of language', *Behavioural and Brain Sciences* 22: 991–1013.

——, ROTHWEILER, M., WOEST, A., and MARCUS, G. F. (1992) 'Regular and irregular inflection in the acquisition of German nouns plurals', *Cognition* 45: 225–55.

CLARK, E. V. (1981) 'Lexical innovations: How children learn to create new words', in W. Deutsch (ed.), *The Child's Construction of Language*. New York: Academic Press, 299–328.

—— (1993) *The lexicon in acquisition*. Cambridge: Cambridge University Press.

—— (1998) 'Lexical creativity in French-speaking children', *Cahiers de Psychologie Cognitive* 17: 513–30.

CLARK, E. V. (2003) *First Language Acquisition*. Cambridge: Cambridge University Press.

—— and BARRON, B. J. S. (1988) 'A thrower button or a button thrower? Children's judgments of grammatical and ungrammatical compound nouns', *Linguistics* 26: 3–19.

—— and BERMAN, R. A. (1984) 'Structure and use in the acquisition of word formation', *Language* 60: 542–90.

—— and —— (1987). 'Types of linguistic knowledge: Interpreting and producing compound nouns', *Journal of Child Language* 14: 547–67.

——, GELMAN, S.A., and LANE, N. M. (1985). 'Compound nouns and category structure in young children', *Child Development* 56: 84–94.

—— and HECHT, B. F. (1982) 'Learning to coin agent and instrument nouns', *Cognition* 12: 1–24.

——, HECHT, B. F., and MULFORD, R. C. (1986) 'Coining complex compounds in English: Affixes and word order in acquisition', *Linguistics* 24: 7–29.

COOLEN, R., VAN JAARSVELD, H. J., and SCHREUDER, R. (1993) 'Processing novel compounds: Evidence for interactive meaning activation of ambiguous nouns', *Memory and Cognition* 21: 235–46.

COSERIU, E. (1975) 'System, Norm und Rede' System, Norm, and Speaking:, in E. Coseriu (ed.), *Sprachtheorie und allgemeine Sprachwissenschaft*. München: Fink, 11–101.

DAI, J. X.-L. (1992) 'Chinese morphology and its interface with the syntax' (Doctoral dissertation, Ohio State University, 1992), *Dissertation Abstracts International* 53: 2792.

DALALAKIS, J. E. (1999) 'Morphological representation in specific language impairment: Evidence from Greek', *Folia Phoniatrica et Logopaedica* 51: 20–35.

DARDANO, M. (1978) *La Comprensione delle Parole nell'Italiano di Oggi*. Roma: Bulzoni Editore.

DE BOT, K., COX, A., RALSTON, S., SCHAUFELI, A., and WELTENS, B. (1995) 'Lexical processing in bilinguals', *Second Language Research* 11: 1–19.

DE GROOT, A. M. B. (1992) 'Determinants of word translation', *Journal of Experimental Psychology: Learning, Memory, and Cognition* 18: 1001–18.

——, and HOEKS, J. C. J. (1995) 'The development of bilingual memory: Evidence from word translations by trilinguals', *Language Learning* 45, 683–724.

—— and KROLL, J. F. (eds). (1997) *Tutorials in Bilingualism: Psycholinguistic perspectives*. Mahwah, NJ: Lawrence Erlbaum Associates.

—— and NAS, G. (1991) 'Lexical representation of cognate and noncognates in compound bilinguals', *Journal of Memory and Language* 30: 90–123.

DE JONG, N. H., FELDMAN, L. B., SCHREUDER, R., PASTIZZO, M., and BAAYEN, R. H. (2002) 'The processing and representation of Dutch and English compounds: Peripheral morphological and central orthographic effects', *Brain and Language* 81: 555–67.

DE KNOP, S. (1987) *Metaphorische Komposita in Zeitungsüberschriften* [Metaphorical compounds in newspaper headlines]. Tübingen: Niemeyer.

DELAZER, M., and SEMENZA, C. (1998) 'The processing of compound words', *Brain and Language* 61: 54–62.

DELL, G. S., SCHWARTZ, M. F., MARTIN, N., SAFFRAN, E. M., and GAGNON, D. A. (1997) 'Lexical access in aphasic and nonaphasic speakers', *Psychological Review* 104: 801–38.

DERWING, B. L. (1976) 'Morpheme recognition and the learning of rules for derivational morphology', *Canadian Journal of Linguistics* 21: 38–66.

DIJKSTRA, T., TIMMERMANS, M., and SCHRIEFERS, H. (2000) 'On being blinded by your other language: Effects of task demands on interlingual homograph recognition', *Journal of Memory and Language* 42: 445–64.

DI SCIULLO, A. M., and WILLIAMS, E. (1987) *On the Definition of Word*. Cambridge, MA: MIT Press.

DOWNING, P. (1977) 'On the creation and use of English compound nouns', *Language* 53: 810–42.

DRESSLER, W. U. (1987) 'Morphological islands: Constraint or preference?', in R. Steele and T. Treadgold (eds), *LanguageTopics, Fs. Halliday*. Amsterdam: Benjamins, 71–9.

—— (1988) 'Preferences vs. strict universals in morphology: Word-based rules', in M. Hammond, and M. Noonan (eds), *Theoretical Morphology*. San Diego: Academic Press, 143–53.

—— (2000) 'Extragrammatical vs. marginal morphology', in U. Doleschal and A. M. Thornton (eds), *Extragrammatical and Marginal Morphology*. München: Lincom Europa, 1–10.

Dressler, W. U. and Denes, G. (1989) 'Word formation in Italian-speaking Wernicke's and Broca's aphasics', in W. U. Dressler and J. Stark (eds), *Linguistic Analyses of Aphasic Language*. Springer, New York, 69–88.

—— and Ladányi, M. (2000) 'Productivity in word formation: A morphological approach', *Acta Linguistica Hungarica* 47: 103–44.

—— and Merlini Barbaresi, L. (1991) 'Interradical interfixes: Contact and contrast', in V. Ivir and D. Kalogjera (eds), *Languages in Contact and Contrast*. Berlin: Mouton de Gruyter, 133–45.

——, Kastovsky, D., Pfeiffer, O., and Rainer, F. (eds) (2005) *Morphology and its Demarcations*. Amsterdam: John Benjamins.

——, Libben, G., Stark, J., Pons, J. C., and Jarema, G. (2000) 'The processing of interfixed German compounds', in J. Van Marle and G. Booij (eds), *Yearbook of Morphology*. Dordrecht: Kluwer Academic Publishers, 186–220.

Duanmu, S. (1998) 'Wordhood in Chinese', in J. Packard (ed.), *New Approaches to Chinese Word Formation: Morphology, Phonology and the Lexicon in Modern and Ancient Chinese*. Berlin: Mouton de Gruyter, 135–96.

Estes, Z., and Glucksberg, S. (2000) 'Interactive property attribution in concept combination', *Memory and Cognition* 28: 28–34.

Fabb, N. (1998) 'Compounding', in A. Spencer and A. M. Zwicky (eds), *The Handbook of Morphology*. Oxford: Blackwell, 66–83.

Fabbro, F., Peru, A., and Skrap, M. (1997) 'Language disorders in bilingual patients after thalamic lesions', *Journal of Neurolinguistics* 10: 347–67.

Fanselow, G. (1985). 'What is a complex word?', in J. Toman (ed.), *Studies in German Grammar*. Dordrecht: Foris, 289–318.

Feldman, L. B. (2003) 'What the repetition priming methodology reveals about morphological aspects of word recognition', in J. S. Bowers and C. J. Marsolek (eds), *Rethinking Implicit Memory*. Oxford: Oxford University Press, 124–38.

Frazier, L. (1987) 'Sentence processing: A tutorial review', in M. Coltheart (ed.), *Attention and Performance, Vol. XII: The Psychology of Reading*. Mahwah, New Jersey: Lawrence Erlbaum Associates, 559–86.

Friederici, A. D. and Frazier, L. (1992) 'Thematic analysis in agrammatic comprehension: Syntactic structures and task demands', *Brain and Language* 42: 1–29.

Fromkin, V., and Rodman, R. (1998) *An Introduction to Language* (6th edn). New York: Harcourt Brace College Publishers.

FUHRHOP, N. (1998) *Grenzfälle Morphologischer Einheiten* [*Borderline Cases of Morphological Units*]. Tübingen: Stauffenburg.
GAGNÉ, C. L. (2000). 'Relation-based combinations versus property-based combinations: A Test of the CARIN Theory and dual-process theory of conceptual combination', *Journal of Memory and Language* 42: 365–89.
—— (2001) 'Relation and lexical priming during the interpretation of noun-noun combinations', *Journal of Experimental Psychology: Learning, Memory and Cognition* 27: 236–54.
—— (2002) 'Lexical and relational influences on the processing of novel compounds', *Brain and Language* 81: 723–35.
—— and Murphy, G. L. (1996) 'Influence of discourse context on feature availability in conceptual combination', *Discourse Processes* 22: 79–101.
—— and Shoben, E. J. (1997) 'The influence of thematic relations on the comprehension of modifier-noun combinations', *Journal of Experimental Psychology: Learning, Memory and Cognition* 23: 71–87.
—— and —— (2002) 'Priming relations in ambiguous noun-noun combinations', *Memory and Cognition* 30: 637–46.
—— and Spalding, T. L. (2003) Relational Priming for Familiar Compounds: A Processing-Based Account. Unpublished manuscript.
—— and —— (2004a) *The Availability of Noun Properties during the Interpretation of Novel Noun Phrases*. Poster presented at the Fourth International Conference on the Mental Lexicon, Windsor, ON, June.
—— and —— (2004b) 'Effect of relation availability on the interpretation and access of familiar noun-noun compounds', *Brain and Language* 90: 478–86.
——, ——, and GORRIE, M. C. in press. 'Sentential context and the interpretation of familiar open-compounds and novel modifier-noun phrases', *Language and Speech*.
GARRETT, M. F. (1990a) 'Levels of processing in sentence production', in B. Butterworth (ed.), *Language Production, Vol. 1: Speech and Talk*, London: Erlbaum.
—— (1990b) 'Review of Levelt: speaking', *Language and Speech* 33: 273–91.
GATHER, A. (2001) *Romanische Verb-Nomen-Komposita*. Tübingen: Niemeyer.
GELMAN, S. A., and MARKMAN, E. (1985) 'Implicit contrast in adjectives vs. nouns: Implications for word learning in preschoolers', *Journal of Child Language* 12: 125–43.
——, WILCOX, S. A., and CLARK, E. V. (1989) 'Conceptual and lexical hierarchies in young children', *Cognitive Development* 4: 309–26.

GLEITMAN, L. R., and GLEITMAN, H. (1970) 'A grammatical sketch of compound nouns', in *Phrase and Paraphrase; Some innovative uses of language*. New York: W. W. Norton.

GOLLAN, T. H. and KROLL, J. F. (2001) 'Bilingual lexical access', in B. Rapp (ed.), *The Handbook of Cognitive Neuropsychology: What Deficits Reveal about the Human Mind*. Philadelphia: Psychology Press, 321–45.

GORAL, M., LIBBEN, G., JAREMA, G., and OBLER, L. K., (in preparation) 'Morphological processing in bilinguals.

GORDON, P. (1985) 'Level-ordering in lexical development', *Cognition* 21: 73–93.

GOTTFRIED, G. M. (1997a). Using metaphors as modifiers: children's production of metaphoric compounds. *Journal of Child Language*, 24, 567–601.

—— (1997b) 'Comprehending compounds: Evidence for metaphoric skill?', *Journal of Child Language* 24: 163–86.

GROSSMANN, M., and RAINER F. (eds) (2004) *La Formazione delle Parole in Italiano*, Tübingen: Niemeyer.

GUSTAFSSON, A. (1978). *Treåringars språkliga kreativitet* [*The linguistic creativity of three year olds*]. Child Language Research Institute, Stockholm University, Paper No. 2.

HAIDER, H. (2001) 'Riesengratulationskompositum—*Kompositumgratulationsriesen or: Why there are no complex head-initial compounds?', in C. Schaner-Wolles, J. Rennison, and F. Neubarth (eds), *Naturally! Fs. W. U. Dressler*. Torino: Rosenberg and Sellier, 165–81.

HARRIS, R. J. (ed.) (1992) *Cognitive Processing in Bilingualism*. Amsterdam: Elsevier Science.

HASKELL, T. R., MACDONALD, M. C., and SEIDENBERG, M. S. (2003) 'Language learning and innateness: Some implications of compounds research'. *Cognitive Psychology*, 47, 119–163.

HERINGER, H.-J. (1984) 'Wortbildung: Sinn aus dem Chaos' [Word formation: Meaning from Chaos], *Deutsche Sprache* 12: 1–13.

HIRAMATSU, K., SNYDER, W., ROEPER, T., STORRS, S., and SACCOMAN, M. (1999) 'Of musical hand chairs and linguistic swing', paper presented at the 24th Annual Boston University Conference on Language Development, Boston, USA, November.

HITTMAIR-DELAZER, M., ANDREE, B., SEMENZA, C., DE BLESER, R., and BENKE, T. (1994) 'Naming by German compounds', *Journal of Neurolinguistics* 8: 27–41.

Ho, K.-C. (1976) 'A study of the relative frequency distribution of syllabic components in Mandarin Chinese', *Journal of the Institute of Chinese Studies* 8: 275–352.

Holyoak, K. (1978) 'Comparative judgments with numerical reference points', *Cognitive Psychology* 10: 203–43.

Hoosain, R. (1992) 'Psychological reality of the word in Chinese', in H.-C. Chen and O. J. L. Tzeng (eds), *Language Processing in Chinese*. Amsterdam: North-Holland, 111–30.

Hsiao, H.-C. S. (2004) 'The role of semantic transparency in the processing of Mandarin compounds', poster presented at the Fourth International Conference on the Mental Lexicon, Windsor, Canada, June.

Hsieh, M.-L. (1989) 'The acquisition and comprehension of lexical entries by Mandarin-speaking children', unpublished master's thesis, Fu Jen Catholic University, Taipei, Taiwan.

Hsu, J. C.-F., Tzeng, O. J.-L., and Hung, D. L. (in press) 'Syntactic effects on constituent components in word recognition: Evidence from compound nouns and compound verbs in Chinese', *Maryland Working Papers in Linguistics* 13: 173–93.

Huang, J.-T. (1979) 'Zhongwen ci lianxiang de yishixing ke fenli jiashe' [Time-dependent separability hypothesis of Chinese word association], *Acta Psychologica Taiwanica* 21: 41–8.

Hung, D. L., Tzeng, O. J. L., and Ho, C.-Y. (1999) 'Word superiority effect in the visual processing of Chinese', in O. J. L. Tzeng (ed.), *Journal of Chinese Linguistics Monograph Series No. 13: The biological bases of language*, 61–95.

Hyltenstam, K., and Obler, L. K. (1989) 'Bilingualism across the lifespan: An introduction', in K. Hyltenstam and L. K. Obler (eds), *Bilingualism Across the Lifespan*. NY: Cambridge University Press.

Iacobini, C. (1998) 'Distinguishing derivational prefixes from initial combining forms', in G. Booij, A. Ralli, and S. Scalise (eds), *Proceedings of the First Mediterranean Conference on Morphology*. University of Patras, 132–40.

Jackendoff, R. (2002) *Foundations of Knowledge*. Oxford: Oxford University Press.

Jarema, G., Busson, C., Nikolova, R., Tsapkini, K., and Libben, G. (1999) 'Processing compounds: A cross-linguistic study', *Brain and Language* 68: 362–9.

JENSEN, J. T. (1990) *Morphology: Word Structure in Generative Grammar*. Amsterdam: John Benjamins.

JI, H., and GAGNÉ, C. L. (2004) 'Lexical and relational influences on the processing of Chinese modifier-noun compounds', poster presented at the Fourth International Conference on the Mental Lexicon, Windsor, Canada, June–July.

KAY, P., and ZIMMER, K. (1976) 'On the semantics of compounds and genitives in English', paper presented at the Sixth California Linguistics Association, San Diego State University.

KEHAYIA, E., JAREMA, G., TSAPKINI, K., PERLAK, D., RALLI, A., and KADZIELAWA, D. (1999) 'The role of morphological structure in the processing of compounds: The interface between linguistics and psycholinguistics', *Brain and Language* 68: 370–7.

KIEFER, F. (2001) 'Productivity and compounding', in C. Schaner-Wolles, J. Rennison, and F. Neubarth (eds), *Naturally! Fs. W. U. Dressler*. Torino: Rosenberg and Sellier, 225–31.

KIM, J. J., MARCUS, G. F., PINKER, S., HOLLANDER, M., and COPPOLA, K. (1994) 'Sensitivity of children's inflection to grammatical structure', *Journal of Child Language* 21: 173–209.

KIPARSKY, P. (1982) 'From cyclic phonology to lexical phonology', in H. van der Hulst and N. Smith (eds), *The Structure of Phonological Representations*. Dordrecht: Foris, 131–75.

—— (1983) 'Word-formation and the lexicon', in F. Ingemann (ed.), *Proceedings of the 1982 Mid-America Linguistics Conference*. Lawrence, KS: University of Kansas, 3–29.

—— (1985) 'Some consequences of lexical phonology' *Phonology Yearbook* 2: 85–138.

KRASHEN, S. (1981) *Second Language Acquisition and Second Language Learning*. Oxford: Pergamon Press.

KROLL, J. F. and CURLEY, J. (1988) 'Lexical memory in novice bilinguals: The role of concepts in retrieving second language words', in M. Gruneberg, P. Morris, and R. Sykes (eds), *Practical Aspects of Memory*, Vol. 2. London: John Wiley & Sons.

KROLL, J. F. and DIJKSTRA, T. (2002) 'The bilingual lexicon', in R. Kaplan (ed.), *Handbook of Applied Linguistics*. Oxford: Oxford University Press.

KROLL, J. F. and STEWART, E. (1994) 'Category interference in translation and picture naming: Evidence for asymmetric connections between bilingual memory representations', *Journal of Memory and Language* 33: 149–74.

KROTT, A., and NICOLADIS, E. (2003) 'Family effects in compound processing start young', paper presented at the Deutsche Gesellschaft für Sprachwissenschaft, Munich, Germany, February.

——, BAAYEN, R. H., and SCHREUDER, R. (2001) 'Analogy in morphology: Modeling the choice of linking morphemes in Dutch', *Linguistics* 39: 51–93.

——, SCHREUDER, R., and BAAYEN, R. H. (2002a) 'Linking elements in Dutch noun-noun compounds: Constituent families as analogical predictors for response latencies', *Brain and Language* 81: 708–22.

——, ——, and —— (2002b) 'Analogical hierarchy: Exemplar-based modeling of linkers in Dutch noun-noun compounds', in R. Skousen, D. Londsdale, and D. B. Parkinson (eds), *Analogical Modeling: An Exemplar-Based Approach to Language*. Amsterdam: John Benjamins, 181–206.

——, LIBBEN, G., JAREMA, G., DRESSLER, W. U., SCHREUDER, R., and BAAYEN, R. H. (2004) 'Probability in the grammar of German and Dutch: Interfixation in triconstituent compounds', *Language and Speech* 47: 83–106.

KUDO, T. (1992) 'Word formation in aphasia: Evidence from Japanese Kanji words', *Journal of Neurolinguistics* 7: 197–216.

LARDIERE, D. (1995) 'L2 acquisition of English synthetic compounding is not constrained by level-ordering (and neither, probably, is L1)', *Second Language Research* 11: 20–56.

—— (1997) 'On the transfer of morphological parameter values in L2 acquisition', in E. Hughes, M. Hughes, and A. Greenhill (eds), *Proceedings of the 21st annual Boston University Conference on Language Development*. Somerville, MA: Cascadilla Press, 366–77.

LAUNEY, M. (1999) 'Compound nouns vs. incorporation in classical Nahuatl', *Sprachtypologie und Universalienforschung* 52: 347–64.

LEE, C.-L., HUNG, D. L., TSE, J. K. P., LEE, C.-Y., TSAI, J.-L., and TZENG, O. J.-L. (2005) 'Processing of disyllabic compound words in Chinese aphasia: Evidence for the processing limitations account', *Brain and Language* 92 (2): 168–84.

LEOPOLD, W. F. (1949) *Speech development of a bilingual child; A linguist's record*, Vol. 4. New York: AMS Press.

LEVELT, W. J. M. (1989) *Speaking. From intention to articulation* Cambridge, MA: MIT Press.

LEVELT, W. J. M., ROELOFS, A., and MEYER, A. (1999) 'A theory of lexical access in speech production', *Behavioral and Brain Sciences* 22: 1–38.

LEVI, J. N. (1978) *The Syntax and Semantics of Complex Nominals*. New York: Academic Press.

LI, C. N., and THOMPSON, S. A. (1981) *Mandarin Chinese: A Functional Reference Grammar*. Berkeley: University of California Press.

LI, P., BATES, E., and MACWHINNEY, B. (1993) 'Processing a language without inflections: A reaction time study of sentence interpretation in Chinese', *Journal of Memory and Language* 32: 169–92.

LIANG, M. Y. (1992) 'Recognition processing in reading compositional and idiomatic words', unpublished master's thesis, National Tsinghua University, Hsinchu, Taiwan.

LIBBEN, G. (1993) 'A case of obligatory access to morphological constituents', *Nordic Journal of Linguistics* 16: 111–21.

—— (1994) 'How is morphological decomposition achieved?', *Language and Cognitive Processes* 9: 369–91.

—— (1998) 'Semantic transparency in the processing of compounds: Consequences for representation, processing and impairment', *Brain and Language* 61: 30–44.

—— (2003) 'Semantic transparency and compound fracture', *CLASNET Working Papers* 9: 1–13.

—— and DE ALMEIDA, R. G. (2001) 'Is there a morphological parser?', in W. U. Dressler and S. Bendjaballah (eds), *Morphology 2000*. Amsterdam: John Benjamins.

—— and JAREMA, G. (2002) 'Mental lexicon research in the New Millennium', *Brain and Language* 81: 2–11.

LIBBEN, G., DERWING, B. L., and DE ALMEIDA, R. G. (1999) 'Ambiguous novel compounds and models of morphological parsing', *Brain and Language* 68: 378–86.

——, JAREMA, G., DRESSLER, W. U., STARK, J., and PONS, J. C. (2002) 'Triangulating the effects of interfixation in the processing of German compounds', *Folia Linguistica* XXXVI: 23–43.

——, GIBSON, M., YOON, Y. B., and SANDRA, D. (2003) 'Compound fracture: The role of semantic transparency and morphological headedness', *Brain and Language* 84: 50–64.

——, BUCHANAN, L., and COLANGELO, A. (2004) 'Morphology, semantics, and the mental lexicon: The failure of deactivation hypothesis', *Logos and Language* 4(1): 45–53.

LIEBER, R. (1983) 'Argument linking and compounds in English', *Linguistic Inquiry* 14: 251–85.
—— (1992) 'Compounding in English', *Rivista di Linguistica* 4: 79–96.
—— (1994) 'Root Compounds and Synthetic Compounds', in R. Asher (ed.), *Dictionary of Language and Linguistics*. Oxford: Pergamon Press, 3607–10.
—— (2004) *Morphology and Lexical Semantics*. Cambridge: Cambridge University Press.
LIU, I.-M. (1988) 'Context Effects on Word/Character Naming: Alphabetic versus Logographic Languages', in I.-M. Liu, H.-C. Chen and M. J. Chen (eds), *Cognitive Aspects of the Chinese Language, Vol. 1*. Hong Kong: Asian Research Service, 81–92.
——, WU, J.-T., and CHOU, T.-L. (1996) 'Encoding operation and transcoding as the major loci of the frequency effect', *Cognition* 59: 149–68.
LIU, Y., and PENG, D. (1997) 'Meaning access of Chinese compounds and its time course', in H.-C. Chen (ed.), *Cognitive Processing of Chinese and Related Asian Languages*. Hong Kong: The Chinese University Press, 219–32.
—— and —— (1995) 'Time-course of Chinese compound word recognition', poster presented at the Seventh International Conference on the Cognitive Processing of Chinese and Other Asian Languages, Hong Kong.
LU, C.-C., BATES, E., HUNG, D., TZENG, O., HSU, J., TSAI, C.-H., and ROE, K. (2001) 'Syntactic priming of nouns and verbs in Chinese'. *Language and Speech*, 44(4), 437–71.
LÜ, C.-C. (1996) 'Zhongwen yuci renzhi licheng' [Chinese word recognition], unpublished doctoral thesis, National Tsinghua University, Hsinchu, Taiwan.
LUZZATI, C., and DE BLESER, R. (1996) 'Morphological processing in Italian agrammatic speakers: Eight experiments in lexical morphology', *Brain and Language* 54: 26–74.
MÄKISALO, J. (2000) 'Grammar and experimental evidence in Finnish compounds'. *Studies in Languages* 35. University of Joensuu, Joensuu.
MÄKISALO, J., NIEMI, J., and LAINE, M. (1999) 'Finnish compound structure: Experiments with a morphologically impaired patient', *Brain and Language* 68: 249–53.
MARKMAN, E. M. (1989) 'Language and richly structured versus arbitrary categories', in *Categorization and Naming in Children: Problems of Induction*. London: The MIT Presss.

MARSLEN-WILSON, W., TYLER, L. K., WAKSLER, R., and OLDER, L. (1994) 'Morphology and meaning in the English mental lexicon', *Psychological Review* 101: 3–33.

MATTHEWS, P. H. (1972) *Inflectional Morphology*. Cambridge: Cambridge University Press.

MATTINGLY, I. G., and HSIAO, P. (1997) 'Constituent superiority in Chinese', in H.-C. Chen (ed.), *Cognitive Processing of Chinese and Related Asian languages*. Hong Kong: The Chinese University Press, 207–18.

—— and XU, Y. (1994) 'Word superiority in Chinese', in H.-W. Chang, J.-T. Huang, C.-W. Hue, and O. J. L. Tzeng (eds), *Advances in the Study of Chinese Language Processing, Vol. 1*. Taipei: Department of Psychology, National Taiwan University, 101–11.

MCEWEN, S., WESTBURY, C., BUCHANAN, L., and LIBBEN, G. (2001) 'Semantic information is used by a deep dyslexic to parse compounds', *Brain and Cognition* 46: 201–6.

MEDIN, D. L., and SHOBEN, E. J. (1988) 'Context and structure in conceptual combination', *Cognitive Psychology* 20: 158–90.

MEL'ČUK, I. (1997) *Cours de Morphologie Générale 4*. Montréal: Les Presses de l'Université de Montréal.

MELLENIUS, I. (1997). 'Children's comprehension of Swedish nominal compounds', in C. E. Johnson and J. H. V. GILBERT (eds), *Children's Language, Vol. 9*. Mahwah, NJ: Lawrence Erlbaum, 167–82.

MENN, L. and OBLER, L. K. (1990). *Agrammatic aphasia: A cross-language narrative sourcebook*. Amsterdam: John Benjamins Publishing Company.

MEREU, L. (ed.) (1999) *Boundaries of Morphology and Syntax*. Amsterdam: John Benjamins.

MEYER, R. (1992) *Compound Comprehension in Isolation and in Context*. Tübingen: Niemeyer.

MICELI, G., SILVERI, M. C., ROMANI, C., CARAMAZZA, A. (1989). 'Variations in the pattern of omissions and substitutions of grammatic morphemes in the spontaneous speech of so-called agrammatic patients', *Brain and Language* 36: 447–492.

MITHUN, M., and G. G. CORBETT (1999) 'The effect of noun incorporation on argument structure', in L. Mereu (ed.), *Boundaries of Morphology and Syntax*. Amsterdam: John Benjamins, 49–72.

MONDINI, S., JAREMA, G., LUZZATTI, C., BURANI, C., and SEMENZA, C. (2002) 'Why is "Red Cross" different from "Yellow Cross"? A neuropsychological study of noun-adjective agreement within Italian compounds', *Brain and Language* 81: 621–34.

MONDINI, S., LUZZATTI, C., and SEMENZA, C. (1999) 'Grammatical gender in an Italian agrammatic patient', *Brain and Language* 69: 278–81.

—— ——, and —— (in press) 'Mental representation of prepositional compounds: Evidence from Italian agrammatic patients', *Brain and Language*.

——, LUZZATTI, C., SALETTA, P., ALLAMANO, N. and SEMENZA, C. (2005). 'Mental Representation of Prepositional Compounds: Evidence from Italian Agrammatic Patients', *Brain and Language* 94: 178–87.

—— LUZZATTI, C., ZONCA, G., PISTARINI, C., and SEMENZA, C. (2004) 'The mental representation of verb-noun compounds in Italian: Evidence from a multiple single-case study in aphasia', *Brain and Language* 90: 470–7.

MONSELL, S. (1985) 'Repetition and the Lexicon', in A. W. Ellis (ed.), *Progress in the Psychology of Language* (Vol. 2). Hillsdale, NJ: Lawrence Erlbaum.

MOTSCH, W. (1994) 'Word formation: Compounding', in R. Asher (ed.), *Dictionary of Language and Linguistics*. Oxford: Pergamon Press, 5017–24.

MOYNA, M. I. (2004) 'Can we make heads or tails of Spanish endocentric compounds?', *Linguistics* 42: 617–37.

MÜLLER, N. (1998) 'Transfer in bilingual first language acquisition', *Bilingualism: Language and Cognition* 1: 151–71.

MURPHY, G. L. (1988) 'Comprehending complex concepts', *Cognitive Science* 12: 529–62.

—— (1990) 'Noun phrase interpretation and conceptual combination', *Journal of Memory and Language* 29: 259–88.

MURPHY, V. A. (1997) 'Level-ordering and dual-mechanisms as explanations of L2 grammars', in E. Hughes, M. Huhges, and A. Greenhill (eds), *Proceedings of the 21st Annual Boston University Conference on Language Development*. Somerville, MA: Cascadilla Press, 410–21.

MYERS, J., and GONG, S. (2002). 'Cross-morphemic predictability and the lexical access of compounds in Mandarin Chinese', *Folia Linguistica* 26: 65–96.

—— and LAI, Y. (2002). 'The auditory lexical access of monomorphemic compounds', paper presented at the Tenth International Conference on the Cognitive Processing of Chinese and Other Related Asian Languages, Taipei, December.

MYERS, J., and GONG, S. DERWING, B., and LIBBEN, G. (2004a). 'The effect of priming direction on reading Chinese compounds', *Mental Lexicon Working Papers* 1: 69–86.

—— LIBBEN, G., and DERWING, B. (2004b). 'The nature of transparency effects in Chinese compound processing', poster presented at the Fourth International Conference on the Mental Lexicon, Windsor, Canada, June.

NICOLADIS, E. (1999) '"Where is my brush-teeth?" Acquisition of compound nouns in a bilingual child', *Bilingualism: Language and Cognition* 2: 245–56.

—— (2002a) 'What's the difference between "toilet paper" and "paper toilet"? French–English bilingual children's crosslinguistic transfer in compound nouns', *Journal of Child Language* 29: 843–63.

—— (2002b) 'When is a preposition a linking element? Bilingual children's acquisition of French compound nouns', *Folia Linguistica* XXXVI: 45–63.

—— (2002c) 'The cues that children use in acquiring adjectival phrases and compound nouns: Evidence from bilingual children', *Brain and Language* 81: 635–48.

—— (2003a) 'What compound nouns mean to preschool children', *Brain and Language* 84: 38–49.

—— (2003b) 'Cross-linguistic transfer in deverbal compounds of preschool children', *Bilingualism: Language and Cognition* 6: 17–31.

—— (2003c) 'Compounding is not contingent on level-ordering in acquisition', *Cognitive Development* 18: 319–38.

—— (submitted) 'Children do not learn compound ordering from phrasal ordering: Acquisition of synthetic compounds by monolingual English- and French-speaking preschoolers'.

—— and MURPHY, V. A. (2002) 'Constraints on English compound production. What is the role of the input?', paper presented at the Third International Mental Lexicon Conference, Banff, Canada, October.

—— and —— (2004) 'Level-ordering does not constrain children's ungrammatical compounds', *Brain and Language* 90: 487–94.

NICOLADIS, E., and YIN, H. (2002) 'The role of frequency in acquisition of English and Chinese compounds by bilingual children', in *Proceedings of the Boston University Conference on Language Development*. Somerville, MA: Cascadilla Press, 441–52.

OLSEN, S. (2000) 'Composition', in G. Booij, C. Lehmann, and J. Mugdan (eds), *Morphology. An International Handbook on Inflection and Word Formation*. Berlin: Mouton de Gruyter, 897–915.

OLSEN, S. (2001) 'Copulative compounds: A closer look at the interface between syntax and morphology', in G. Booij and J. van Marle (eds), *Yearbook of Morphology 2000*. Dordrecht: Klewer, 279–320.

PACKARD, J. L. (1993) *A Linguistic Investigation of Aphasic Chinese Speech*. Dordrecht: Kluwer.

—— (1999) 'Lexical access in Chinese speech comprehension and production', *Brain and Language* 68: 89–94.

—— (2000) *The Morphology of Chinese: A Linguistic and Cognitive Approach*. Cambridge: Cambridge University Press.

PARADIS, J., and GENESEE, F. (1996) 'Syntactic acquisition in bilingual children: Autonomous or interdependent?', *Studies in Second Language Acquisition* 18: 1–25.

PENG, D., LIU, Y., and WANG, C. (1999) 'How is access representation organized? The relation of polymorphemic words and their morphemes in Chinese', in J. Wang, A. W. Inhoff, and H.-C. Chen (eds), *Reading Chinese Script: A Cognitive Analysis*. Mahwah, NJ: Lawrence Erlbaum Associates, 65–89.

PINKER, S. (1999) *Words and Rules: The Ingredients of Language*. New York: Basic Books.

PLAG, I. (2003) *Word-Formation in English*. Cambridge: Cambridge University Press.

POTTER, M. C. (1979). 'Mundane symbolism: The relations among objects, names, and ideas', In N. R. Smith and M. B. Franklin (eds), *Symbolic functioning in childhood*. Hillsdale, NJ. Erlbaum, 41–65.

——, SO, K.-F., VON ECKHARDT, B. and FELDMAN, L. B. (1984). 'Lexical and conceptual representation in beginning and more proficient bilinguals'. *Journal of Verbal Learning and Verbal Behavior* 8: 295–301.

RAINER, F. (1993). *Spanische Wortbildungslehre [Spanish Word Formation]*. Tübingen: Niemeyer.

—— and VARELA, S. (1992) 'Compounding in Spanish', *Rivista di Linguistica* 4: 117–42.

RALLI, A. (1992) 'Compounding in Modern Greek', *Rivista di Linguistica* 4: 143–174.

—— (2003) 'Prefixation vs. compounding', in G. Booij and J. van Marle (eds), *Yearbook of Morphology 2003*. Dordrecht: Klewer, 37–63.

RAVID, D., and AVIDOR, A. (1998) 'Acquisition of derived nominals in Hebrew: Developmental and linguistic principles', *Journal of Child Language* 25: 229–66.

REICHER, G. M. (1969) 'Perceptual recognition as a function of meaningfulness of stimulus material', *Journal of Experimental Psychology* 81: 275–80.

ROCHFORD, G., and WILLIAMS, M. (1965) 'Studies in the development and breakdown of the use of names. Part IV. The effect of word frequency', *Journal of Neurology, Neurosurgery and Psychiatry* 28: 407–13.

ROEPER, T., and SIEGEL, M. E. A. (1978) 'A lexical transformation for verbal compounds', *Linguistic Inquiry* 9: 199–260.

ROOD, D. S. (2002) 'Polysynthetic word formation: Wichita contributions to the morphology/syntax debate', in S. Bendjaballah, W. Dressler, O. Pfeiffer, and M. Vœikova (eds), *Morphology 2000*. Amsterdam: Benjamins, 293–304.

ROSCH, E., MERVIS, C., GRAY, W. D., JOHNSON, D. M., and BOYES-BRAEM, P. (1976) 'Basic objects in natural categories', *Cognitive Psychology*, 8: 382–439.

SADOCK, J. M. (1998) 'On the autonomy of compounding morphology', in S. G. Lapointe, D. K. Brentari, and P. M. Farrell (eds), *Morphology and its Relation to Phonology and Syntax*. Stanford, CA: Center for the Study of Language and Information, 161–87.

SANDRA, D. (1990) 'On the representation and processing of compound words: Automatic access to constituent morphemes does not occur', *The Quarterly Journal of Experimental Psychology* 42: 529–67.

SCALISE, S. (1992) 'Compounding in Italian', *Rivista di Linguistica* 4: 175–99.

SCHANER-WOLLES, C., RENNISON, J., and NEUBARTH, F. (eds.). (2001) *Naturally! Festschrift for W.U. Dressler*. Torino: Rosenberg and Sellier.

SCHREUDER, R., and BAAYEN, R. H. (1997) 'How complex simplex words can be', *Journal of Memory and Language* 37: 118–39.

—— NEIJT, A., VAN DER WEIDE, F., and BAAYEN, R. H. (1998) 'Regular plurals in Dutch compounds: Linking graphemes or morphemes?', *Language and Cognitive Processes* 13: 551–73.

SEIDENBERG, M. S., HASKELL, T., and MACDONALD, M. C. (1999) 'Constraints on plurals in compounds: Some implications of compounds research', *Abstracts of the Psychonomic Society: 40th annual meeting*, 81.

SEILER, H. (1975) 'Die Prinzipien der deskriptiven und der etikettierenden Benennung' [The principles of descriptive and labelling denotation], in E. Seiler (ed.), *Linguistic Workshop 3.* München: Fink, 2–57.

SELKIRK, E. O. (1982) *The Syntax of Words.* Cambridge, MA: MIT Press.

SEMENZA, C., BUTTERWORTH, B., PANZERI, M., and FERRERI, T. (1990) 'Word formation: New evidence from aphasia', *Neuropsychologia* 28: 499–502.

——BUTTERWORTH, B., PANZERI, M., and HITTMAIR-DELAZER, M. (1992) 'Derivational rules in aphasia', *Berkeley Linguistic Society 18,* Berkeley, CA, 435–40.

——, LUZZATTI, C., and CARABELLI, S. (1997) 'Morphological representation of nouns: A study on Italian aphasic patients', *Journal of Neurolinguistics* 10: 33–43.

SHAW, J. H. (1979) *Motivierte Komposita in der deutschen und englischen Gegenwartssprache* [*Motivated Compounds in Current German and English*]. Tübingen: Narr.

SHOBEN, E. J., CECH, C., and SCHWANENFLUGEL, P. (1983) 'The role of subtractions and comparisons in comparative judgments involving numerical reference points', *Journal of Experimental Psychology: Human Perception and Performance,* 9: 226–41.

SÖDERBERGH, R. (1979). 'Barnets språkliga kreativitet belyst av exempal från ordböjning och ordbilding' [The linguistics creativity of children: word-inflection and word-formation], *Språkform och Språknorm,* Svenska språknämnden, 67: 236–45.

SPENCER, A. (1991) *Morphological Theory.* Oxford: Blackwell.

SPRINGER, K., and MURPHY, G. L. (1992) 'Feature availability in conceptual combination', *Psychological Science* 3: 111–117.

SPROAT, R., and SHIH, C. (1996) 'A corpus-based analysis of Mandarin root compounds', *Journal of East Asian Linguistics* 5: 49–71.

STACHOWIAK, F. J. (1979) *Zur semantischen Struktur des Subjektiven Lexikons* [*On the Semantic Structure of the Individual's Lexicon*]. Wilhelm Fink, München.

STARK, J., and STARK, H. K. (1990) 'On the processing of compound nouns by a Wernicke's aphasic', *Grazer Linguistische Studien* 35: 95–113.

STAROSTA, S., KUIPER, K., NG, S., and WU, Z. (1998) 'On defining the Chinese compound word: Headedness in Chinese compounding and Chinese VR compounds', in J. L. Packard (ed.), *New Approaches to Chinese Word Formation.* Berlin: Mouton de Gruyter, 347–70.

STORMS, G., and WISNIEWSKI, E. J. (in press) 'Does the order of head noun and modifier explain response times in conceptual combination?', *Memory & Cognition*.

SU, Y.-C. (1998) 'The representation of compounds and phrases in the mental lexicon: Evidence from Chinese', *Web Journal of Modern Language Linguistics*, 1: (4). http://wjmll.ncl.ac.uk/issue04-05/su.htm.

TAFT, M. (2003) 'Morphological representation as a correlation between form and meaning', in E. Assink and D. Sandra (eds), *Reading Complex Words*. Amsterdam: Kluwer, 113–38.

—— (1997) 'Using masked priming to examine lexical storage of Chinese compound words', in H.-C. Chen (ed.), *Cognitive Processing of Chinese and Related Asian Languages*. Hong Kong: The Chinese University Press, 233–41.

—— and FORSTER, K. I. (1975) 'Lexical storage and retrieval of prefixed words', *Journal of Verbal Learning and Verbal Behavior* 14: 638–47.

—— (1976) 'Lexical storage and retrieval of polymorphemic and polysyllabic words', *Journal of Verbal Learning and Verbal Behavior* 15: 607–20.

—— and ZHU, X. (1995) 'The representation of bound morphemes in the lexicon: A Chinese study', in L. B. Feldman (ed.), *Morphological Aspects of Language Processing*. Hillsdale, NJ: Lawrence Erlbaum Associates, 293–316.

—— HUANG, J.-T., and ZHU, X. (1994) 'The influence of character frequency on word recognition responses in Chinese', in H.-W. Chang, J.-T. Huang, C.-W. Hue, and O. J. L. Tzeng (eds), *Advances in the Study of Chinese Language Processing, Vol. 1*. Taipei: Department of Psychology, National Taiwan University, 59–73.

—— LIU, Y., and ZHU, X. (1999) 'Morphemic processing in reading Chinese', in J. Wang, A. W. Inhoff, and H.-C. Chen (eds), *Reading Chinese Script: A Cognitive Analysis*. Mahwah, NJ: Lawrence Erlbaum Associates, 91–113.

TEES, R. C. and WERKER, J. F. (1984) 'Perceptual flexibility: Maintenance or recovery of the ability to discriminate non-native speech sounds', *Canadian Journal of Psychology*, 38: (4), 579–90.

TEN HACKEN, P. (1994) *Defining Morphology: A Principled Approach to Determining the Boundaries of Compounding, Derivation, and Inflection*. Hildesheim: Olms.

—— (2000) 'Derivation and compounding', in G. Booij, C. Lehmann, and J. Mugdan (eds), *Morphology. An International Handbook on Inflection and Word Formation*. Berlin: de Gruyter, 349–59.

TSAI, C.-H. (1994) 'Effects of semantic transparency on the recognition of Chinese two-character words: Evidence for a dual-process model', unpublished master's thesis, National Chung Cheng University, Chia-Yi, Taiwan.

—— MCCONKIE, G. W., and ZHENG, X. (1998) 'Lexical parsing by Chinese readers', poster presented at the Advanced Study Institute on Advances in Theoretical Issues and Cognitive Neuroscience Research of the Chinese Language, University of Hong Kong.

TSAI, P. (1998) 'Auditory access of disyllabic words in the Chinese mental lexicon', unpublished master's thesis, National Chung Cheng University, Chia-Yi, Taiwan.

TSAY, J., MYERS, J., and CHEN, X.-J. (1999) 'Tone Sandhi as evidence for segmentation in Taiwanese', in E. V. Clark (ed.), *Proceedings of the Thirtieth Annual Child Language Research Forum*. Stanford, CA: Center for the Study of Language and Information, 211–18.

TSENG, C.-H., HUANG, K.-Y., and JENG, J.-Y. (1996) 'The role of the syllable in perceiving spoken chinese', *Proceedings of the National Science Council, Part C: Humanities and Social Sciences* 6: 71–86.

TURCO, S. (2000) '*Determination de la Frequence des Relations thematiques des Concepts constituant d'une Combinaison conceptuelle*' [Determination of the frequency of thematic relations of constituent concepts of a conceptual combination]. Unpublished manuscript.

TYLER, L. K., BEHRENS, S., COBB, H. and MARSLEN-WILSON, W. (1990) 'Processing distinctions between stems and affixes: Evidence from a non-fluent aphasic patient', *Cognition*, 36: 129–53.

TZELGOV, J., HENIK, A., and LEISER, D. (1990) 'Controlling Stroop interference: Evidence from a bilingual task', *Journal of Experimental Psychology: Learning, Memory and Cognition* 16: 760–71.

UNSWORTH, S. (2000) 'Testing Hulk and Muller (2000) on crosslinguistic influence: Root infinitives in a bilingual German/English child', *Bilingualism: Language and Cognition*, 2003: 6,(2), 143–58.

VAN JAARSVELD, H. J. and RATTINK, G. E. (1988) 'Frequency effects in the processing of lexicalized and novel compounds', *Journal of Psycholinguistic Research* 17: 447–73.

VAN MARLE, J. (1985) *On the Paradigmatic Dimension of Morphological Creativity*. Dordrecht: Foris.
WANG, W. and MYERS, J. (2004) 'The processing of affixation and compounding in Chinese', paper presented at Fourth International Conference on the Mental Lexicon, Windsor, Canada, June.
WARREN, B. (1978) *Semantic Patterns of Noun-Noun Compounds*. Goteborg: Acta Universitatis Gothoburgensis.
WEINREICH, U. (1953) *Languages in contact: Findings and problems*. New York: Humanities Press.
WILDGEN, W. (1987) 'Dynamic aspects of nominal composition', in T. Ballmer and W. Wildgen (eds), *Process Linguistics*. Tübingen: Niemeyer, 128–62.
WILLIAMS, E. (1981) 'Argument structure and morphology', *Linguistic Review* 1: 81–114.
WISNIEWSKI, E. J. (1996) 'Construal and similarity in conceptual combination', *Journal of Memory and Language* 35: 434–53.
WOLFF, S. (1984) *Lexical Entries and Word Formation*. Bloomington: Indiana University Linguistics Club.
WONG, K. F. E., and CHEN, H.-C. (2002) 'Morphemic ambiguity resolution in reading Chinese two character words: An eye-monitoring study', paper presented at the Tenth International Conference on the Cognitive Processing of Chinese and Other Related Asian Languages, Taipei, December.
WUNDERLICH, D. (1986) 'Probleme der Wortstruktur' [Problems of Word Structure], *Zeitschrift für Sprachwissenschaft* 5: 209–52.
WURZEL, W. U. (1998) 'On the development of incorporating structures in German', in R. Hogg and L. van Bergen (eds), *Historical Linguistics 2*. Amsterdam: John Benjamins, 331–44.
XUE, N. (2001) 'Defining and automatically identifying words in Chinese'. Unpublished doctoral thesis, University of Delaware, Newark, DE.
YIN, H., DERWING, B. L., and LIBBEN, G. (2004) 'Branching preferences for large lexical structures in Chinese', poster presented at the Fourth International Conference on the Mental Lexicon, Windsor, Canada, June.
ZHANG, B. (1997) 'Zhongwen shuangzici zai xinli cidian zhong de chucun moshi' [Storage model of Chinese two-character words in the mental lexicon], in R. Peng, H. Shu, and H. Chen (eds), *Hanyu renzhi yanjiu* [Chinese Cognitive Research]. Jinan, China: Shandong Jiaoyu Publishers, 217–30.

ZHANG, B. and PENG, D. (1992) 'Decomposed storage in the Chinese lexicon', in H.-C. Chen and O. J. L. Tzeng (eds), *Language Processing in Chinese*. Amsterdam: North-Holland, 131–49.

ZHOU, X. (1995) 'Morphological structure in the Chinese mental lexicon', *Language and Cognitive Processes* 10: 545–600.

—— (2000) 'Lexical representation of compound words: Cross-linguistic evidence', *Psychologia* 43: 47–66.

—— and MARSLEN-WILSON, W. (1994) 'Words, morphemes, and syllables in the Chinese mental lexicon', *Language and Cognitive Processes* 9: 393–422.

—— MARSLEN-WILSON, W., TAFT, M., and SHU, H. (1999) 'Morphology, orthography, and phonology in reading Chinese compound words', *Language and Cognitive Processes* 14: 525–65.

——, OSTRIN, R. K., and TYLER, L. K. (1993) 'The noun-verb problem and Chinese aphasia: Comments on bates et al. (1991)', *Brain and Language* 45: 86–93.

——, ZHUANG, J., and YU, M. (2002) 'Phonological activation of disyllabic compound words in the speech production of Chinese'. *Acta Psychologica Sinica* 34:(3), 242–7.

ZWANENBURG, W. (1992a) 'Compounding in French', *Rivista di Linguistica* 4: 221–40.

—— (1992b) 'La composition dans les langues romanes et germaniques: essuie-glace/wind-shield wiper' [Compounding in romance and germanic languages: wind-shield wiper/essuie-glace], *OTS Working Papers* OTS-WP-TL-92–103.

ZWITSERLOOD, P. (1994) 'The role of semantic transparency in the processing and representation of Dutch compounds', *Language and Cognitive Processes* 9: 341–68.

Index

Figures and notes are indexed as **f** and **n**.

Ackema, P. 29
Ahrens, R. 53, 54, 72, 73
Albert, M. L. 126, 143
Alegre, M. A. 99, 117
Anderson, S. R. 24, 173
Andree, B. 53, 73, 75, 78, 79, 80, 94
Andrews, S. 137, 146, 195, 195
Aronoff, M. 25
Avidor, A. 114

Baayen, R. H. 15, 19, 30, 40, 52, 58, 66, 67, 141, 179, 192
Badecker, W. 53, 76, 81, 82, 84, 85, 94
Baker, M. 35, 108
Barron, B. J. S. 111, 112, 114, 115, 123
Bates, E. 172, 188, 189
Bauer, L. 25, 28, 29, 30, 36, 40
Beauvillain, C. 140
Becker, T. 42, 112, 113, 120
Behrens, S. 142
Benke, T. 53, 73, 75, 78, 79, 80, 94
Berman, R. A. 43, 58, 96, 99, 100, 102, 103, 105, 107, 108, 110, 114, 115, 117, 119, 120, 121, 124, 146
Bialystok, E. 143
Bickerton, D. 2
Bisetto, A. 26, 28, 39
Blanken, G. 53, 72, 73, 76, 81, 83, 84, 94, 95, 137

Blekher, M. 130
Bloomer, R. K. 31
Bloomfield, L. 172
Bock, K. 127
Booij, G. 26, 27, 28, 29, 36, 38, 39, 42
Borer, H. 136
Boyes-Braem, P. 154
Brekle, H. 37, 40
Brones, I. 127
Buchanan, L. 14, 86
Burani, C. 59, 88, 89
Busson, C. 56, 132, 135, 182
Butterworth, B. 77, 147

Caplan, D. 77
Carabelli, S. 53, 75, 76, 80, 188
Caramazza, A. 85, 127, 137
Cech, C. 158
Chang, L.-P. 172
Chao, Y.-R. 171, 14
Chen, H.-C. 128, 191
Chen, J.-Y. 176, 194
Chen, K.-J. 172
Chen, S. 172, 188, 189
Chen, S.-C. 186
Chen, S.-T. 182, 183
Chen, T.-M. 194
Chen, X.-J. 194
Cheng, C.-M. 176
Chomsky, N. 4

Chumbley, J. 158
Clahsen, H. 31, 60, 61, 116, 117, 138
Clark, E. V. 43, 58, 96, 98, 99, 100,
    101, 103, 104, 105, 107, 108,
    110, 111, 112, 113, 114, 115, 117,
    119, 120, 121, 122, 123, 124, 146
Cobb, H. 142
Colangelo, A. 14
Coolen, R. 49
Coppola, K. 61
Corbett, G. G. 35
Coseriu, E. 36
Cox, A. 126, 127
Curley, I. F. 128

Dai, J. X.-L. 173
Dalalakis, J. E. 59
de Almeida, R. G. 14, 49, 137, 139,
    167
de Bleser, R. 53, 59, 73, 75, 78, 79, 80,
    87, 88, 89, 90, 94, 136
de Bot, K. 126, 127
de Groot, A. M. B. 126, 127, 128,
    129, 135, 143
de Jong, N. H. 15, 52, 58, 141
de Knop, S. 41
Delazer, M. 53, 76, 79, 81, 82, 84,
    85, 95
Dell, G. S. 127
Denes, G. 73, 74
Derwing, B. L. 49, 137,
    139, 167, 176, 182, 183, 192,
    193
Di Sciullo, A. M. 33
Dijkstra, T. 126, 128, 129, 135
Downing, P. 104, 148, 151
Dressler, W. U. 2, 8, 15, 24, 26, 30, 31,
    38, 42, 45, 50, 52, 57, 62, 64,
    66, 73, 74, 92, 97, 129, 131, 135,
    136, 137, 145, 160, 172, 192
Duanmu, S. 172

Estes, Z. 50

Fabb, N. 24, 97, 142
Fabbro, F. 142
Fanselow, G. 36, 37, 38
Feldman, L. B. 52, 58,
    127, 141, 186
Ferreri, T. 77
Forster, K. I. 20, 48, 177
Frazier, L. 142, 192
Friederici, A. D. 142
Fromkin, V. 172
Fuhrhop, N. 29, 30, 39, 42

Gagné, C. L. 50, 149, 150, 151, 152,
    153, 154, 155, 157, 158, 159, 160,
    165, 166, 190
Gagnon, D. A. 127
Garrett, M. F. 77, 127
Gather, A. 38
Gelman, S. A. 58, 59, 99, 101, 104,
    107, 110, 111, 119, 121, 152
Gibson, M. 47, 132, 135, 147, 192
Gleitman, H. 151
Gleitman, L. R. 151
Glucksberg, S. 50
Gollan, T. 128
Gong, S. 180, 186
Gordon, P. 61, 99, 111, 116, 117, 118,
    124, 138
Gottfried, G. M. 105, 106, 121
Grainger, J. 140
Gray, W. D. 154
Griffin, Z. M. 127

Haider, H. 33
Hakuta, K. 143
Harris, R. J. 126
Haskell, T. 116, 117, 118
Hecht, B. F. 108, 111, 112, 119, 120, 123
Henik, A. 128
Hiratmatsu, K., 121
Hittmair-Delazer, M. 53, 73, 75, 78, 79, 80, 94
Ho, C.-Y. 175, 176
Ho, K.-C. 128, 170
Hoeks, J. C. J. 128
Hollander, M. 61
Holyoak, K. 158
Hoosain, R. 172
Hsiao, H.-C. S. 179, 192
Hsieh, M.-L. 194
Hsu, H.-L. 172
Hsu, J. C.-F. 191
Huang, C.-R. 172
Huang, K.-Y. 174
Huang, J.-T. 177, 178, 179, 182, 190, 191
Hung, D. L. 175, 176, 189, 191
Hyltenstam, K. 143

Iacobini, C. 25, 29

Jackendoff, R. 2
Jarema, G. 6, 12, 15, 51, 54, 56, 59, 63, 64, 67, 89, 131, 132, 135, 182, 192
Jeng, Y.-J. 174
Jensen, J. T. 38
Ji, H. 190
Johnson, D. M. 154

Kadzielawa, D. 51, 54, 63, 64, 131, 135
Kay, P. 151
Kehayia, E. 51, 54, 63, 64, 131, 135
Kellar, L. 77
Kiefer, F. 30
Kim, J. J. 61
Kiparsky, P. 61
Krashen, S. 129
Kroll, J. F. 126, 128, 129, 143
Krott, A. 35, 66, 113, 192
Kudo, T. 50
Kuiper, K. 173

Lai, Y. 181, 186
Laine, M. 54, 55
Landányi, M. 30, 31
Lane, N. M. 99, 101, 104, 107, 110, 111, 119, 121
Lardiere, D. 99, 117, 138
Laudanna, A. 88, 137
Lee, C. Y. 182, 187
Leiser, D. 128
Leopold, W. F. 136, 137
Leung, Y.-S. 128
Levelt, J. M. 82, 84, 126, 127
Levi, J. N. 36, 38, 151, 156
Li, C. N. 172
Li, P. 172, 182
Liang, M. Y. 182
Libben, G. 13, 14, 18, 21, 41, 42, 45, 47, 48, 49, 52, 53, 56, 57, 64, 67, 82, 85, 86, 121, 124, 131, 132, 135, 137, 139, 147, 163, 166, 167, 176, 182, 183, 192, 192, 193
Lieber, R. 24, 27, 35, 36, 37, 39, 98
Liu, I.-M. 176
Liu, Y. 169, 182, 184, 185

Lock, J. 77
Lü, C.-C. 179, 180, 181 [Lü]
Lupker, S. J. 135
Luzzati, C. 53, 59, 75, 80, 87, 88, 89, 90, 136, 188

MacDonald, M. C. 116
MacWhinney, B. 172
Mäkisalo, J. 54, 55, 136, 139
Marcus, G. F. 60, 61, 138
MarkmanE. M. 152
Marslen-Wilson, W. 50, 137, 142, 171, 178, 180, 183, 186, 187, 195
Martin, N. 127
Matthews, G. 146
Matthews, P. H. 39
Mattingly, I. G. 175, 179, 181
Mayer, A. 81, 85
McEwen, S. 86
Medin, D. L. 149, 151
Mel'cuk, I. 24, 39 [hachek]
Mellenius, I. 99, 115, 118
Menn, L. 142
Merlini Barbaresi, L. 42
Mervis, C. 154
Meyer, R. 36, 40
Miceli, G. 137, 142
Miller, D. 146
Mithun, M. 35
Monsell, S. 146
Mondini, S. 80, 88, 89
Motsch, W. 38
Moyna, M. I. 28
Mulford, R. C. 111, 112, 119, 120, 123 check
Müller, N. 111
Murphy, G. L. 149, 150, 151, 153, 154, 161

Murphy, V. A. 113, 117, 118, 137, 149
Myers, J. 180, 181, 182, 183, 186, 192, 193, 194, 195

Nas, G. 127
Neijt, A. 65
Ng, S. 173
Nicoladis, E. 66, 99, 101, 102, 104, 105, 106, 107, 108, 110, 111, 113, 115, 117, 118, 120, 121, 123, 125, 134, 135, 137, 142
Niemi, J. 54, 55
Nikolova, R. 56, 132, 135, 182

Obler, L. K. 126, 142, 143
Older, L. 187, 195
Olsen, S. 24, 30, 34
Opie, M. 172, 188
Ostrin, R. K. 185, 188

Packard, J. L. 172, 173, 174, 178, 186, 194
Panzeri, M. 75, 77
Pastizzo, M. 52, 58, 141
Peng, D. 182, 184, 185, 189, 190, 191
Perlak, D. 51, 54, 63, 64, 131, 135
Pinker, S. 4, 61
Pistarini, C. 80
Pons, J. C. 64
Potter, M. C. 127

Rainer, R. 24, 25, 28, 32, 33, 38, 39
Ralli, A. 29, 42, 51, 54, 63, 64, 131, 135
Ralston, S. 126, 127
Rattink, G. E. 137
Ravid, D. 114
Reicher, G. M. 176
Rochford, G. 53, 73

Rodman, R. 172
Roelofs, A. 82, 84
Roeper, T. 98n, 110, 121
Rood, D. S. 35
Rosch, E. 154
Rothweiler, M. 60, 61, 138

Saccoman, M. 110, 121 check
Saffran, E. M. 127
Sandra, D. 13, 47, 48, 131, 132, 135, 146, 147, 192
Scalise, S. 26, 28, 32, 34, 39
Schaufeli, A. 126, 127
Schreuder, R. 15, 30, 40, 49, 52, 58, 65, 66, 126, 141, 179
Schriefers, H. 135
Schwanenflugel, P. 158
Schwartz, M. F. 127
Seidenberg, M. S. 116
Seiler, H. 42
Selkirk, E. O. 97, 98n, 100, 116, 120, 124
Semenza, C. 26n, 28, 32, 42, 53, 59, 73, 75, 76, 77, 78, 79, 80, 81, 82, 84, 85, 87, 88, 89, 188
Shanon, B. 127
Shaw, J. H. 41
Shih, C. 173
Shoben, E. J. 50, 149, 150, 151, 152, 153, 155, 157, 158, 159, 160
Sholl, A. 128
Shu, H. 186
Siegel, M.E.A. 98
Silveri, M. C. 137
Snodgrass, J. G. 127
Snyder, W. 110, 121 check
So, K.-F. 127
Spalding, T. L. 154, 165, 166

Spencer, A. 28
Springer, K. 149, 154
Sproat, R. 173
Stachowiak, F. J. 73
Stark, H. K. 55, 74, 75
Stark, J. 55, 64, 74, 75
Starosta, S. 173
Stewart, E. 129, 130
Storms, G. 159
Storrs, S. 110, 121 check
Su, Y.-C. 182

Taft, M. 20, 48, 169, 170, 171, 175, 177, 178, 179, 180, 182, 184, 185, 190
Tees, R. C. 143
Ten Hacken, P. 24, 26, 30
Thompson, S. A. 172
Timmermans, M. 135
Tsai, C.-H. 172, 179, 181, 182, 187
Tsapkini, K. 51, 54, 56, 63, 64, 131, 132, 135, 182
Tsay, J. 194
Tse, D. L. 189
Tseng, C.-H. 174
Turco, S. 159
Tyler, L. K. 142, 185, 187, 188, 195
Tzelgov, J. 128
Tzeng, O. J. L. 172, 175, 176, 188, 189, 191

Ullman, M. 60
Unsworth, S. 142

van der Weide, F. 65
van Jaarsveld, H. J. 39, 49, 137
van Marle, J. 30
Varela, S. 38

von Eckhardt, B. 127
Waksler, R. 187, 195
Wang, C. 182, 184
Wang, W. 195
Warren, B. 151
Weinreich, U. 126, 143
Weltens, B. 126, 127
Werker, J. F. 143
Westbury, C. 86
Wilcox, S. A. 58, 59
Wildgen, W. 37
Williams, E. 32, 33
Williams, M. 53, 72
Wisniewski, E. J. 150, 159, 161
Woest, A. 60, 61, 137
Wolff, S. 28, 40
Wong, K. F. E. 191
Wu, Z. 173
Wunderlich, D. 34
Wurzel, W. U 29, 35

Xu, Y. 176

Yin, H. 102, 123, 176, 192
Yoon, Y. 48, 132, 135, 147, 192

Zhang, B. 173, 174, 189, 190, 191
Zheng, X. 172
Zhou, X. 50, 137, 169, 171, 177, 178, 180, 183, 185, 186, 187, 188, 194
Zhu, X. 169, 177, 178, 179, 180, 182, 184, 190
Xu, Y. 191
Xue, N 172
Zwanenburg, W. 28, 32
Zwitserlood, P. 13, 47, 48, 146, 147, 166
Zimmer, K. 151
Zonca, G. 80

Subject Index

abstract words 128
    Chinese 171
accentedness rating 141
accessibility 67, 69
acoustic duration 181
acoustical analysis 141
acquisition *see* language acquisition
activation 9–10, 12, 152, 165, 166, 177, 185;
    see also compounds, components; constituents, activation
    constituents 14, 135
    morphemes 186, 190
    patterns 12–13
    semantics 14, 183
    word 179, 181–182
adjectival compounds 35, 44, 121
adjective-adjective compounds 32, 145
adjective-noun compounds 32, 56, 59–60, 89, 111, 124;
    see also under other compounds
adjective-verb compounds 32
adjectives 25, 29, 33, 34, 65, 90–91, 111, 121;
    see also relational adjectives
adverbs 136
affixation 142, 194–195
    Chinese 169, 172
    derivational 2, 42, 172
    inflection 172
    internal 90
    words 174
affixes 4, 18, 20, 28, 60, 90, 102, 112, 119
agents 108, 111, 113
agrammatism 59, 88, 89, 91, 93, 94
agreement markers 43, 65
ambiguous compounds 49, 139, 155
analogical processes 63, 64, 66
anaphoric islands 26
Ancient Greek 42
anomics 50, 72, 73, 76, 81, 82
aphasia 14, 50, 53, 75–76, 85, 141–142, 175, 188
aphasics 62, 69, 70, 72, 73, 75, 77, 78, 80, 83, 130, 141–142, 163, 189
    Chinese 194
    performance 18, 50, 59, 85
aphasiology 72–75, 81, 85, 127, 169
    evidence 52–54, 69, 75, 163, 188–189
automatic progressive parsing and lexical excitation (APPLE) 48, 85, 86, 121
appositional compounds 34
Arabic 140
atoms 26, 43, 90–91

base constituents 31, 38, 39, 44, 46, 59
bilingual memory stores *see* lexical memory stores
bilinguals 43, 67, 125–144
    activation 135

bilinguals (cont.):
  adults 133
  brains 142, 144
  children 66, 101–102, 105, 110, 111, 113, 117, 118, 121, 134, 135
  lexicon 126–128, 129–130, 133, 138, 140–141, 143
  processing 134
  speakers 137
  studies 135
binary compounds 35, 39, 44; see also coordinate compounds; subordinate compounds
binding words 174, 178–181; see also nonbinding words
brain imaging 142
British English 113, 117
Broca's aphasia 50, 53, 72, 73, 74, 76, 78, 80, 88, 188, 189
bound morphemes 77; see also morphemes
Bulgarian 56, 57, 67, 68, 132, 182

Canadian English 113, 117
CARIN see Competition-Among-Relations-in-Nominals (CARIN)
characters 170, 171, 174, 175–176, 177, 179, 180, 181–182, 183, 184, 185, 186–187, 189–194
  bound 179–180
  frequency 178–179, 180–183, 186, 189
child language 3, 58
Chinese 19, 51, 54, 67, 68, 102, 140, 196t; see also Mandarin Chinese; Pinyin
  compounds 169–196
  morphemes 169–194
clitics 24, 68
closed-class vocabulary 77
cognates 140–141; see also noncognates
  compounds 40
  status 128–129
cognitive processing 12, 67, 70
cohort competition 178
cohort size 180, 181
Competition-Among-Relations-in-Nominals (CARIN) 150–153, 155–162, 168
  lexicalized compounds 162–167
complex words 80, 84–85, 174; see also monomorphemic words; words
componentiality 45; see also endocentric compounds; exocentric compounds; noncomponential words
composition 23, 81, 131
  on-line 133, 135
  processes 79–81
compositionality 40
compound-internal variables 138
compounding 145
  nominal 148, 151
compounds 5, 6, 8, 10, 11, 15, 24, 29, 124, 129, 131, 135, 173
  classification 31–35
  components 95, 177, 191–192, 194
    activation 185, 188, 190
  constituents, activation 14
  form 58–59
  neologisms 79, 82, 85
  ordering 110–114, 124

representation 45–70
recognition 141
retrieval 57, 84
status 77, 138
structure 62, 75, 77–79, 125, 130
   meaning of 10–16
   words 5, 11, 75, 120–121, 126, 146, 147, 149, 155, 160, 163, 166, 168
      mental lexicon 6f, 9;
      status 75–77
comprehension 16, 58, 74, 101, 103, 104, 113, 114–116, 122, 130, 155, 160, 161
   children's 105
computation 3–6, 6f, 7–10, 19, 21, 22; see also storage
concatenation 64, 68
conceptual combination 145, 148–149, 152, 167–168
   theories 149–154, 155–162
conceptual levels 147, 148
conceptual representation see representation, conceptual
conceptual system 53, 82, 84, 85, 86, 88, 126–128, 149, 151, 166
concrete words 128
concreteness 128–129
connectionist modeling 4, 13
constituent activation 47–57, 51, 52, 69, 135
constituent morphemes 3, 5, 6, 8, 9, 10, 11, 12
constituent representations 10, 10f, 11
constituent transparency 57
constituents 2, 6f, 7, 13f, 14–17, 18, 21, 45, 46, 47, 48, 49, 50,
51–53, 54, 55, 58, 62, 63, 64, 65, 66, 69, 88, 94, 96, 125, 132, 137, 143, 146, 149, 151, 152, 154, 162, 163, 167;
see also whole-words
activation 9, 13, 14
first 135
identification 129, 141
meaning 11, 16
mental lexicon 13, 86, 148
morphological 81
movement 90–91
ordered 134
syntactic 29, 135
transparency 86, 131, 132
   semantic 131
words 3
constructional idioms 27–28
constructional phrases see idiomatic phrases
conventionality 119, 120
coordinate compounds 34, 35, 44;
see also binary compounds;
subordinate compounds
coordinative compounds 189–190
count nouns 127; see also nouns
cross-language differences 127, 136,
perspectives 45–70
priming 129, 140
cross-linguistic differences 124, 125, 138, 194
compound variations 125, 131, 136
differences 100
investigations 23, 24, 46, 51, 54, 57, 67, 69, 70, 114
patterns 142
priming 141

Subject Index

decomposition 8, 11, 46,
  47–48, 50, 51–52, 121, 131, 132,
  133, 147, 162–163, 164–165,
  167, 174;
  see also morphological
  decomposition
deep dyslexia 54, 86, 88
derivation 23, 24, 38, 59, 77, 78,
  124
derivatives 28, 29, 39
derived nouns 88; see also nouns
derived words 45, 88
descriptiveness 42, 72, 73
deverbal compounds 108–110,
  123, 135
discrete compounds 30
distributional effects 51–52, 66, 68,
  69, 177, 181, 194
disyllables 50–51, 171, 174, 180
Dutch 19, 29, 29, 38, 42, 47, 48, 49,
  51, 52, 54, 65, 66, 67, 68,
  127, 192
dysphasic children 60

endocentric compounds 33–34, 44,
  61, 90, 173
errors 73–74, 75, 76–77, 78, 79,
  81, 82, 83, 84, 107, 110,
  114, 129, 130, 137, 138,
  188, 189
etymology 140–141, 143
exocentric compounds 33–34, 36,
  37, 44, 61, 87, 90, 173

facilitation 132, 177–178, 184, 186,
  187–188
familiar compounds 163, 165, 167,
  168

family size 178–179, 180; see also
  morphological family
Finnish 54, 55, 56, 67, 68, 136, 139–
  140
first constituents 56–57, 60–61, 64,
  65, 138, 160, 165–166
  see also second constituents
French 8, 17, 28, 35, 40, 55, 56,
  66–67, 68, 99, 101, 102, 105,
  109, 110, 111, 113, 117, 118, 121,
  123, 125, 132, 133, 134, 135, 136,
  137, 139–140, 141, 159, 182
frequency 30, 32, 50, 52, 53,
  72–73, 82, 83, 100, 101–103,
  113, 122, 122t, 123, 124, 131,
  133, 136, 137, 153, 155, 156, 178,
  182, 194;
  see also character, frequency;
  word, frequency
of relations 152–153
Friulian-Italian 142

gender:
  agreement 33, 34, 59–60, 84
  assignment 87–89
  grammatical 127
  marker 91
German 8, 19, 20, 24, 26, 27, 28, 29,
  34, 35, 36, 37, 38, 39, 41, 42,
  46, 53–54, 55, 56, 57, 60, 62,
  64, 67, 68, 72, 73, 74, 75, 77,
  78, 79, 80, 83–84, 116, 117,
  136, 137, 138, 192
Germanic languages 50, 65, 68, 99
grammaticalization 2, 28, 29
grapheme-phoneme
  correspondences 140
graphemes, changes in 141

Subject Index

Greek 23, 46, 51, 54, 55, 56, 59, 62, 63, 64, 67, 68, 135

Hanyu Pinyin 170
head 15, 17, 28, 31–35, 36, 37, 40–41, 50, 56, 58, 61, 80, 83, 87, 104, 107, 110, 112, 116, 132, 190–191;
see also non-head
morphological 16, 17, 34, 56, 69, 131
nouns 27, 49–50, 58, 104–105, 107, 146, 149, 150, 152, 155–156, 157, 158, 159, 160, 161–162, 166–167
syntactic 84, 90
verbs 26
headedness 17–18, 19, 31–32, 44, 69
Chinese 189
effects 48, 55–57
Hebrew 38, 55, 58, 59, 62, 67, 68, 99, 102–103, 105, 107, 108, 110, 114–115, 117, 122, 123, 134, 136, 141
script 140
hierarchical morphological structure 18, 19;
see also morphological structure; structure
homographs 65
homophones 51, 170, 185
priming 187–188
homophony 63, 194
Chinese 170, 174, 185, 186
morphemes 51
horse-race models 9
hyphenation 141

impaired population 55, 62, 69, 84, 88
incorporating compounds 35, 44
Indonesian 159
infinitives 78, 79
inflection 4, 23, 27, 31, 32, 33, 38, 45, 59, 60, 62, 63, 65, 68, 77, 77, 87, 88, 89, 90–91, 101, 116–118, 124
instruments 108, 111, 113
interdependence of languages 126
interfixes 29, 39, 42–43, 44, 46, 62–63, 64, 66, 67, 69, 84, 101, 118
isolating languages 171
Italian 18, 27, 28, 30, 32, 33, 53–54, 57, 59, 62, 67, 68, 74, 75–76, 77, 80, 87, 89–91, 136, 140, 142, 188, 189

Japanese 67, 68
juxtapositions 27, 28, 29, 104

kanji compounds 50
Korean 68

L2–learners 100–108, 111, 117, 118, 128–130, 133–134, 136, 138, 139–140, 142, 144
labeling 58–59, 73, 77, 146
language acquisition 4, 60, 114–116, 136–137, 138, 143, 144
by children 58–59, 61–62, 69, 96–114, 117, 119–124
history 2, 143
morphological 116
of compounds 100, 119–122, 122t, 123
processing 15, 22, 143

language-specific properties 129, 169
Latin 23, 42
left-branching compounds 44, 50;
see also right-branching compounds
left-headed compounds 17, 19, 32, 33, 34, 35, 43, 56, 59–60, 88, 90, 105, 111, 130, 134, 135;
see also head; headedness; right-headed compounds
lemmas 85, 126–128, 130, 133, 144
level-ordering 116, 117–118
lexemes 24, 126–128, 144
lexical access 47, 54, 68, 84–85, 92, 183, 187, 194
Chinese 194
lexical decision 15, 50, 52, 64, 88, 141, 177, 180, 182, 186
auditory 186
experiments 178, 185, 187, 189, 190
tasks 47, 47n, 48, 51, 56, 129, 135, 165, 175, 177, 181, 182–183, 187, 189, 192
lexical entries 10, 80, 133, 147
lexical gaps 120
lexical items 2, 24, 52, 55, 59, 64, 67, 79, 81, 85, 109, 125, 129, 130, 133, 125, 166, 176;
see also monomorphemic lexical items
lexical levels 126, 127–128, 147, 148
lexical memory stores 126
lexical processing 4, 7, 9–10, 11, 12, 13, 14–15, 21, 22, 50, 68, 79, 82, 143, 144

lexical representations 5, 17–18, 68, 147, 178
bilingual 128–129
lexical structures 101, 114, 123
lexical status 57–58, 176, 177
lexical units 25, 46, 57, 69, 82, 175
lexicalization 40, 43, 136, 140, 145
compounds 117, 124, 150, 155, 165, 168;
see also Competition-Among-Relations-in-Nominals (CARIN), lexicalized compounds
lexicon 40, 48, 60, 128, 133, 145, 148, 166
bilingual 125
linking elements see interfixes
literal compounds 106–107
loan words 30–31
locatives 37
interpretation 157
relations 152, 155
logographics 68
loose compounds 27–28

Mandarin Chinese 50–51, 101–102, 170, 187–188, 194
compounds 178, 180
markers:
overt 141
plurals 61
maximization of opportunity system 6, 9, 12, 14
meaning 126, 140, 154, 155, 163–164, 170, 174, 187, 192
lexicalized 163
of compounds 146, 173

memory stores *see* lexical memory stores
mental architecture 12, 21
mental lexicon 4, 6, 6f, 7, 9, 10, 13, 15, 16–17, 21–22, 45, 46, 60, 67, 68, 70, 86, 131, 145, 146, 148, 163, 165, 166, 167, 168
  models 126
metaphoric compounds 106–107
misordering 81, 130
modalities 143, 144, 183–184, 187, 194
models (of mental lexicon) 126, 128, 144
Modern Greek 42
modifier-noun compounds 107, 148, 149, 151–152, 158, 161, 173, 189, 190, 191
modifiers 17, 27, 37, 39, 50, 58, 90, 104, 107, 121, 145, 149, 150, 152, 153, 154, 155–156, 157–160, 161–162, 163, 165–167, 191
  relations:
    frequency 159–160;
    pairing 161
  relational distribution 152, 153, 157, 167
monolinguals 129, 131, 133, 136, 137
  children 101, 105, 110–111, 113, 117, 123, 135
  studies 67, 68, 69
monomorphemic compounds 173, 174
monomorphemic representation 6–7, 17
monomorphemic sentences 3–10
monomorphemic words 3–10, 52, 58, 76–77, 81, 82, 84, 125–126, 134, 136, 141, 171, 173, 192; *see also* complex words; words
nonbinding 186
morphemes 2, 4, 6, 8, 9,13f, 14, 15, 17, 18, 19, 20, 21, 45, 52, 60, 62, 63, 64, 65, 66, 72, 79, 85, 91, 99, 125, 135, 139, 140–141, 142, 171, 173–174, 178, 179, 183, 184, 185, 186–187, 189, 190, 191, 194;
  see also Chinese, morphemes; constituent morphemes; homophonic morphemes
  activation 178, 187
  bound 77, 172, 173, 176, 172, 173, 176
  frequency 50, 177, 178, 195
  meaning 10, 11, 12, 86
  priming 184, 185, 186–187
  recall 49
  root 12
  transparent 172
morphological complexity 102, 141
morphological decomposition 5, 6, 13, 132
morphological family 15, 51–52
morphological headedness 16, 17, 34, 131–134, 135, 143
morphological parsing 9, 14, 20–21, 22, 88;
  see also parsing; phonological parsing
morphological processing 2, 3, 9, 65, 90, 126, 131, 139, 142, 193–195
  Chinese 176–177, 184
morphological productivity 30, 81

morphological representations 14, 21
morphological structures 6–7, 14, 16–20, 22, 45, 46, 52, 53, 76, 81, 130, 191
morphology 3, 14–15, 18, 28, 58, 62, 79, 99, 103, 108, 115, 140, 142, 170–171, 177, 178, 186, 188
  Chinese 169, 172, 174–175
  constituents 81
  constraints 62, 143
  derivational 59, 114
  distinctions 100
  forms 103, 114
  representation 3
  studies 183
  word-based 173
morphosemantic transparency 40–41, 44
morphotactic transparency 42–43, 44; see also transparency
Multi-Level Cluster Representation Model 51
multilexical units 27–28
multimorphemic strings 10, 16, 131
multimorphemic words 1, 2, 4, 10, 16, 18, 45, 46, 47, 62, 125, 131

neo-classical compounds 25, 28, 39
neologisms 75, 78, 79, 82, 83
  compound 76
neologistic compounds 54–55
neurolinguistics 17, 43, 46, 53–54, 55, 60, 141–142
neuropsychology 70–95
nominal compounds 36, 37, 44, 65, 90, 173, 188, 190, 191

nominal morphemes 188; see also morphemes
nominalization:
  morphology 114–115
  verbs 37
non-head 18, 28, 31, 32, 33–34, 35, 36–37, 38, 39, 40–41, 99, 100, 111, 116–117, 190
nonbinding words 179–181, 192; see also binding words
noncognates; see also cognates
  homographic 15, 140
nonimpaired adults 194
nonwords 63, 88–89, 176, 178
noun compounds 31, 72, 73, 74, 87, 99, 101, 105, 107, 110, 111, 112, 115, 117, 119, 121, 148, 151
  meaning 101, 103–108
  novel 105, 115, 121–122
noun phrases 28, 33, 34, 35, 39, 40, 139
noun-adjective compounds 32, 59–60, 89
noun-noun compounds 23, 50, 110, 32, 43, 66–67, 72, 78, 87, 88, 89, 90, 100, 102, 105, 107, 110, 111–113, 119, 121, 123, 136, 145, 189, 191
  novel 100, 104, 155
noun-preposition-noun compounds 66–67, 118
noun-verb compounds 78, 119, 136
nouns 18, 23, 25, 26, 29, 31, 32, 36, 38, 60–61, 65, 67, 72, 74, 80, 87, 90–91, 99, 110, 115, 121, 123, 135, 152, 153, 154, 157, 163, 164–165, 166, 188, 188, 190;
  descriptive 73

forms 109
gender 88
plural 60, 79, 138
novel compounds 5, 8, 49, 57, 58, 59, 66, 86, 100–101, 103, 105, 107, 108, 110, 113, 115, 116–117, 118, 119, 121, 122, 124, 125, 136, 137, 145, 148, 162, 163, 164, 165, 166, 167, 168, 192
novel forms 120, 121
numerals 25

object-verb-er compounds 100, 108–109, 111–112, 123
objects 104, 105, 107, 108, 110–111
  ordering 112
off-line processing 66
on-line processing 18–19, 66, 144, 149
opacity 15–16, 40, 41, 47, 86, 132, 181–182, 192
opaque compounds 14, 44, 47, 48, 49, 53, 74, 76, 81, 85, 86, 100, 124, 133, 147, 174, 182–183, 193
  semantically 131–132, 173, 181, 182
open-class vocabulary 77
ordering errors 123, 135
ordering of compounds 5, 19, 121, 124
orthography 9, 19, 26, 52, 58, 86, 127–128, 131, 139, 140, 141, 143, 169, 178, 186
  Chinese 170–172, 174, 181, 193
  representation 181

paradigms 15, 170, 176, 178, 183, 184, 188, 192
parallel constituent processing 10f

paraphasias 73, 75, 77–78, 82, 83
paraphrasing 141–142, 163
parsing 8, 21, 42–43, 47, 48, 49, 50, 54, 65, 88, 89, 121, 139, 141, 148, 167, 176–177, 192;
  see also morphological parsing; phonological parsing
  recursive 85–86
particles see prefixes
Persian 140
phonemes, detection tasks 174
phonological parsing 139;
  see also morphological parsing; parsing
phonology 77, 79, 83, 85, 127–128, 131, 139–140, 174, 186
  components 4
  deletions 39
  distinctions 26–27, 100
  errors 74
  levels 75
  rules 99
phrasal compounds 28
phrases 26, 27, 38–39, 57, 99, 109, 113, 114, 127, 149, 154, 164
  based 44
  Chinese 171–172
  familiar 163, 164
Pinyin 196t; see also Chinese
plausibility 167
pluralization 38, 138–139
plurals 27, 32, 33, 34, 61, 99, 100, 116, 117
  form 90, 116–117
  formation 61–62
  irregular 60, 69, 116, 137, 138
  markers 61, 65, 139
    overt 127

plurals (cont.):
  regular 61, 99, 116–118, 138
pleonastic compounds 31–32
Polish 27, 42, 51, 54, 55, 56, 62, 63, 64, 66, 67, 68, 135
polyglot aphasia 141, 142; see also aphasia
polysemous compounds 36, 43
position-in-the-string 30, 51, 54–55, 56, 69, 72, 131, 132, 143, 192–193
prefixes 18, 19, 20, 29, 79
prepositional compounds 67 check
prepositional phrases 57, 67
prepositions 29, 67, 99, 102, 118
preschool children see L2 learners, children
primes 131–132, 158–159, 165, 166, 189–190, 193
  Chinese 184–186, 187, 190, 195
  combination 165, 166
  compounds 165, 166
  nonbinding 188
  opaque 184, 185, 188
  transparent 184, 186, 187–188
priming 47, 47n, 48, 51, 54, 56, 63, 64, 70, 127, 129, 132, 135, 140–141, 160, 162, 166, 183–189, 194
  auditory-auditory 184
  cross-modal 184
  differential 56–57
  morphological 183, 186
  paradigms 186, 188
  semantic 127, 184, 186
  visual-visual 183–184
processing 19–20, 45–70; see also on-line processing

agreement 89–91
production 16, 46, 58, 59, 79, 81, 82, 101, 103, 113, 114–116, 122, 130, 134, 137, 138, 142
productivity 30–35, 44, 100, 101–103, 119, 120, 122, 131, 136–137, 143, 181
proficiency 128–129, 143
pronouns 26
pronunciation 140, 170, 171, 174, 177, 179, 180, 187
proper nouns 12
prosodic accents 139–140
prosodic form 27, 76
prototypical compounds 24–25, 27, 29–30, 43–44
psycholinguistics 3, 4, 11–12, 17, 20, 21–22, 23, 24, 40, 41, 43, 46, 54, 55, 58, 60, 67, 70, 71, 125–126, 128, 139, 170, 174, 175
putative compounds 57
Putonghua see Mandarin Chinese

reaction times 132, 134, 137, 141, 143, 179, 183
reading 65, 86, 115, 169, 176, 180, 181, 194
  Chinese 174, 178, 191–192
real-world knowledge 126–127
recursion 35, 43
redundancy 9, 10, 21
reduplication 2, 172
referents 104, 107, 109
regression 158
regularity effects 31, 60–62
relational adjectives 37; see also adjectives

relational nouns 37, 151; *see also* nouns
relations 145, 148–149, 150, 152, 153–154, 155–158, 161, 162, 163, 166
   availability 158–159, 162, 164–165
   compounds 165
   information 146, 147, 151, 159, 160, 161, 166, 167
   multiple 154–155
   priming 159, 162, 165, 166
   selection 152
   use 146–147, 154, 159, 161
representation 6–7, 9, 12, 13, 14, 16–17, 21, 43, 48, 51, 52, 53, 59, 68–70, 86, 126, 127–128, 130, 131, 134, 139, 144, 145, 146, 163, 167, 174
   compound 21, 131, 134, 144, 162, 164
   conceptual 127, 128, 147, 148, 149, 155, 163
   levels of 126, 127–128, 155
   mental 126
   pre-morbid 142
   semantic 153
   shared 130
   stored 166
   unified 164–165
response latencies 52, 66; *see also* reaction times
right-branching compounds 44, 50; *see also* left-branching compounds
right-headed compounds 17, 32, 33, 34, 35, 43, 56, 59–60, 105, 111, 130, 132, 134, 135; *see also* head, headedness; left-headed compounds
Roman alphabet 140
Romance 28, 38, 42, 50, 68, 99, 117
root compounds 35–36, 44
root nouns 99, 102
root-based morphology 39, 44
rules 24, 30–31, 63, 66, 73, 75, 78–79, 82, 90, 111, 116, 117
   ending 89
   morphological 38, 80
   word-building 77–79

schema-modification theories 149–150, 155–162
schwa 65
second constituents 56–57, 59, 159, 160; *see also* first constituents
semantic opacity 11–12, 13, 13f, 14, 15–16, 53, 147
semantic radicals 170–171
semantic relatedness 187, 190
semantic representations 14, 85
semantic transparency 11, 13, 15, 22, 45, 46, 69, 85–86, 119, 121, 131–134, 137, 143, 147, 175, 181–183, 192, 193, 194
   effects 47–57, 69
semantics 3, 14–15, 81, 82–83, 84, 182, 183
   associates 131–132
   effects 182
   levels 126–127
   priming 184
semi-compounds 136
Semitic languages 68; *see also* Hebrew

sense-nonsense judgments 157, 158, 159, 165
sentences 3, 4, 16, 39, 77, 108, 155, 176
  prime 163–164
  syntactic relations 35
sequencing 82–86, 134
simplicity 119–120
Sinitic languages 170, 194
Sino-Tibetan 68
Slavic 28, 38, 42, 68
Spanish 28, 138, 140
specific-language impaired (SLI) children 59–60
speech 1, 60, 75, 76, 80, 92, 97, 100, 102, 139, 140
speed-accuracy trade-off 190
spelling 140
spoken compounds 178, 181, 186, 187, 194
spoken words 180, 181, 194
Standard Chinese *see* Mandarin Chinese
stem-based/compounding morphology 39, 44
stems 20, 31, 39, 44, 46, 58, 60, 63, 78, 79, 88, 90, 102, 114
  verb 78, 90
stereotypical relations 37–38
stimuli 128, 140, 188, 194
  spoken 186
stimulus-onset asynchrony (SOA) 182–183, 185, 186, 193
storage 3–6, 6f, 10, 22, 67, 79; *see also* computation
strength ratio 157–158
stress 26, 27, 29, 73, 99, 118–119, 136, 139
Stroop tests 128

structure 33–34, 35, 36, 37, 57, 58–60, 69, 77–78, 108, 113, 120–121, 123, 135, 136, 138, 149, 152, 154, 160, 167, 175, 189–193
  features 134–135
  word 172
  word-internal 68, 188
subcategorization role 103, 105, 107, 108, 110, 112, 115, 146, 154, 160, 163, 166–167
subordinate compounds 33–34, 35, 36, 44, 58, 59;
  see also binary compounds; coordinate compounds
suffix-er 108, 120
suffixes 19, 20, 29, 36, 87, 88, 91, 173, 195
  derivational 88, 89
  plural 60, 65, 138
Swedish 99, 104, 105, 115–116, 118, 122
syllables 50–51, 139, 171, 174, 177, 178, 180, 181
symbolic modeling 4, 13
synonyms 74
syntactic categories 25, 127, 135–136, 143, 189, 191
syntactic phrases 27–28, 42
syntax 18, 26, 100, 140, 192
synthetic compounds 35, 36, 37, 38–39, 44;
systematicity 137

templates 111, 121, 130
thematic relations 39, 50, 151; *see also* relations
times 37, 83
  response 131–132

transfer errors 130, 134, 135, 138, 141, 143, 144 check
transition probability 179–181
translation 127, 128, 128, 129, 131, 133
 tasks 134, 137, 141
translation equivalents 128–129, 130, 133–134, 137
transparency 15, 16, 31, 40–43, 147, 181, 182–183, 192, 193
transparent compounds 11, 13, 41, 42, 47, 48, 49f, 73, 74, 76, 81, 85, 86, 133, 147, 148, 175, 182–183, 185
 Mandarin Chinese 180
 semantically 131–132, 147, 182
 written 180–181
transparent words 15, 45
Turkish 26

unimpaired population 55, 62, 69, 142, 191
units, single 147, 166
Universal Grammar (UG) 138
Uralic 68
use *see* relations, use

verb phrases 28, 112, 188
 nominalizations 36
verb-noun compounds 32, 72, 78, 80, 87, 88, 89, 90, 111, 189
 see also adjective-noun compounds; noun-noun compounds
 neologisms 78
verb-object compounds 109, 135
verb-verb compounds 32, 102, 112, 145, 191

verbal compounds 35, 44, 174, 189, 191
verbal morphemes 188
verbs 18–19, 25, 29, 36, 37, 65, 73, 79, 108, 109–110, 112, 126, 138, 188
 base 111, 112
 ordering 112
 stems 78, 90
vowels 27, 39, 59, 62, 89
 linking 63–64 check

Wernicke's aphasia 50, 55, 72, 73, 74, 76, 78, 80, 188, 189
whole-words 7–8, 10, 13, 15–16, 80, 81, 133, 134, 146, 147, 163, 183, 184, 185
 activation 9
 Chinese 179–180
 first architecture 8
 frequency 51
 meaning 11, 12, 82, 83, 86
 processing 8–9, 10f, 131
 relatedness 185
 relational information 148
 representations 9, 10–11, 12–13, 18, 132
 status 133
word-based morphology 38, 39, 44
word-level semantic compounds 186; *see also* priming
wordhood 172
words 10–11, 13, 14, 15–16, 17, 18, 19, 24, 32, 42–43, 46, 50, 51–52, 57–58, 63, 73–74, 75–76, 77, 79–81, 88–89, 90–91, 100, 103, 120, 127, 134,

words (*cont.*):
    135–136, 137, 140, 141, 145, 173, 178, 182, 188, 191;
    see also complex words; monomorphemic words
  access 178, 181–182, 191, 194
  boundary 74–75
  Chinese 171–172, 174, 175, 176, 177, 179, 180–181, 193
    level 175–177
  compound status 75–77
  formation 2, 8, 21, 24, 45, 50, 77, 79, 81, 84, 94, 99, 100, 119, 120, 145
  frequency 50, 177, 178, 180–182
  hyphenated 141
  length 72, 74–75
  meaning 108, 173–174, 184
  reading of 194
  recognition 7, 10, 22, 52, 79, 86, 178
  single 128–129, 130, 133, 141
world knowledge 150–151
writing systems 169
written text, in Chinese 171
    150–151